FINANCIAL GUIDANCE FOR CHRISTIANS

PRESENTED TO: _____

ON: _____

MESSAGE: _____

_____

_____

_____

_____

_____

_____

_____

_____

PRESENTED BY: _____

FROM $00 to $30,000 IN THREE YEARS

There is a young man who has three small children and is a typical working individual. Three years ago, if he had sold all of his assets, paid off all of his debts, his net worth would have been zero.

Following the principles in this book and in the financial newsletter that I edit, he recently told me, three years later, that if he sold everything and paid off all of his debts, he would have $30,000 left!

Three years earlier he had decided to become a good steward and to bring his financial affairs into a shape that would glorify God. This book can help you do the same thing. My prayer is that as you read these pages, God will give you fresh and new insights and that when you stand before the judgment seat of Christ and give an account for your stewardship, you will hear Him say, "Well done, good and faithful servant."

Much love in Christ,

Jim McKeever

FINANCIAL GUIDANCE
FOR
CHRISTIANS

by Jim McKeever

Omega Publications
P.O. Box 4130
Medford, Oregon 97501

FINANCIAL GUIDANCE FOR CHRISTIANS
formerly
THE ALMIGHTY AND THE DOLLAR

Omega Publications
P.O. Box 4130
Medford, Oregon 97501

Printed in the United States of America
First printing — February, 1981
Major revision and second printing — March 1984
Third printing — September 1986

ISBN 0-931608-09-0 (Hardbound)
ISBN 0-931608-10-4 (Softbound)

TABLE OF CONTENTS

This book is dedicated first and foremost to the
glory of God; it is also dedicated
to those Christians who will become better stewards
through following the advice herein.

FOREWORD

BY PAT ROBERTSON

This is not just another "Christian money book." There have been many Christian books written on financial affairs, but none of them by a man like Jim McKeever who has a wide reputation as one of the top economists and investment advisors in the world.

Jim McKeever has spoken in monetary conferences in the Orient, London, Amsterdam, Zurich, as well as all over North and Latin America. He has shared the platform with such men as Ronald Reagan, Gerald Ford, William Simon, William Buckley, Harry Schulz, Harry Browne, Howard Ruff, Louis Rukeyser, Alan Greenspan, and many other outstanding leaders including heads of foreign governments, U.S. senators and congressmen, and economists and writers of renown.

He is editor of *The McKeever Strategy Letter,* a financial newsletter with readers on every continent. Many of the wealthy and powerful people of the world look forward to his regular advice in this newsletter. *The McKeever Strategy Letter* has been acclaimed as one of the top newsletters of the world and recently received the "Outstanding Newsletter Award" by the *Hard Money Digest.*

In addition to being an author, world traveler, and lecturer, Jim McKeever is also a dedicated Christian. As a Christian leader he has shared the platform with such men as Pat Boone, Dr. Bill Bright, Ted Engstrom, Dr. Bob Turnbull, and a host of other Christian leaders.

He is editor of *End-Time News Digest* and author of several top-selling Christian books including *Now You Can Understand the Book of Revelation, Close Encounters of the Highest Kind, Why Were You Created?, Only One Word,* and *Christians Will Go Through the Tribulation and How to Prepare For It.*

As a deep Bible researcher and teacher, Jim has come up with some outstanding insights as to how the scriptures relate to an individual Christian's financial situation. It is fortunate for the body of Christ that a man who is a top level economist and investment advisor and also a Christian with deep scriptural knowledge can combine his wisdom into a single volume to help guide Christians through the troubled economic times that lie ahead of us.

I have followed Jim's economic writings through the years and have been impressed with the diligence of his research, the accuracy of his forecasts, and the special insight and wisdom that God gives to him.

PAT ROBERTSON,
President of CBN
Host of "The 700 Club"

MEET THE AUTHOR

Jim McKeever

Jim McKeever is an international consulting economist, lecturer, author, world traveler, and Bible teacher. His financial consultations are utilized by scores of individuals from all over the world who seek his advice on investment strategy and international affairs.

Mr. McKeever is the editor and major contributing writer of *Financial Guidance,* the financial newsletter for the middle-income Christian. He is also editor of the highly awarded and acclaimed newsletter for investors with above-average net worth, *The McKeever Strategy Letter (MSL).* He was formerly editor of

Inflation Survival Letter (now *Personal Finance*). For five years after completing his academic work, Mr. McKeever was with a consulting firm which specialized in financial investments in petroleum. Those who were following his counsel back in 1954 invested heavily in oil.

For more than ten years he was with IBM, where he held several key management positions. During those years, when IBM was just moving into transistorized computers, he helped that company become what it is today. With IBM, he consulted with top executives of many major corporations in America, helping them solve financial, control and information problems. He has received many awards from IBM, including the "Key Man Award" and the "Outstanding Contribution Award." He is widely known in the computer field for his books and articles on management, management control and information sciences.

In addition to this outstanding business background, Mr. McKeever is an ordained minister. He has been a Baptist evangelist, pastor of Catalina Bible Church for three and a half years (while still with IBM) and a frequent speaker at Christian conferences. He has the gift of teaching and an in-depth knowledge of the Bible.

Mr. McKeever is president of Omega Ministries, which is a nonprofit organization established under the leading of the Holy Spirit to minister to the body of Christ by the traveling ministry of anointed men of God, through books, cassettes, seminars, conferences, and the newsletter, *End-Times News Digest.* The various ministries of Omega Ministries are supported by the gifts of those who are interested.

ACKNOWLEDGEMENTS

I would like to start off by acknowledging the whole host of people who have contributed to my personal spiritual growth and insights and to my economic education and understanding. Unfortunately, they are far too numerous to mention, but I am deeply appreciative to every one of them.

I would like to single out for special acknowledgement my son, Mike McKeever. He has edited this book, rewritten sections of it, and contributed ideas and constructive criticisms. I could not have found a more perfect editor. He has taught English and has a deep understanding of economics and investments.

My heartfelt thanks go to my wife, Jeani, who has inspired me and provided loving encouragement. She also served as the official proofreader and coordinator for the typesetting of the book.

Of course at the top of the list I would have to put my appreciation to God who gave me the wisdom and the courage to write this book in a way that I trust will glorify Christ.

Jim McKeever
P.O. Box 4130
Medford, OR 97501

PART 1

PLANNING AND ACTION

1

THE FOUNDATION IS FIRST

As I travel all over North America, Latin America, Europe and the Orient, I talk with many people from all levels of society—from very wealthy to very poor. Most of them seem to be viewing the world this way:

- Prices keep going up, so I can buy less of the things that I need and want. My standard of living appears to be declining, and I am not sure why.

- Everybody else seems to be making out better than I am. I want more of my share of things. I feel I have a right to this.

- Taxes are really getting to be a burden. Why do we have to give so much money to the government when all they do is waste it?

- I am not sure where I should invest my money. Savings accounts do not pay enough; I have lost money in the stock market.

- This whole economic thing is very confusing, but I am assuming and hoping that our government will do something about it and solve the problems.

- On the other hand the government appears to be more corrupt and less capable than I thought. In fact it appears too helpless to do anything about our current problems.

Most people are confused about the economic situation. They assume that the government will be able to solve their problems and, therefore, they take no action themselves. I would like to suggest that they are wrong—that government will not solve the problems. But there are many things that you can do to help solve your personal problems. This book gives many detailed suggestions to help you.

LET'S FIRST LAY A FOUNDATION

If we are going to build a building, the foundation is the first thing we must lay down. Before we can discuss ways that you can protect yourself from inflation and things that you can do to better your financial situation, we need to first lay a foundation to help you understand the basics of why things are as they are. This will help you not only to understand the things that we discuss in this book but also to understand new economic events and how they will affect you as they occur in the future.

Even though this book is being written primarily for Christians, the principles and advice given here will be of great value regardless of your personal faith and beliefs.

In laying our foundation, we are going to first go back and look at what the Bible has to say about money and wealth. There are many valuable principles that we find there that are applicable to anyone, Christian or non-Christian. We will then, in the first part of the book, examine some vital trends, particularly the trend of inflation. We will also look at planning techniques for your own financial situation (whether you are rich or poor or anywhere in between), and we will cover establishing your financial goals. It is necessary to have a blueprint of what we want to build on this foundation before we charge off and build it.

This is the weakness of many investors today. They read a particular newsletter which is proclaiming some investment vehicle or another, and they dash off and dabble in that for a while. Then, perhaps, they attend an investment conference and hear something else that sounds good, and they move into that. Then along comes a good book on investments or finances, and they're off in another direction. They tend to act on the emotion of the moment rather than clearly selecting a path that will move them toward their financial goals. As Christians we need to determine whether or not our actions are moving us toward goals that have been established by seeking the Lord's guidance through prayer.

Speaking of prayer for God's guidance, did you know that the Bible says that God does not hear the prayers of those who are unbelievers? In Psalm 66, we read this: "If I regard wickedness in my heart, the Lord will not hear," (verse 18). Most people need some divine guidance, and maybe even some divine intervention, in their financial affairs. If you find yourself unsure as to whether or not you are a believer, I would encourage you to read Appendix A entitled "How To Become A Christian" before proceeding with this book.

THE ALMIGHTY AND THE DOLLAR

We are going to be looking at what our heavenly Father has to say about money and wealth as a basis for conducting our financial affairs. I am writing this book because I have long felt that there is an incredible vacuum of sound financial information available to Christians.

As an economist and investment consultant, who wrestles with the world economy each day in the battle for financial survival and prosperity, I am utterly appalled at the counsel available to most Christians today from the typical Christian bookstore shelf. There is a broad spectrum of books and tapes authored by well-meaning pastors and Christian laymen available to the Christian public. As I read many of these, I shudder at the thought of what will happen over the coming years to those people who follow the advice I find there. I have no doubt that these authors are upright and well-intentioned in providing their counsel. However, the vast majority of what I read in these Christian investment guides is diametrically opposite to a sound investment strategy for today. Some of it even violates biblical principles.

I have written this book to counteract this wealth of bad information and advice that Christians are consuming. The world economy in the coming years will remain extremely complex and turbulent and will drive the vast majority of Christians and non-Christians into utter confusion. God is not the author of confusion, and it is my prayer that this book can help clear the fog and enlighten your understanding of the stage on which your financial stewardship will be played out.

PROVIDE FOR YOUR FAMILY

If you are a Christian reading this, I must first ask you if you would be interested in denying your faith? In addition, would you like the Lord to consider you worse than an unbeliever? The Bible says that you *are* worse than an unbeliever and you *have* denied the faith if you do not provide for your own family.

This truth is found in a personal letter that Saint Paul wrote to Timothy—a young man he evidently helped to become a Christian. In the first letter to Timothy, Chapter 5, Paul says:

> 8 But if anyone does not provide for his own, and especially for those of his household, he has denied the faith, and is worse than an unbeliever.

Does providing for your family mean just while you are able to work? Does it mean only while you are alive? Perhaps God wants you to provide for your family even if you become incapable of working and perhaps even after your death.

You may be the father of small children, and if you were to die accidentally, how would they be provided for? As we go through this book, we will look at various methods that would allow you to provide for them even after your death.

Today, you can provide food for your family because the trucks bring it in to the big cities daily. How would you provide food for your family if the trucks stopped running? How would you provide for your family if you were unemployed and there was no unemployment insurance available from the government? Providing for your family means providing for them regardless of the future circumstances. Again, in this book I will help you to understand ways that you can take care of these and other emergencies.

CHRIST TAUGHT PLANNING AND BUDGETING

Did Christ teach that we should plan and budget? Some Christians would respond, "No, He said that we should take no thought for tomorrow."

This is true, Christ did teach this; however, it had nothing to do with planning and budgeting. He was talking about worry and anxiety. We find this teaching in His "sermon on the mount" in Matthew 6:

31 "Do not be anxious then, saying, 'What shall we eat?' or 'What shall we drink?' or 'With what shall we clothe ourselves?'

32 "For all these things the Gentiles eagerly seek; for your heavenly Father knows that you need all these things.

33 "But seek first His kingdom and His righteousness; and all these things shall be added to you.

34 "Therefore do not be anxious for tomorrow; for tomorrow will care for itself. *Each* day has enough trouble of its own. . . ."

Here, we see that Christ does not want us to experience anxiety, pressure, or worry. As a matter of fact, He came to give us peace instead. Peace is the opposite of anxiety. When you are anxious, someone or something has robbed you of the peace that Jesus gave you—a peace that is rightfully yours in all circumstances.

The passage above does not deal with planning and budgeting, so we need to find out what Christ *did* teach on those subjects. In fact, it is interesting to note that over half of Christ's parables and teachings dealt with the financial and material side of life. He seemed to be just as concerned about that side of his followers' lives as He was about the spiritual side.

For Christ's teaching on planning and budgeting, we turn to Luke 14:

28 "For which one of you, when he wants to build a tower, does not first sit down and calculate the cost, to see if he has enough to complete it?

29 "Otherwise, when he has laid a foundation, and is not able to finish, all who observe it begin to ridicule him,

30 saying, 'This man began to build and was not able to finish.'

31 "Or what king, when he sets out to meet another king in battle, will not first sit down and take counsel whether he is strong enough with ten thousand *men* to encounter the one coming against him with twenty thousand?

32 "Or else, while the other is still far away, he sends a delegation and asks terms of peace. . . ."

In this parable, Christ teaches us to first sit down and "calculate the cost," that is to develop a budget. Counting the cost involves budgeting and planning to ensure that one has sufficient resources to accomplish his goal; otherwise, when he has begun a work and can't finish it, everyone ridicules him.

Incidentally, I have seen this scriptural principle violated by top Christian leaders, as well as fledgling Christians who are new to a biblical lifestyle. I've seen Christian organizations set out to build something "operating on faith," not calculating the cost first. They worked on the assumption that God was miraculously going to provide, and in some instances He did not. There may be an occasional man of faith, like George Mueller, whom God leads to operate in this way, but for most Christian organizations and churches He expects them to first calculate the cost. I have seen Christian organizations go bankrupt and others totter on the verge of bankruptcy because of a lack of planning and budgeting. We can use faith as an excuse for being sloppy and slothful in business. In no way does this glorify God.

I have seen wealthy investors make investments in the commodity market and not have enough money to cover the margin calls. They did not count the cost before they began to build.

I have seen young newly-married Christian couples buy homes that were far too expensive for them, or buy furniture and appliances on credit which they later had to let "go back."

I have seen them strap themselves financially such that they could not do the things God wanted them to do. I have seen Christians abuse their credit cards like Visa, BankAmericard, Diners Club, and American Express. They charge far too much and pay a great deal of interest, making it almost impossible to pay down the balances owed.

In many of these cases, a month of unemployment, an illness, or an accident could bring total financial disaster to these families, simply because they have not followed Christ's principles of sitting down first to calculate the cost to be sure that they have adequate resources.

I'll have more to say about planning and budgeting in the chapters to come, but I wanted to point out now that planning and budgeting are principles taught by Christ in the Bible. This is true whether it be for a business, for an investment decision, or for our own personal family finance management. Violations of this principle prevent most Christians from being able to tithe, save, or invest. I believe that the first 10 percent of an income should go to the Lord's work, and the second 10 percent should be saved. An individual family should then live within the remaining 80 percent, and out of that 80 percent give extra "offerings" to the Lord's work.

I've had so many Christians say to me, "That is impossible for me." My response is, "No, it's not. All you have to do is sell that four-bedroom home and rent a two-bedroom apartment, and you can do it." But they would rather attempt to live in luxury than to follow God's principles. They have new cars and staggering car payments. They could sell their cars and buy used cars that are completely paid for. However, they would miss the luxury of the new car.

Life is full of choices. I have never seen anyone who could not, by slightly lowering his standard of living, live within 80 percent of his income. Normally, the problem is unwillingness rather than inability. It may mean living in an older apartment and not having a dishwasher or air conditioning, but it can be done. It is often simply a choice between our personal desires and God's principles.

Before we move on to our next biblical principle, I should point out that when I say one should save 10 percent, that does not necessarily mean it should be put into a savings account or a money market fund or any of the traditional savings vehicles. Most of these methods of saving will pay less than the rate of inflation, when inflation worsens. There are other viable ways to save which will be discussed in Chapter 5.

YOU WON'T BELIEVE WHAT CHRIST TAUGHT ABOUT INVESTMENTS

Stewardship is a word used loosely in the Christian community. Most people don't understand the word, much less the concept. In former times, a *steward* was the equivalent of a modern-day manager. Today, if I let someone run my business for me for a few years while I took a sabbatical, I would call him the *manager* of the business. In biblical times, he would have been called the *steward* of the business.

I would prefer to use a term like *managership* or *shepherdship* rather than *stewardship*. But since *stewardship* is a term ingrained in the modern Christian world, I will use it. Unfortunately, when most Christians think of stewardship today, they see images of someone saying, "Please donate," or "Please give," or "Please include us in your will." It is certainly valid to give to good Christ-centered churches and organizations, but that has nothing to do with stewardship.

Personally, I have never heard a sermon on stewardship; I have never read a book on stewardship; and I have never seen a stewardship Sunday in a church or a stewardship department in a Christian organization. I have heard a lot of sermons and read a lot of books on tithing and giving, but tithing and giving have to do with your income, while stewardship has to do with your assets. I believe that stewardship has to do with *all* of your assets, including your time, but we will apply it, as Christ did in one of his teachings on this subject, just to the financial area of life.

So tighten your seatbelts; you're probably going to experience the first real teaching on stewardship that you've ever had. In the teaching we are about to review, let me first explain something. A *talent* is not an ability. A talent in biblical days was seventy-five to one hundred pounds of silver. At a silver price of $15, that would be roughly equivalent to $30,000. So when someone received five talents, he was receiving approximately $150,000. Two talents would be worth approximately $60,000, and one talent, of course, would be worth $30,000. Now let's see what Christ has to say in Matthew 25 about handling the money (assets) that He gives to us:

14 "For *it is* just like a man *about* to go on a journey, who called his own slaves, and entrusted his possessions to them.

15 "And to one he gave five talents, to another, two, and to another, one, each according to his own ability; and he went on his journey.

16 "Immediately the one who had received the five talents went and traded with them, and gained five more talents.

17 "In the same manner the one who had *received* the two *talents* gained two more.

18 "But he who received the one *talent* went away and dug in the ground, and hid his master's money.

19 "Now after a long time the master of those slaves came and settled accounts with them.

20 "And the one who had received the five talents came up and brought five more talents, saying, 'Master, you entrusted five talents to me; see, I have gained five more talents.'

21 "His master said to him, 'Well done, good and faithful slave; you were faithful with a few things, I will put you in charge of many things, enter into the joy of your master.'

22 "The one also who had *received* the two talents came up and said, 'Master, you entrusted to me two talents; see, I have gained two more talents.'

23 "His master said to him. 'Well done, good and faithful slave; you were faithful with a few things, I will put you in charge of many things; enter into the joy of your master.'

24 "And the one also who had received the one talent came up and said, 'Master, I knew you to be a hard man, reaping where you did not sow, and gathering where you scattered no *seed*.

25 'And I was afraid, and went away and hid your talent in the ground; see, you have what is yours.'

26 "But his master answered and said to him, 'You wicked, lazy slave, you knew that I reap where I did not sow, and gather where I scattered no *seed*.

27 'Then you ought to have put my money in the bank, and on my arrival I would have received my *money* back with interest.

28 'Therefore take away the talent from him, and give it to the one who has the ten talents.'

29 "For to everyone who has shall *more* be given, and he shall have an abundance; but from the one who does not have, even what he does have shall be taken away.

30 "And cast out the worthless slave into the outer darkness; in that place there shall be weeping and gnashing of teeth.

I hope you read all of that passage; if you have not, I would encourage you to go back and read it before proceeding. Notice in verse 16 that one steward had $150,000 and went out and "traded" and made 100 percent on his money. He gained an additional $150,000. Trading implies having some knowledge as to how to trade and spending the time and energy necessary to trade. Trading also implies taking risks.

However, when the master came back and talked to his stewards (managers), he praised the one who had taken risks and had spent the time and energy to trade, making 100 percent on his money. The other steward, who was given $60,000, made 100 percent on his money, gaining another $60,000 and the approval of his master.

However, the third steward (manager) told his master that he hadn't wanted to take any risks and that he had preferred to play it completely safe. Therefore, he had rented a safe deposit box and put the $30,000 into it and was simply returning that $30,000 to his master. That steward simply broke even and, therefore, was thrown into "outer darkness" where there was "weeping and gnashing of teeth."

If Christ was that harsh on a steward who broke even, I wonder what He would have to say to a person who puts his money in a savings account at 5 percent while inflation is going at 15 percent. That person is losing 10 percent on his money, actually doing *worse* than breaking even. What do you think

Christ would have said in this parable to a person whose inactivity resulted in a 10 percent loss?

I believe He would have had extremely harsh words to say to him. Remember, this is not my teaching; this is the teaching of Jesus Christ. He applauded the man who took risks, who spent time and energy, and made 100 percent. He condemned the man who made no profit.

There are many wonderful Christians who love the Lord and who have saved their money by putting it into savings accounts, savings bonds, and so forth, but they are losing money every year. None of the Christian leaders and teachers have made them aware that they are poor stewards according to Christ's teaching.

It is possible that even if a minister were to try to teach on this subject, he would not know what to tell the members of his congregation to do with their money if they drew it out of their savings accounts. Thus, it would be very difficult for him to give a teaching on how to become a good steward.

That is the real purpose of this book—to help Christians clearly understand how they can be good stewards. You need to be a good steward regardless of whether you have $50, $500, $50,000, or $50 million. We are all going to have to stand before Christ and give an account of our stewardship. You need what's in the rest of this book in order to understand how to be a good steward.

THE PARABLE OF THE TALENTS AND GOD'S WILL

Most of the parables of Christ have both a "content" truth and a "kingdom" truth. I believe in the vast majority of cases Christ would have us apply both of these truths.

For example, in the parable of the good Samaritan, I think Christ intended to teach us to physically help those who were in difficulty as well as to apply the spiritual principles of that parable. Similarly, in the parable of building the tower, I believe that Christ was clearly teaching that we should plan and budget. Of course on the spiritual side, He was teaching that before we decide to follow Him we need to count the cost.

In the same way, the parable of the talents has some spiritual (Kingdom of God) lessons for us to learn, and I believe that Christ also wants us to apply the "content" portion of the parable to our financial affairs.

There may be some who would not agree with this and would try to make everything that Christ taught apply only to His spiritual kingdom. I believe that this is a mistake because Christ is also interested in the practical everyday well-being of His followers.

Looking at stewardship, and at the parable of the talents in particular, I am in no way trying to impose this teaching upon anyone so that they follow the teaching rather than God's guidance. It is possible that God would lead someone to give away all or most of what he has. Once that individual gives his assets to a Christian organization or to some other individual, the recipient has the responsibility for being a good steward of them.

What I am emphasizing here is that as long as *you* have the assets under your control (until the Lord tells you to give them away), then God holds you accountable for being a good steward of them. You're going to have to seek God to find out what being a good steward means in your particular case. What I'm trying to do is to help you understand what the Bible says.

If you feel God leading you in a way that is contrary to this teaching, then I would encourage you to follow what God is telling you to do. However, unless God clearly and specifically leads you to the contrary, I believe that what He has outlined in the scriptures about your stewardship is what He expects you to follow.

SUMMARY AND CONCLUSION

We have said that there are outstanding principles in both the Old Testament and the New Testament for managing your financial and material assets. The Jewish people have found that following these principles produces financial well-being.

We have looked at basically three principles:

Principle #1: Provide for your family both now and during hard, turbulent times, even times of famine, and provide for them even after your death.

In order to do this, and do it well, Christians need to apply the second biblical principle, and that is:

Principle #2: Plan and budget your financial affairs. Give the first 10 percent to God; save the second 10 percent; and live on the remaining 80 percent.

If principle #2 is followed, there will be surplus funds from your savings that the Lord wants you to handle properly. This takes us to the third principle:

Principle #3: A good steward is willing to spend the time and energy to learn how to "trade" and is willing to take risks so that he does not just break even (that is, just keep up with inflation). Rather, he makes a substantial gain on his savings (investments) in the process.

It does not matter if you are a high school student with $50, a young married couple with a net worth of $5,000, a middle-aged family with a net worth of $50,000, or a retired business tycoon with $50 million. We will all have to stand before our Maker, and He will ask questions concerning how good a steward (manager) we were of the assets over which He gave us responsibility. The remaining chapters of this book will help you understand the economic environment in which we are living and how you can apply these principles to your everyday financial affairs.

First, we will begin to understand our economic environment by looking at three very important trends that point out the direction of the future of our economy.

2

THREE CRITICAL TRENDS

I think any observer of the U.S. and world economies would have to say that things are getting progressively more chaotic. We have wide swings in interest rates as well as in the inflation rate. Stocks and bonds move upward and then fall with the same rapidity. Gold and silver used to be the stables of the investment world, but now they too have shown tendencies toward large and erratic movements. These things seem to be pointing toward an economic crisis.

Why do I think we are facing a potential economic crisis? Before I answer that, I would like to state that I am not the type of economist who looks at a crystal ball and comes up with predictions. I basically extrapolate trends, determine whether these trends are likely to continue, and, if so, ascertain where they will take us. I would like to examine three trends, each of which could create an economic crisis.

THE FIRST TREND—
THE VALUE OF PAPER DOLLARS

The first trend is the pattern of continually rising prices (which, viewed in another way, is simply our paper money becoming worth less). To illustrate this, let's look back a number of years to the time when either a silver dollar or a paper dollar would buy eight loaves of bread. Bread was about twelve cents a loaf. Today bread is about $1 a loaf.

But it is interesting to note that a silver dollar will still buy eight loaves of bread (a silver dollar costs about ten or more paper dollars today). When gold was $42 per ounce, a barrel of oil cost about $2. Thus, an ounce of gold would be worth roughly twenty barrels of oil. In 1980, we found gold at about $600 per ounce and a barrel of oil at roughly $30. So in 1980, an ounce of gold would still buy roughly twenty barrels of oil. We can see from these two examples that the ratio between silver dollars and bread has not changed, and the ratio between gold and oil has not changed. What has changed? Paper money has become worth much less.

If this trend continues, even more significant are the problems we will probably face in food supply. In most major cities today there is roughly a two-week supply of food in the stores and warehouses. They rely on trucks and railroads to bring a continuous stream of additional food. If paper money eventually becomes totally worthless, will farmers sell their grains, vegetables and meats for it? Will truck drivers be willing to drive their trucks into the cities for worthless money? Not likely. If the money becomes worthless we could see a breakdown of services in the major cities, and we could see the cities running out of food.

What would be likely to occur then in these cities? Unfortunately, there would probably be massive riots, with large numbers of people dying from either the bullets of rioters and looters, or from starvation or disease.

Dr. Franz Pick, a fellow economist, tells a story from his experiences as a boy during the German runaway inflation in the early 1920's. He and his brother took a bushel basket full of money down to the store to see if it would buy anything. They set the basket down on the sidewalk to look in the window. When they turned back around someone had stolen the basket.

The thieves had dumped the money out on the sidewalk and left it, but they had taken the basket since the basket was of more value than the money. If you can imagine taking a basketful of U.S. $100 bills to the store and having someone steal the basket, leaving the pile of $100 bills, you can imagine what it is like in a country where the money has become worthless.

Another man I know went through that same German run-away inflation. His father had taken out an annuity policy which was going to see him through college. He made the investment before the bad inflation really started. During the middle of the inflation, he cashed in this annuity policy. Not only would it not see him through four years of college; it wouldn't even buy his breakfast.

On the following three pages are photographs of old German marks starting with twenty marks and going up through 100 million marks. It is interesting that as the inflation progressed, each of these bills would buy approximately the same thing. The twenty marks would buy as much at the beginning of Germany's inflation as 100 million would buy toward the middle of it. By the end of the inflation, it took 100 trillion marks to buy what twenty would buy before the inflation began.

Can you imagine holding a $100 million bill in your hand? Can you imagine spending it to buy what $20 would buy today? It happened in Germany, and it could happen here in the U.S.

As we look at the rise in U.S. prices, it is interesting to note that in 1960 coffee was five cents per cup. Today, in most cities in the U.S., coffee is thirty cents per cup. In the intervening twenty years, the price of a cup of coffee has risen 600 percent. This gives an average rate of price increase of 30 percent per year.

The inflation rate that our government gives us is actually much lower than the true rate of inflation. For example, in the old days, if an automobile cost more one year than the other, that was added to the inflation rate. Now the government says that the new model has features the old model didn't; thus there is a "quality improvement," not a price increase. As they throw out things like this and mortgage rates, they are artificailly showing a lower inflation rate than what exists in reality.

Not long ago, a national accounting firm went back and calculated the inflation rate based on the government's formula for calculating inflation ten years ago. They came up with the fact that inflation was actually about twice what the government was reporting to us. So you see that today we still have significant real price inflation.

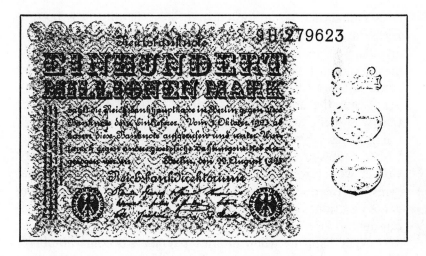

In light of this kind of real price inflation, it is important to realize that if you are making less than 5 percent per year above the inflation rate on your investments, you are losing part of your capital. If you wish to make a true increase of 5 percent on your wealth, you are going to need to make a minimum of 5 percent on your investments above the rate of inflation as measured in U.S. dollars.

So if inflation is at 20 percent, you must make an average of 25 percent on your investments. Believe me, there are ways to achieve this. We will have more to say about this in our chapters on investments.

So with this upward trend in prices, as with any trend, we must assume the trend will continue until it tells us it's leveling off and turning in the other direction. This present inflationary trend is still moving up strongly but might reach a breaking point sometime between now and the year 2000.

THE SECOND TREND—
TOTAL AMOUNT OF INTEREST

You should be interested in interest, because it is becoming critical. In the early days of America, both the citizens (individuals) and the governments felt it was honorable to spend no more than their income. Many of our fathers felt that if you could not pay cash you should not spend. Therefore, not many years ago, the amount of our Gross National Product (GNP) that was spent to pay interest was less than 5 percent. Today, the interest payments on public and private debt within the United States are 40 percent of the GNP. This means that every worker works from January to June just to pay off the financial "sins" of the past. This 40 percent figure will certainly grow because additional borrowing is necessary to pay interest on previous debts.

What happens when interest payments become 50-60-70-80-90 percent of the GNP? At some point the burden becomes unbearable. When this has happened in the past, governments have simply been forced to cancel all debts. If this were to occur it would mean that those holding bonds, Treasury bills, and any other debt instrument would wind up holding worthless pieces of paper. What impact would that have on the economy, the banks, insurance companies, colleges, retired people? It would cause our economic institutions, as we know them, to come crashing down. It would close Wall Street, since four-fifths of Wall Street's volume is in bonds and only one-fifth in stocks. Wall Street could not function if bonds became worthless.

Normally, along with debt repudiation would come a new currency and, hopefully, monetary reform and balanced government budgets. With the institution of a new currency, as has happened with many countries who have gone through this, the citizens normally turn in ten or a hundred (or even more) of their old "dollars" to get one new one. For example, at the end of the runaway inflation in Germany in the 1920's the people turned in five trillion old marks in order to get one new mark. This would be equivalent to Americans turning in five trillion of our current U.S. paper dollars to get one new dollar.

It is interesting to note that in the Old Testament God provided an automatic solution for this problem. Every seventh year the Israelites had to let their land go fallow and plant no crops. After seven cycles of seven years (which is forty-nine years) there was an additional year or the fiftieth year called the year of Jubilee, in which they had to let their fields remain fallow a second year. Also, during that year of Jubilee all property returned to the original owners, and all indentured servants were set free. This caused an automatic flush-out of the economy every fifty years.

It is likely that a piece of property had progressively less value as the year of Jubilee approached, since the new temporary owner would have only a short period of time in which to use it. After the year of Jubilee the prices of everything probably went to a very high point since there would be fifty more years in which to utilize the property. In modern economics it has also been found that about fifty years of compound interest takes an economy to a breaking point. Jubilee cancelled all of that debt and compound interest and allowed the economy to start over again.

If we take 1930-35 as the beginning of the present fifty year cycle, it would end in 1980-85. It could well be that the interest payments by that point in time will be reaching a critical point. They certainly will be by the year 2000.

THE THIRD TREND—
THERE IS SUCH A THING AS A FREE LUNCH!

The third trend I would like to extrapolate concerns welfare, social security, and unemployment. In 1935 when the social security and welfare program was first instituted there was one beneficiary for every 143 workers. Today, there is one beneficiary for every 1.7 workers. If you include government employees, who are nonproductive, we have one beneficiary for every one productive worker. The number of people who are receiving benefits is not likely to decrease. Rather, it is definitely continuing to increase. What happens when there are two beneficiaries per worker, or three, or four? At what point do the workers either resign or revolt?

According to Dr. Hans Sennholz, professor at Grove City College, it may not be the workers who revolt, but the beneficiaries. His analysis goes like this. In the early days of America there was only one way to make a living and this was by working. In the 1930's a new way to make a living was found. You could pass a law which would take money from people who were working and give it to people who were not. Once this new way of making a living became known, the lines of people who wanted a free ride began to get longer and longer.

The money to pay these people had to come from someone else. At first it was the rich. They were taxed heavily to pay these welfare and social security recipients. Now, there is no more money to be gained from taxing the rich. Someone has estimated recently that if the government took 100 percent of every annual salary over $25,000, the money would operate the government for only two days. Once the rich were taxed to the point that they could no longer support the government programs, then the government began to tax the middle class.

Now the middle class people's savings and ability to bear taxation has just about run out. Dr. Sennholz estimates that it *will run out* soon. At that time there will be few resources from which to get money to give to those on social security and welfare.

Many of these recipients have been hearing for two generations that they have a moral right to be supported by the government whether they want to work or not. Rightly or wrongly, these beneficiaries feel that this is their due and that the government owes them a living. Once payments to them stop or, because of hyperinflation, become inadequate to support them in the style to which they have become accustomed, we will have a very mean and angry lower class. If the government cannot or will not give them what they want, Dr. Sennholz feels that they will take it by force. They will break into stores and take what they feel they have a right to.

However this trend works out, it appears that there will be a time of revolt either by the workers themselves or by the beneficiaries who are living off of the efforts of the productive workers. Revolution in this day and age will probably not come peacefully but rather will be accompanied by violence, massive social upheaval, and what I term "wall to wall rioting" in the cities.

This trend looks like it too will reach a breaking point sometime between now and the year 2000.

VIEWING ALL THREE TRENDS

All three of these trends appear to be continuing with little if any chance of reversal, regardless of what governmental changes are made and regardless of who is President. Any one of these trends that reaches a breaking point could create a major economic calamity for everyone in the United States. If the interest rate trend reaches a breaking point, we could have a stock market panic. If the inflation trend reaches a breaking point, we could see total disruption of our system for buying and selling and possibly an end to services of all kinds. If the beneficiary load on the workers reaches a breaking point, we could easily see looting and rioting, at least in the cities.

According to my projections, it looks as if each of these will come to a breaking point sometime between now and the year 2000. Unfortunately, there is a good likelihood that two or all three of them will come to a breaking point at about the same time. If we are going to provide for our families and be good stewards, we need to be prepared and protected against such an eventuality.

THE COMING DEPRESSION

Many years ago, before governments began attempting to control and manipulate our economy, the economy would go up and then adjust itself downward, go up again and adjust naturally downward, in a somewhat sawtoothed formation. Politicians (being very "clever" fellows) decided that the simplest thing to do would be to not let the economy go down. So beginning in the 1930's, as the economy would attempt its natural downward adjustment, they would "stimulate" it by hiring additional government workers, putting out additional government contracts, lowering interest rates, and so on. If the government needed to deficit spend in order to do these things, it did so. Our government officials were guilty of very faulty thinking at that time, feeling deficit spending did not matter because "we owed it to ourselves."

If we are going to dance, eventually the fiddler must be paid, and that time is rapidly approaching. For forty years the government has been pumping up the economy, and now the economy is insisting on its natural adjustment. This adjustment is going to be so gigantic that it will make 1929 look like a Sunday School picnic. This means we will probably have an economic crash or depression.

However, there are two kinds of depressions. One is the depression like Germany experienced in the early 1920's. Along with their depression, they had runaway inflation. Theirs was an inflationary-depression. The other type is the one the U.S.

economy experienced in the 1930's—a deep depression with prices falling dramatically. A period of decreasing prices is commonly called a *deflation,* so we had a deflationary-depression.

In both the German and American depressions there were bread lines. In Germany, people were hungry, but their money was worthless and would not buy food. In the U.S., people did not have any money, and they, too, were hungry. In both instances there were bread lines, and people were willing to stand quietly in line for many hours in order to get a few loaves of bread. I question whether this would occur today. Would people quietly stand in line for a few loaves of bread? My feeling is that the times are much more violent, as was shown by the Patty Hearst food giveaway program where people attacked the trucks on the way to the distribution points; they weren't even hungry. No matter how the economy adjusts itself we are probably in for violence.

SUMMARY AND CONCLUSION

There are many other trends we could have examined, such as the price of energy, higher taxes, the growing power of labor unions, the increasing lack of capital in America to rebuild industries and so forth. All of these trends look ominous. We examined only three trends, all of which look as if they will continue and probably come to a breaking point sometime between now and the year 2000. If any one of these trends reaches a breaking point, it could throw our entire economy and social order into an upheaval. Unfortunately, it looks as if they all might be coming to a breaking point at about the same time within the next ten to twenty years. In later chapters, we will discuss how you can protect yourselves against the results of these trends.

We saw that there are two kinds of depressions. There is a deflationary-depression, where the standard of living goes down and prices fall. There is also an inflationary-depression, where the standard of living goes down but the prices skyrocket. Our economy could adjust itself in either of these two ways as we move toward a depression.

My strong feeling is that we will experience an inflationary-depression and that it will be a surprise to most people. In fact my definition of a depression is: a protracted period of time in which the general standard of living in a country declines. Based on that definition we *are* in a depression now. We are keeping our buildings hotter in the summer and colder in the winter. We are driving smaller cars and fewer miles. We are paying more for food and have less of it. Thus, I must conclude that we are in a depression, and yet we see inflation continuing to rise. This gives further credence to the fact that the depression (crash) that we are going to experience will be of the inflationary type. However, a Christian who understands how much God loves him should have no fear of this coming depression.

Since inflation can easily be the monster that catches us unaware and causes Christians to be very poor stewards, we need to look at inflation in detail in the next chapter.

3

HURRICANE INFLATION

I gave a talk in Hong Kong a few years ago just after a violent tropical storm had hit that area, doing an incredible amount of damage. In my talk I pointed out that there is an economic storm approaching of intense velocity, and there are four kinds of people who will face it:

1. Those who are totally unaware that the storm is coming and who will be completely wiped out by it. (Christians should not be unaware!)

2. Those people who see the storm coming but think it will turn and miss them. In this category are primarily the government economists, the Keynesians, the eternal optimists, and those simply unwilling to face reality. They too will be destroyed by the storm and will have no excuse for not foreseeing it.

3. Those people who see the storm coming and are busy building storm cellars. These people are basically adopting a defensive strategy similar to the farmers in the Midwest where there are frequent tornadoes. Even though they can't completely protect their homes and farms, they build storm cellars so at least their family members will be safe.

4. Those people who realize that in the power of the storm there is immense energy that can be harnessed.

Thus, they are out busily building windmills to take advantage of the storm.

Which type of person are you right now? Which type would you like to be? Keep reading; we will try to help you chart your course.

The name of the storm? I believe the name of the storm is "hurricane inflation." Hopefully, with what you will gain from the rest of this book, you will be able to move yourself from the first category to at least the third category and possibly the fourth.

WILL INFLATION CONTINUE?
WILL IT GET OUT OF CONTROL?

These two questions have to be burning in the mind of every thinking individual who is concerned about the financial future of his family. And if you are a Christian, you should be even more concerned. Even though inflation ran low in 1983–1984, by conservative government figures, if and when inflation resumes, everyone's financial life will be affected either for the better or for the worse. (Yes, there is a way inflation can affect your financial life for the better! We'll talk about that later.) But first let's examine these two fundamental questions concerning inflation.

McKEEVER'S RULE #1 FOR THE 1980's:

INFLATION WILL CONTINUE AND WORSEN

First, I need to say a few words about inflation itself to lay the foundation for rule #1. To an economist, the definition of inflation is very clean and simple: it is the increase in the money supply over and above the increase in productivity. Since that is not the way the word "inflation" is normally used, keep in mind that in this book we will use the terms "true inflation" or "monetary inflation" to mean an increase (inflation) in the money supply. We will use the term "inflation" by itself to refer to the rise in the prices of goods and services. According to Webster's dictionary, inflation is "expansion due to the injection of hot air or gas." This is what the government is doing to our money supply. Monetary inflation causes price inflation.

In order to help you understand why this is true, I would like to use my familiar (and famous?) illustration. If there was a group of people assembled in your living room, and I passed out Monopoly money to them and held an auction of the items in the room (pictures, lamps, tables, chairs, vases, etc.), a general level of prices would emerge. However, if we had the same group of people in the same living room, and I passed out twice as much Monopoly money and held the same auction, what would happen to the prices? The answer is they would double. The passing out of additional money (monetary inflation) *causes* prices to rise (inflation). It's as simple as that.

When you read that the government is deficit spending by $130 billion, by and large this means that they are creating much of this "out of thin air" and are passing this money out. As these additional dollars flow through the economy, the prices will rise proportionately. This is why those who understand the economy are clamoring for a balanced federal budget. They think that it will bring inflation under control. It would certainly help if a law balancing the budget were passed *and* implemented. However, there are a number of ways that the government can continue to create this money without deficit spending, such as off-budget deficits, fractional banking ratios, and guaranteed loans. I believe that with or without a constitutional amendment, we will continue to have deficit spending in the federal government.

In 1980, when Reagan was elected, there was a great deal of talk about balancing the federal budget. On April 10th of that year I was on the television program "The 700 Club," and Pat Robertson asked me if I felt the government was going to balance the federal budget. At that time, on nationwide television, I said the balancing of the budget was pure fantasy. Everybody wanted to balance the budget, but in such a way that it wouldn't hurt the old people, wouldn't hurt the farmers, wouldn't hurt the unemployed youths in the ghettos, wouldn't hurt our defense, and the exceptions went on and on. Everybody is *for* the general theory of balancing the budget.

However, what most people do not realize is that the government is spending about 20-30 percent more than it is taking in in taxes. (Incidentally, any family or business that spent 25 percent more than it took in year after year would eventually go bankrupt.) Today, the U.S. Government would be bankrupt if it did not have the ability to create money out of thin air.

In order to balance the federal budget, assuming a 25 percent annual deficit, the government would either have to raise taxes by 25 percent or would have to cut expenses by 25 percent. I don't think the politicians will vote for a tax increase so let's look at the likelihood of their cutting expenses by 25 percent. If they were to do this, this would mean firing 25 percent of the government employees, canceling 25 percent of all government contracts, removing 25 percent of all the recipients on the welfare and social security rolls, reducing the pensions paid to retired military personnel by 25 percent, and on and on. What do you think is the likelihood of politicians passing that type of legislation? I believe it is basically zero. Even if they did pass it, it would throw our country into an incredible depression because of the economic dislocation.

Viewed from every direction I can think of, I believe we will continue to see the government spending more than it takes in. There are other reasons for this. One is that the beneficiaries now outnumber the producers. (Remember, the beneficiaries include all government workers, the military personnel, subsidized farmers, welfare recipients, social security recipients, and the list goes on and on.) As long as the beneficiaries can vote, they will vote themselves a bigger and bigger share of the national pie.

Another reason why I believe inflation will continue is that our elected representatives like to play Santa Claus. When special interest groups come to them with requests, they like to hand out the goodies so that they can get reelected. Rather than being statesmen and raising taxes to cover the additional expenditures, most elected representatives would by far rather inflate the money supply by simply creating dollars out of nothing.

The Bible says we are to use "just" weights and measures (Lev. 19:36). To do otherwise is really stealing. For example, if your butcher used a "pound" weight that was really less than a pound to weigh the meat you were buying, he would be overcharging you. In reality he would be stealing from you.

When a government creates extra money out of thin air, it is not using consistent weights and measures; it is therefore actually stealing from all of the people who have and use its currency.

THE GOLD STANDARD AND INFLATION

You may have heard references to a "gold standard" for the U.S. and not understood its significance. The lack of a gold standard is one of the reasons that I conclude that inflation will continue. Initially, the U.S. dollar was an I.O.U. for gold. A promise was actually printed on the currency to pay the bearer on demand in gold coins. A photograph of one of these bills is shown in Figure 3.1.

Figure 3.1

At that point in time, the dollar was "as good as gold" for everyone, both U.S. citizens and foreigners. In 1933, the United States abandoned the gold standard as far as its own citizens were concerned, but internationally the dollar was still convertible to gold.

After World War II was over, there was considerable confusion in the international monetary system. With Japan, Germany and Italy reeling from a military defeat and most of the industrial capacity of many of the European nations destroyed, what was the correct relationship of the Japanese yen or German mark to the U.S. dollar or to the British pound? Stability was needed.

The major nations of the free world met at Bretton Woods and eventually came up with an agreement. (As far as I'm concerned, the agreement was a "slick deal" by the U.S.). The U.S. convinced the rest of the nations that instead of pegging their currencies to gold, they should each peg their currencies to the U.S. dollar. Since the U.S. had most of the gold in the world at that time, they could convert the U.S. dollars that they held to gold at any time. Thus, they claimed, if the central bank of any other country held U.S. dollars in its national treasury, this was just like holding gold.

Out of this Bretton Woods agreement came the International Monetary Fund. This organization was to act as the stabilizing agency for the world's currencies. Once there was a "fixed exchange rate" between each of the currencies and the U.S. dollar, a country could not change this exchange rate without notifying the IMF and getting its approval.

With this agreement, we entered an era of almost thirty years of prosperity and stability. You might say, "That sounds great! What could possibly have gone wrong?"

All the other countries in the world played this game by the rules, but the U.S. cheated. Other countries would sell goods to the U.S. and receive for them U.S. dollars. These U.S. dollars would go into the treasuries of the various countries and become part of their "reserves" or national store of wealth. They looked at these U.S. dollars as though they were gold because they believed that at any time they could convert them to gold at $35 per ounce.

The U.S. meanwhile began to print excessive amounts of U.S. dollars. Since the exchange rates with the currencies of these other countries were fixed, and there was a flood of U.S. dollars, this meant that we could buy things very cheaply from these other countries. This is why back in the 1950's and 1960's Japanese radios, cameras, and other products were dirt cheap here in the U.S. By inflating our currency, we were in effect siphoning off the productive wealth of these other countries. Thus, the standard of living in the U.S. rose very high while that of our "neighbors" remained much lower.

Toward the end of the 1960's, some of the other countries, primarily France, began to get suspicious. They were accumulating vast amounts of U.S. dollars while the U.S. was still "pretending" that these could be exchanged for gold. France began to cash in its dollars for gold, as did some of the other European countries. As this "run on the gold bank" gained momentum, the U.S. Government officials realized that they did not have nearly enough gold to redeem all of those dollars held in Europe and Asia. So in August of 1971, Nixon closed the gold window. That is, he said that those dollars were no longer redeemable in gold. The U.S. at last confessed to the great farce that it had been pulling on the rest of the world and defaulted on its promise. This promise to always redeem U.S. dollars for gold had been the basis for the world monetary system.

Shortly after Nixon closed the gold window, the European countries announced that they would no longer attempt to maintain the fixed exchange rates with the U.S. dollar but would let their currencies float against the U.S. dollar. So we entered into the era of international monetary instability. The international monetary scene has been getting progressively less stable every day.

Once the gold backing was removed from the U.S. dollar, it became a commodity like any other product with value. Since the other currencies in the world were backed by the U.S. dollar, they too became commodities. These currencies were no

longer simply money so they became subject to the laws of supply and demand just like any other commodity. As with any
commodity, if the demand exceeds the supply, the price or value
will increase. If the supply exceeds the demand, the price or
value will decrease.

At the time the currencies began to float against each
other, there were approximately $300 billion in Europe. These
U.S. dollars were essentially stuck in Europe and became known
as "Eurodollars." They could no longer be returned to the U.S.
in exchange for gold. It should be obvious that at that point
there was a much bigger supply of U.S. dollars in Europe than
there was demand. Therefore, it was inevitable that the U.S.
dollar would decline significantly in value. The problem today
is that that huge supply of U.S. dollars overseas still exceeds the
demand. Until these come into equilibrium, we will see a continued fall in the worth of the U.S. dollar. There may be times
of temporary strength in the U.S. dollar, but the overall trend
will be down. About the only thing that I can see that will halt
this downward trend of the dollar is for something to occur to
make the dollar more desirable (increase the demand) because
the supply is going to remain monstrous. There are a number of
things that the U.S. could do to make the dollar more desirable,
such as balance the federal budget, increase interest rates, make
the dollar convertible to gold, and so on.

Some individuals in foreign countries are beginning to conclude that since they cannot trade this huge supply of U.S. dollars for gold, they will trade it for whatever is of value in the
U.S. We have had a tremendous influx of Japanese buying, using
U.S. dollars to buy up land along the west coast of the U.S. We
have seen the Swiss buying shopping centers in Texas and the
Arabs buying everything in sight. However, I do not think that
these "small" purchases are going to really diminish the supply
of overseas U.S. dollars. If the demand for U.S. dollars does not
increase, the dollar will continue to fall.

To be sure, the dollar will cyclically become strong and
then weak and then strong and then weak again. But overall in
purchasing power and in relation to the commodities of the
world, it continues to lose value.

Back in 1933 when the U.S. went off the gold standard domestically, it then backed the currency with silver. The U.S. currency then became an I.O.U. for silver. U.S. dollars were called "silver certificates" and had printed on them, "will pay the bearer on demand in silver." A copy of one of these silver certificates is printed below.

Figure 3.2

Then in 1967, the silver backing for the U.S. dollar was removed, and our paper money became an I.O.U. for nothing. Because it is not backed by anything, it is called a "fiat" currency. During the time the U.S. dollar was backed by gold or silver, there were restrictions on how much paper money the government could print because there had to be enough precious metal in the U.S. Treasury to redeem these paper dollars. (That was not always the case, but it should have been if the U.S. Government had been honest.) However, now there is absolutely no restriction on how much paper money the U.S. Government can print or create with checks. So our current inflation is a result of ever-increasing deficit spending by the federal government, financed by the creation of new money. As we pointed out earlier, this increase in the money supply (which can now be done without limit) forces prices to rise. Our current dollar is an I.O.U. nothing and is not even issued by the U.S. Government. The Federal Reserve is a private institution owned by banks. Our dollar today is simply a Federal Reserve note, as is shown below.

Figure 3.3

Let's summarize. I believe that inflation is going to continue because of some basic low moral and ethical values that exist in the United States. The work ethic is gone. We give incentives to people not to work. Our elected representatives really don't represent us. The beneficiaries outnumber the producers. There is no gold backing for our currency; and every fiat (unbacked) currency in history has ultimately become worthless. My warning to all is to get prepared for higher and worse inflation. To be sure, there will be ups and downs in the inflation rate, but as we look at the 1980's, the trend is up, up and maybe away.

WILL INFLATION GET OUT OF CONTROL?

The answer to this question is not nearly as clear. There are a number of alternatives that could come about. One possibility is that we could have total wage and price controls. This means we could eventually move basically into a totally controlled economy, much like Russia's. Another alternative is that we could go the route of the Latin American countries that have rocked along with 100-360 percent inflation per year. (I call this hyperinflation.) Some of these Latin American countries have been doing this for many years without *runaway* inflation occurring.

The third possibility would be that we could evolve into a runaway inflation. I would not consider inflation to be out of control (runaway) until prices were escalating more than 1 percent per day (360 percent per year). At that point in time, there would probably be an inflationary blow off, with money becoming worthless quickly. I believe we are quite a way from a runaway inflation and that before it occurs we would have plenty of warning, enabling us to change our strategies.

At present we need to be concerned about regular inflation (10-29 percent per year), severe inflation (30-99 percent per year), and hyperinflation (100-360 percent per year). We need to look at how we can protect ourselves against and even benefit from inflation.

YOUR ESTIMATED RATE OF PRICE INFLATION

Now, I would like for you to take a moment and do some estimating for me. Determine the average annual rate of price inflation that you think we will have for approximately the next twenty years. To make this easier for you, I would like you first to write your "optimistic" view. This is the percentage of price inflation you think we'll have if everything goes well. Next, write in your "pessimistic" view—the worst figure that you could reasonably see inflation reaching across the next twenty years. Somewhere in between these two extremes is the inflation rate that you would consider "most likely." Let's take a minute to actually write down these three numbers:

Optimistic   _____ %

Most Likely   _____ %

Pessimistic   _____ %

In order to get your estimated inflation rate, multiply the "optimistic" by 2, the "pessimistic" by 2, and the "most likely" by 6. Then add these three sums together and divide by 10 for your estimated price inflation rate.

Let's take an example. Perhaps you feel the best possible conditions would have us at 6 percent inflation. The worst possible rate would be 20 percent, and the most likely rate, 10 percent. Multiplying 6 by 2 we have 12, and 20 by 2 equals 40. Multiplying 10 by 6 we have 60. The sum of 12, 40 and 60 is 112. After dividing by 10 we come up with 11.2 percent. Now take a minute and do the same calculation with your numbers and come up with your estimated percentage:

Optimistic _____ % X 2 = _____

Most Likely _____ % X 6 = _____

Pessimistic _____ % X 2 = _____

Total   _____ ÷ 10

Estimated inflation _____ %

We will use this estimated inflation percentage later in the chapter. Just as an aside, I might mention that this formula is an excellent tool for other types of estimating. If you need to complete a project (such as building a house), write down the length of time in which you optimistically think that it can be built, followed by your pessimistic appraisal, and finally the length of time that you think it will most likely take. Then calculate your estimate using this formula. You could use the same formula for estimating the cost of completing a project at work.

As I have traveled around the world, speaking at monetary conferences and Christian meetings, I have frequently asked the audience what they felt the average inflation rate would be across the next twenty years. In the early 1970's, I would get figures like 5 percent. Later in the '70's I began to get 10 percent responses from the audiences. In 1978 I began to get figures at about 15 percent. In 1979, it was 20 percent, and in 1980 I began to get figures such as 25-30 percent. What people do not realize is the incredible impact of that kind of inflation upon their expenses.

THE EFFECT OF PRICE INFLATION ON YOUR EXPENSES

Christians have a need to provide for their families in spite of inflation. With an average inflation rate of 25.9 percent, in twenty years the cost of everything is multiplied by 100. Thus, if eggs cost $1 a dozen now, they would cost $100 per dozen in twenty years. If a house is worth $50,000 now, twenty years later that same house would cost $5 million. If a man is making a $20,000 per year salary today, in twenty years he would have to be making $2 million per year just to break even.

Now you are beginning to see why I call this "hurricane inflation"—the economic storm that will destroy most people. At an average inflation rate of 25.9 percent, what will be the value of a $50,000 life insurance policy twenty years from now? The answer is that it will be almost worthless. If you buy a bond for $1,000 that comes due in twenty years, that $1,000 will be worth the equivalent of $10 at the beginning of the twenty year period. If any individual, and in particular a Christian, does not take the effects of inflation into account, his financial situation is liable to be wiped out.

Provided is a tabulation of expenses with inflation (Table 3.1). Across the top you will see various average annual inflation rates and underneath each percentage you will see the effect that rate of inflation will have on $1,000 worth of expenses over the next twenty years.

So you can understand how to use this table, year 0 (zero) is the current year; year 1 would be one year from now; and year 8 would be eight years from now. If you take, for example, 6 percent as the average annual inflation rate, you can see that you would have to spend $3,207 twenty years from now to buy the same goods and services that cost you $1,000 today. At a 13 percent average inflation, in twenty years expenses would have to be multiplied by a factor of 10. So if an individual were

Table 3.1–Expenses with Inflation
AVERAGE INFLATION RATES 6%–18%

YEAR	YOUR AGE	6%	8%	10%	12%	14%	16%	18%
0.		$1,000	$1,000	$1,000	$1,000	$1,000	$1,000	$1,000
1.		1,060	1,080	1,100	1,120	1,140	1,160	1,180
2.		1,123	1,166	1,210	1,254	1,299	1,345	1,392
3.		1,191	1,259	1,331	1,404	1,481	1,560	1,643
4.		1,262	1,360	1,464	1,573	1,688	1,810	1,939
5.		1,338	1,469	1,610	1,762	1,925	2,100	2,288
6.		1,418	1,586	1,771	1,973	2,194	2,436	2,700
7.		1,503	1,713	1,948	2,210	2,502	2,826	3,185
8.		1,593	1,850	2,143	2,475	2,852	3,278	3,759
9.		1,689	1,999	2,357	2,773	3,251	3,802	4,435
10.		1,790	2,158	2,593	3,105	3,707	4,411	5,234
11.		1,898	2,331	2,853	3,478	4,226	5,117	6,176
12.		2,012	2,518	3,138	3,895	4,817	5,936	7,287
13.		2,132	2,719	3,452	4,363	5,492	6,885	8,599
14.		2,260	2,937	3,797	4,887	6,261	7,987	10,147
15.		2,396	3,172	4,177	5,473	7,137	9,265	11,974
16.		2,540	3,425	4,594	6,130	8,137	10,748	14,129
17.		2,692	3,700	5,054	6,866	9,276	12,467	16,672
18.		2,854	3,996	5,559	7,689	10,575	14,462	19,673
19.		3,025	4,315	6,115	8,612	12,055	16,776	23,214
20.		3,207	4,660	6,727	9,645	13,743	19,422	27,393

AVERAGE INFLATION RATES 20%-60%

YEAR	YOUR AGE	20%	25%	26%	30%	40%	60%
0.		$ 1,000	$ 1,000	$ 1,000	$ 1,000	$ 1,000	$ 1,000
1.		1,200	1,250	1,260	1,300	1,400	1,600
2.		1,440	1,562	1,587	1,690	1,960	2,560
3.		1,728	1,953	2,000	2,197	2,744	4,096
4.		2,073	2,441	2,520	2,856	3,841	6,553
5.		2,488	3,051	3,175	3,712	5,378	10,485
6.		2,985	3,814	4,002	4,826	7,529	16,777
7.		3,583	4,768	5,042	6,274	10,541	26,843
8.		4,299	5,960	6,352	8,157	14,757	42,949
9.		5,159	7,450	8,005	10,604	20,661	68,719
10.		6,191	9,313	10,085	13,785	28,925	109,951
11.		7,430	11,641	12,707	17,921	40,495	175,921
12.		8,916	14,551	16,012	23,298	56,693	281,474
13.		10,699	18,189	20,175	30,287	79,371	450,359
14.		12,839	22,737	25,420	39,373	111,120	720,575
15.		15,407	28,421	32,030	51,185	155,568	1,152,921
16.		18,488	35,527	40,357	66,541	217,795	1,844,674
17.		22,186	44,408	50,850	86,504	304,913	2,951,479
18.		26,623	55,511	64,072	112,455	426,878	4,722,366
19.		31,948	69,388	80,731	146,192	597,630	7,555,786
20.		38,338	86,735	101,721	190,050	836,682	12,089,258

making $25,000 a year today, and the inflation rate were 13 percent, in twenty years he would have to be making $250,000 a year just to stay even.

Let's take another example. Suppose that things get worse, and the average inflation rate runs at about 20 percent. Let's also suppose that a typical American father and mother give their son a $12,000 savings bond that will mature in twenty years, thinking that the bond will provide him with about one year's income (at $1,000 per month). However, what they have not realized is that when he cashes it in in twenty years, it will be worth less than one week's income! It will take $38,338 to purchase what $1,000 will purchase today!

I think you can see that it is absolutely *essential* to take inflation into account in planning your future, and particularly your future retirement. Most of us would like to retire someday (the sooner the better). Unfortunately, if we do not take inflation into account in our retirement planning, we could be in dire financial difficulty.

Now I would like for you to turn to Table 3.1 and write in your age all the way down the second column. After you have done that, circle the inflation rate percentage at the top that is nearest to your estimated inflation rate, which you calculated earlier in this chapter. In our example, the estimated inflation rate was 11.2 percent. Therefore, in Table 3.1 we would circle 12 percent. Use either 10 percent or 12 percent, but don't try to fiddle with averaging the two. What we are after here is a rough estimate for planning purposes, not a detailed financial statement.

INFLATION AND YOUR PERSONAL
FINANCIAL FUTURE

Obviously everyone's expenses are not exactly $1,000 per month; they may be more or less. In Table 3.2 you will find a form that will be of help to you in projecting the potential effects of inflation on your personal situation. The form is shown in greatly reduced form in Table 3.2. You may wish to draw a

Table 3.2–Income and Expense Projection with Inflation

For _____   Date _____

| | (1) | (2) EXPENSES BASIS NOW | (3) FROM INFL. TABLE | (4) EXPENSES ___ % INFL. | (5) INCOME FROM: | (6) INCOME FROM: | (7) INCOME FROM: | (8) TOTAL INCOME | (9) SURPLUS (DEFICIT) |
YEAR	AGE								
0.									
1.									
2.									
3.									
4.									
5.									
6.									
7.									
8.									
9.									
10.									
11.									
12.									
13.									
14.									
15.									
16.									
17.									
18.									
19.									
20.									

bigger copy of this form or try to write small and utilize the one in the book. Multiple copies of this form in full size are contained in *The Almighty And The Dollar Personal Planning Workbook,* which we suggest you get to assist you in planning and investing. (Information on how to obtain this workbook is found in the back of this book in Appendix B.) It's important that you complete this form; however, I would suggest that you complete your reading of this chapter and then come back and complete the form.

When you are ready to complete Table 3.2, first write your age in column 1, starting with year 0 as the current year. Then copy into column 3 the entire column that you selected as your estimate of the future inflation rate from Table 3.1. That is the easy part. Now you need to do some estimating. For column 2, estimate your expenses as though there were not going to be any price escalation (inflation). You can do this column on either a monthly or an annual basis. Start with year 0 as the current year. It may be that your expenses will be a constant number—perhaps $2,000 per month—all the way down. On the other hand, it is more likely that your expenses would start out at $2,000 per month but would increase or decrease with time. For example, if you knew your house would be paid for in 1988, your expenses might then drop to $1,700 per month. Then maybe your children would be out of college and on their own by 1992, and your expenses would drop again.

Don't forget that it is very likely that your expenses will increase if you think you are going to be moving into a nicer home or driving nicer cars as time goes by.

After you have thought through and completed column 2, multiply each entry in column 2 by the corresponding entry in column 3 and put the results in column 4. Column 4 will be your projected expenses, taking into account the average inflation percentage that you think we will have between now and the end of the century.

After taking care of the expense side, we need to analyze the income side. We have three columns left for income. It may be that in column 5 you wish to include both your salary and your company retirement benefits. On the form I would call this "S & R" (salary and retirement). In looking at your salary, you should take into account raises that you anticipate along the line. If your retirement is a fixed percentage of your highest income year(s), enter that as a constant figure (same each year) from the year of your retirement forward. It may be that in column 6 you would also like to show your anticipated social security income. Possibly in column 7 you have rental income, dividend income, or income you anticipate from the sale of gold or silver coins. After you have completed these three columns, total them into column 8. Now comes the simplest step but the one where the rubber meets the road. To calculate column 9, subtract column 4 (your expenses) from column 8 (your total income). This will give you how much surplus you have left over, or how much you will go in the hole. If it is a negative number, put it in parentheses to indicate a deficit.

A few things about your personal situation should now be very apparent to you. One thing that you have probably realized is that at any point that your income becomes fixed while your expenses continue to increase because of inflation, you will be in bad trouble.

Unfortunately, many of our retired people already fall into this category; they have a constant income while expenses are continuing to increase. Now is the time to prepare for being able to meet your retirement needs in spite of the ravages of inflation.

I might add that the Bible has much to say about Christians taking care of the widows and helpless and providing for them. I do not think we should rely on the federal government to take over the responsibilities the Bible says are clearly ours. We cannot expect financial prosperity or even stability unless we are living in tune with God's financial guidelines.

WHAT TO DO TO PREPARE FOR HURRICANE INFLATION

Don't let a lull in inflation fool you. Inflation will return.

There are many things you can do to prepare for the inflationary storm that is coming. I will present five here in a very general way, and we will deal with them in detail later in the book:

1. Don't have your money (except on a temporary basis) in anything that is denominated in a fixed amount of U.S. dollars. This would include bonds, whole life insurance (not term insurance), savings accounts, and cash. (Although I still recommend keeping a certain amount in a savings account and about three months' worth of your monthly expenses in pure cash.)

2. Invest in ways that will make, on the average, 5-10 percent over the rate of inflation. Anything making less than that today is causing you to fall behind.

3. If you are a sophisticated invester, consider opening a commodity account with risk capital, possibly handled by a money manager; this can also help increase your average profits. This may help offset inflation losses in purchasing power on your savings accounts and cash positions.

4. Buy hard assets, such as gold coins, silver coins, and real estate to help keep your average yearly profits higher than inflation.

5. Inflation transfers wealth from lenders to borrowers; be an intelligent borrower for investment purposes that can give you the leverage that will help transfer wealth to you.

Many investment considerations will be covered in the next section, so I will not deal with those here. Now let's expand a little on the last suggestion for preparing to survive inflation.

McKEEVER'S RULE #2 FOR THE 1980's:

WEALTH WILL BE TRANSFERRED FROM LENDERS TO BORROWERS

I will use a simple example to show what I mean by this. Table 3.3 shows the present financial status of three men. Note what happens to their financial status after the prices of everything double. Neil Neutral had a $10,000 loan against his house and $10,000 in a savings account. In reality, this $10,000 in a savings account says that he has loaned this amount to a local savings and loan association. The amount of money that he owes and the amount of money owed to him are the same. His lending/borrowing ratio is 1/1, which is 1.00. This puts him in a neutral position. Thus, if the price of his house doubles, his net worth will also exactly double. This means that his net worth would have the same amount of purchasing power as it did before the prices of everything, including his house, doubled.

Benny Borrower has a $60,000 loan against his house and his lending/borrowing ratio is 1/6, or 0.17. He is in good shape to take advantage of the transfer of wealth by inflation. His net

Table 3.3

NEIL NEUTRAL (1/1 = 1.00)	NOW	WHEN PRICES DOUBLE
ASSETS		
Savings (Lending)	$ 10,000	$ 10,000
House	80,000	160,000
LIABILITIES AND NET WORTH		
Loan (Borrowing)	10,000	10,000
Net Worth	80,000	160,000
BENNY BORROWER (1/6 = 0.17)		
ASSETS		
Savings (Lending)	10,000	10,000
House	80,000	160,000
LIABILITIES AND NET WORTH		
Loan (Borrowing)	60,000	60,000
Net Worth	30,000	110,000
LARRY LENDER (8/1 = 8.00)		
ASSETS		
Savings (Lending)	80,000	80,000
House	80,000	160,000
LIABILITIES AND NET WORTH		
Loan (Borrowing)	10,000	10,000
Net Worth	150,000	230,000

worth starts out at $30,000, but after the price of everything doubles, his net worth is $110,000. This is an increase in net worth of almost four times, while prices only doubled. Therefore, his real purchasing power has almost doubled.

Larry Lender is exactly the opposite. He has just about paid off his house, and has a large amount of money in a savings account. His lending/borrowing ratio is 8/1, which is equal to 8.00. He is in bad shape as far as inflation goes. When the prices of everything double, his net worth does not even *double;* it only goes from $150,000 to $230,000. It needed to go to at least $300,000 for him to simply break even. His net worth only increased 44 percent while prices increased 100 percent. Thus, Larry Lender *lost* wealth because of inflation, while Benny Borrower *gained* net worth because of inflation.

Let us point out that what we have labeled as "savings" is really any asset measured in a fixed amount of paper dollars. This could be a mortgage you took back when you sold a piece of property, a whole life insurance policy, bonds, a retirement policy, money you loaned to relatives. Under the category "loan" could be a mortgage against your house, money borrowed for an investment in a farm, personal loans, credit cards, and so forth.

I would encourage you to sit down and calculate your own personal lending/borrowing ratio. If it is above 1.00, inflation will steal wealth from you. The bigger the number, the worse you will fare under inflation. In this case (just like in golf scores), the smaller the number, the better. Therefore, if your number is below 0.4 you should be set all right for inflation. Before you erroneously charge out and recklessly borrow money, or run up credit card bills, we need to take a look at credit.

WISE USE OF CREDIT

It will vary from family to family and individual to individual how much indebtedness one should have. Remember, we are talking about indebtedness for purchasing appreciating assets. The mortgage on your home would fit into this category of borrowing for purchasing appreciating assets, whereas borrowing to buy furniture or an automobile would not fit this category.

As a rule of thumb, an individual should owe on these types of appreciating investments from one up to five times his annual salary. If inflation rates are higher than interest rates, this type of borrowing is far more attractive than if the interest rates are higher than the inflation rates. God can lead you to get totally out of any kind of debt and, if He does this, you certainly should. However, intelligent borrowing for investments makes good sense in an inflationary environment.

Another possibility for increasing our borrowing is through our credit cards. Most people use credit cards in a very stupid way. (If I offend you, I'm glad. Perhaps it will jolt you into wise use of credit cards.) Credit cards can either give you a handy source of funds for true emergencies (car breakdown on a trip, etc.), or they can eat you alive, forcing you to pay a ridiculous 18 percent or more in interest. Credit cards used properly must be paid in full *every time* you receive a bill. If you cannot use credit cards in this way, my advice would be to take out the scissors, cut the cards in half and throw them away. Even if you have to borrow the money to initially pay them off, you would be paying less interest than you would be paying to the credit card companies. Once you've paid off the balances owed against these accounts you must then discipline yourself every month to totally pay off the credit cards. If for any reason some month you are not able to pay all charges, you should lock that credit card away somewhere and not use it again until you have paid it off completely.

It is interesting to note that Sears & Roebuck basically breaks even on the merchandise they sell. Almost *all* of their profit comes from the interest payments that their credit card customers pay to them. Therefore, companies like Sears will do everything they can to encourage you to charge and to charge more.

In short, paying off credit cards monthly is essential. If you can't pay them off *every month,* destroy the cards.

HOW TO BORROW ON YOUR HOME EQUITY

Be very sure that God is leading you if you borrow against your home. If He tells you to do this, you need to do it wisely. *Personal Finance* (P.O. Box 2599, Landover Hills, MD 20784), in the December 20, 1978 issue, had an excellent write-up on this subject. They said:

"The best investment most people have made in recent years is their home. But how do you capitalize on that appreciation when you need the money for, say, investment purposes, a second home, or to pay off pressing debts? Most people are apparently cashing in on the equity in their homes by refinancing their mortgages, which isn't always a wise idea. In many cases, a second mortgage may end up being a lot cheaper than refinancing your original mortgage.

"To begin with, you'll save substantial paperwork and legal fees by getting a second mortgage. When you refinance, you usually have to go through the whole business of closing again. That means pretty hefty costs —just to get a new mortgage drawn up can cost you $2,000. And if there's a prepayment clause, you may also have to pay what could be a substantial sum as a penalty for prepaying your original mortgage.

"By contrast, second mortgages don't disturb your original mortgage —which means you won't have to pay new closing costs or a penalty fee. The only fee you'll probably have to pay is a one-time charge that ranges from $15 to $150 to cover the paperwork. One of the reasons why the costs are low is that the lender is concerned mainly with your ability to meet the payments, and hence won't spend considerable sums analyzing the value of the property.

"And even the interest rates on a second mortgage—which range anywhere from 11.5 to 18 percent—may not be as bad as they seem at first glance. That's especially true if you recently took out a first mortgage and haven't yet made much of a dent in the principal repayments. In fact, refinancing your original mortgage would probably be cheaper only if you have paid it down to the point where you have considerably reduced the amount of principal that you owe—which usually takes over 10 years. (A typical mortgage is structured so that the early payments—say, for the first 10 years—are heavily weighted toward the interest. If you refinanced, you'd have to start paying interest on the amount now outstanding as well as the additional money you borrow. Over the long-term, that could be costlier than a second mortgage.)

"Here's how the numbers look: Let's assume that you bought your home 10 years ago for $55,000. Let's say you took out a 25-year mortgage for 90 percent of the value of the house, or $50,000, at an interest rate of 6½%. Now assume that 10 years later your house has appreciated at an annual rate of 3 percent (a very conservative figure) and is currently worth $38,689—which gives you an equity of $33,311. That's a lot of money to have sitting idle.

"If you refinanced or went in for a second mortgage, most lenders today would probably lend you only 80 percent of the value of your house, rather than the 90 percent you got when mortgage money was available on easier terms. That means you could borrow a total of $57,600 on the house (80 percent of its present value of $72,000). Since the outstanding balance on your mortgage is $38,689, you can raise an additional $18,911 by refinancing your current mortgage, or by taking out a second one.

"As you can see from the chart below, you'll end up saving $53,353 in interest costs if you take out a second mortgage. Granted, your combined monthly payments for the second mortgage and the original mortgage will be $131 a month higher than what you'd have to pay if you refinanced your mortgage. (But you'll be able to increase your tax deductions for interest.)

	Refinancing Your Mortgage vs.	Combination Original &	Second Mortgage
Amount of loan	$57,600	$38,689*	$18,911
Interest rate	9%	6.5%	12.5%
Length of loan	25 years	15 years	10 years
Monthly payment	$484	$338	$277
Interest cost over term of loan	$87,034	$19,386	$14,295
Fees	$2,000**	None	$15 to 150
Total monthly payments at beginning	$484		$615
Total interest cost	$87,034		$33,681

*Balance of original mortgage outstanding

**Fees could amount to $2000 for new closing costs and the possibility of a prepayment penalty.

"However, before you get a second mortgage, look into other alternatives. Be sure to check out, for instance, the terms on a loan for the special purpose you have in mind. For example, education loans are often less costly than a second mortgage loan might be, but might not be made for as long a period."

OWE NO MAN ANYTHING?

You may say, "Wait a minute, I thought a Christian should not be in debt." Many religious leaders—such as Pat Robertson, whom I love and support—are advising people to be out of debt. I think that is a valid concern so we will deal with that next.

Let's first begin by going back and looking at the passage in the Bible that says; "Owe nothing to anyone. . . ." It is found in Romans 13:

> **8   Owe nothing to anyone except to love one another; for he who loves his neighbor has fulfilled** *the* **law.**
>
> **9   For this, "YOU SHALL NOT COMMIT ADULTERY, YOU SHALL NOT MURDER, YOU SHALL NOT STEAL, YOU SHALL NOT COVET," and if there is any other commandment, it is summed up in this saying, "YOU SHALL LOVE YOUR NEIGHBOR AS YOURSELF."**
>
> **10   Love does no wrong to a neighbor; love therefore is the fulfillment of** *the* **law.**

If you read this paragraph (all three verses) as a unit, you will probably, as I have, conclude that the passage is not talking about *money* at all but is indeed talking about *love.* In its complete context, there is no way this passage can be applied to a broad financial situation. In verse 7 there is instruction on taxes, so the most one could do would be to conjecture that that passage means not to owe anyone taxes.

Just as an aside, I find that many of the books written for Christians about their finances are written by pastors, ministers, or at best Christians fresh out of college with a degree in economics. With love and compassion for these brothers who have good intentions, I must say that they are simply not professionals in the financial world. As well meant as their advice may be, it is frequently either poor or misleading. This is especially true in this area of "owe nothing to anyone" which many ministers and "advisors" are so adamant about. This kind of financial advice can mean your financial destruction in the coming inflation.

I had one T.V. interviewer ask me concerning this subject if a person wouldn't sleep better if he were totally out of debt. I answered, "Yes, of course a person would sleep better." Then I asked him which of the men in the parable of the talents probably slept best—the one with the five talents who went out and took risks and traded or the one who buried his talents in the ground. He replied red-faced, "I guess the one who buried it in the ground." Sleeping better was not one of Christ's criteria for being a good steward.

I once had a long discussion with an author of one of the Christian money books. He maintained strongly that every Christian should be out of debt. He said that being debt-free was the way to "play it safe." He then asked me if I agreed and was surprised when I answered with a quiet no. I asked him about the parable of the talents and which one of the three he felt "played it safe." He had to admit it was the one who buried the money in the ground.

Now let me emphasize something. I am not talking about abusive use of credit cards. As I said, some people use credit cards poorly, charging on them to their full limits with no prospects of paying them down. They wind up giving away 18 percent of that portion of their income as interest charges on these credit cards. That is being a poor steward. What we are talking about here is intelligent borrowing for investment purposes, such as a mortgage on a property as we discussed earlier. These are the kinds of decisions a Christian should pray about, seeking God's specific guidance concerning whether or not to borrow for investments. But keep in mind that "hurricane inflation" is coming. One of the ways to dampen this destructive force is with intelligent borrowing because borrowing transfers wealth from the lender to the borrower.

McKEEVER'S RULE #3 FOR THE 1980's:

BE SURE YOUR INCOME STAYS AHEAD OF THE INFLATION RATE

Let's assume for the moment that the average salary in the United States increases at the same rate as inflation (by the way, it doesn't). If the average salary is keeping even with inflation, those whose salaries increase at less than the average lose purchasing power to inflation, and those whose salaries increase at a rate greater than the average, gain purchasing power as related to inflation. This means that at this minute if your salary is not increasing at least at the same percentage as the inflation rate, you are losing ground to inflation.

If you are a professional individual, you might look at your fee schedule and determine whether your fees are higher by an amount equal to inflation than they were last year. If they are not, you are losing ground to inflation. If you own your business, be sure to give yourself raises that will compensate for inflation. If you are paid a salary by someone else, let your employer know that you are aware of the inflation situation. For example, if you are making $2,000 per month, and the inflation rate is 15 percent, with a $300 raise you would simply break even with inflation. The amount of the raise that is over $300 is really your increase. If you are bashful about discussing these things with your employer, inflation will move income from you to someone else who is not so bashful.

If you are not yet retired, be sure and examine your retirement program, and be sure that it is indexed to the cost of living. This means that your benefits will go up as inflation goes up.

Even if you have to put a little more into the retirement policy to get it indexed to the cost of living, it would be well worth it.

SUMMARY AND CONCLUSION

We have looked at what inflation is and what really causes it. The government passing out unbacked fiat money forces prices up. It looks as if this is going to continue because of the welfare programs, the attitudes of the politicians. Continued inflation is simply the nature of a fiat (unbacked) currency.

When Ronald Reagan became President, I asked the question: "Can he change or stop this inflationary future?" My answer then was this: "I've known Ronald Reagan since before he was Governor of California and I've shared the platform with him frequently at various conferences. I know of no one I would rather have as President of the United States. I believe that he will do the best possible job of slowing inflation down a bit, but I do not think that he will be able to reverse things."

Even with all of Reagan's efforts, we have incredibly large federal deficits. The percent of the GNP that the government spends has risen under him. The only reason that inflation is not roaring now is the recession and the huge inflow of foreign funds to buy U.S. bonds, thus financing the federal deficit. Those funds will run out and back will come inflation, worse than ever.

Reagan has been able to slow down the approach of "hurricane inflation" but the hurricane moves on and is going to hit us in spite of the best efforts of Ronald Reagan and his administration. With all my heart I wish I could believe otherwise. I will gladly change my mind when I see two consecutive years when federal revenues exceed federal expenditures. Until then, we need to assume that inflation will return and eventually worsen.

We then looked at the impact "hurricane inflation" is going to have on our finances. At an average inflation rate of 25.9 percent, everything goes up by a factor of 100 by the year 2000. Thus, a loaf of bread costing $1 now would cost $100 then.

We then saw that anything denominated in a fixed number of U.S. dollars, such as savings accounts, bonds, and whole-life insurance, will lose purchasing power and will be worth very little by the year 2000. I encouraged you to take this into account in your financial planning.

We then looked at a couple of rules for protecting ourselves against inflation. The first was that wealth would be transferred from the lenders to the borrowers, so God-guided, intelligent borrowing is wise. The second was that we must watch our incomes and try to make sure they increase at least as much as inflation.

Some additional rules will be discussed in Chapter 5 as we begin to get into investments. However, before one can possibly think about making wise investments, he must first get an accurate picture of his present status and establish his goals. This is the subject we will take up in the next chapter.

4

HOW TO GET MONEY TO INVEST

After reading about the need to invest money profitably in order to beat inflation, the average reader of this book may be thinking, "That's all very interesting, but I'm barely making ends meet and don't have any money at all left over to invest."

This may be true, but I have good news for you. There are ways to bring your financial condition into order so that you will have surplus funds that you can invest for the Lord's glory.

The principles found in this chapter apply both to those who are barely making it and to those who are wealthy. People who have surplus money and who just spend without any thought to a budget or conserving their money need to think through their expenditures to be sure they are glorifying the Lord. Those just barely making it need to think through their expenditures for survival purposes.

Perhaps, the Lord has already blessed you financially and you have ample funds for investments. Since this chapter is primarily directed toward people who are having problems accumulating capital for investment, you may want to skip it and go on to Chapter 5. My suggestion is that you read it anyway; you may find some thoughts that will help you get even better mileage from your income and assets.

A CHANGE IN LIFESTYLE

People can do just about anything they want to do. However, since life is full of choices, significant changes in one's lifestyle may be required in order to accomplish certain things.

When I lived in Costa Rica, the average wage there was about $400 per year. People in the U.S. looked at that with dreamy eyes and thought, "Oh, if I could be there and live on only $400 per year." Actually they could if they wanted to live like the natives there in Costa Rica. The natives live very simply; many of them do not have electricity; they wash their clothes in the creek, and in general live rather primitively. But the person who, with stars in his eyes, wants to live on $400 per year likely wouldn't consider adopting a lifestyle like those natives. In order to have a lifestyle similar to the one he enjoys in the United States, it would cost him just as much if not more in Costa Rica.

But let's bring this closer to home as I share a couple of examples of the kinds of problems Christians describe to me as I travel around the country. There was a young, single man whom I met during an appearance on "The 700 Club" who heard me talk on Christians and their finances. He said to me that there was no way that he could save 10 percent of his salary. In fact, he said he didn't even have enough to tithe. He said, almost with tears in his eyes, that he was just barely able to keep his head above water and pay his bills.

Having been through this many times, you must forgive my skepticism for not sympathizing with this young man. Since he had come to me with his problem, I felt free to ask him a couple of questions. I asked him how much he paid for his apartment and he told me $600 per month. I asked him if he lived alone and he said, "yes." When I asked him why he didn't get a roommate to share the rent and utilities with him, he replied that roommates were a lot of trouble. They kept the place messy, and he wouldn't have much time alone. It is very possible that these reasons were of the Lord and that God actually did want him to live alone. It is also equally possible that these were very selfish motives.

I then asked the young man if there were any apartments in the city that he could rent for $200 per month. His reply to me was, "Yes, but I wouldn't want to live in one of them." So I shared with him that at last we had gotten down to the bedrock problem. He could not tithe and obey God because he didn't want to live in a lifestyle that was below his current one. This was a clear case of his will as opposed to God's will.

Another case was that of a young Christian woman who had just come through a tragic divorce. She, too, told me that she could barely make ends meet and couldn't save or even tithe. I then asked her if she owned her home, to which she replied, "Yes." In looking at the monthly payments, which were in excess of $700, I began to inquire about the value of the home when they purchased it, how long they had had it, and so forth. It turned out that the home was probably worth close to $90,000 and that she probably had about $50,000–$60,000 equity in it.

I asked her why she didn't sell the home and rent an apartment. She would certainly have been able to find a nice apartment for her and her young daughter for less than $700 per month. She said that she couldn't do that because her daughter viewed their house as her home. I commented that people with children often move and the children adjust, but this did not seem to register on her at all so I dropped the subject. However, this again was a clear case of a person's desires (wants) preventing her from being a good steward and also from obeying the Lord with her financial tithe.

If you find yourself in a similar position—barely able to keep your head above the water financially, with nothing left to save or even tithe—you need to face the fact that if you lowered your standard of living, even a little, you could indeed give your full tithe to the Lord and also be able to save 10 percent. This lowering of the standard of living may not even require moving from the place where you live, but it will require changes.

If you find yourself in this state, I would encourage you to pause right now and ask the Lord to help you to be willing to change. If you are not willing to change, then the rest of this chapter, and probably the rest of this book, will not be of any value to you.

Lord, help all of us to be willing to change our lifestyles and live more like Jesus so that we can be good stewards and pay at least the tithe to the Lord's work.

FIND OUT YOUR PRESENT FINANCIAL STATUS

I believe that finding out your realistic financial status is a wise thing for anyone to do, regardless of whether you are poor, wealthy, or anywhere in between. It is difficult for God to lead us to make changes unless we clearly know where we are at present.

I've read many books and seen many systems on budgeting and other related financial subjects. However, almost no one ever uses these because they are so complicated. What I am going to suggest to you is simplicity itself. It will require almost no extra effort on your part.

This method utilizes your regular checkbook. If you do not have a checking account, I would encourage you to open one so you can have a record of your expenditures. If you are married and have only one checking account, I would encourage you to open a second one for your spouse. If the husband is the one who primarily handles the finances, he could periodically move money over to his wife's account. The reason why this is necessary is that we are going to be writing checks for *everything,* including those things your wife buys.

The idea is to take a one-month period (it does not have to be a calendar month; it can start tomorrow) and write checks for absolutely everything. Do not charge anything and spend as little cash as you can. This way you can know exactly where your expenditures are going.

NEEDS AND WANTS

Before I tell you about the slight change I would recommend you make in your checkbook, I need to touch on another subject. That is the difference between "needs" and "wants." In many expenditure categories there are things that we need for our daily sustenance, and there are also things that we want. One way to differentiate between these is to use what I call the "basket shopping system."

Go to the supermarket you always go to and shop as you always do. Then before you go to the checkout counter, stop by and get a second basket. Into this empty basket place all of the things that you "want" but really don't need to sustain your life. In this category might be soft drinks, candies, gadgets, potted flowers, and anything that is obviously not necessary for the sustenance of your life.

There are some things that are on the margin line between wants and needs, such as toothpaste. One can clean his teeth just as well (or possibly better) using salt and baking soda. In many countries of the world, toothpaste is a sheer luxury. It is obviously a matter between you and the Lord as to which of these marginal items you want to include in the "want" category. When you have completed this separation, go to the checkout stand, and have them check out and total the two baskets separately. *Write two checks,* not one. In your check register, the check for the essential items will be entered as *food-need,* and the items of an optional nature would be entered as *food-want* (more on this later).

We could apply this same shopping technique to buying clothing or just about any other items. For example, a lady might go to a clothing store to buy a dress that she really needs in order to replace one that she has worn out. While she is there she might see other items she "wants" such as a silk scarf, a fancy apron, or some other item of clothing that is very pretty but is not really something that she needs. My counsel to her would be to write two checks in an effort to try to find out the true status of her financial situation. In her checkbook she should label one check *clothing-need* and the other one *clothing-want.*

The same procedure should be followed for your household. There are some appliances and items of furniture that fall into the "need" category, and there are also many things that we buy for our homes that are purely in the "want" category. Again, these should be entered in the checkbook in the appropriate categories.

You may encounter some checkout clerks who think you are absolutely bananas when you take the time to write two checks. However, if the Lord wants you to find out your present financial status so you can bring your financial affairs into order, that's a small price to pay.

Your check register may look something like the check register below shown as Figure 4.1. Please take a moment to examine this check register. You will see that checks have been

CHEQUE NO.	DATE	CHEQUE ISSUED TO CAT	AMOUNT OF CHEQUE	√	DATE OF DEP.	AMOUNT OF DEPOSIT	BALANCE
953	10/5	FOOD – NEED	43 12				
954	10/5	FOOD–WANT	26 52				
955	10/5	RENT	620 00				
—	10/7	MY SALARY	→			300 00	
—	10/8	WIFE'S SALARY	→			200 00	
956	10/9	FILM	8 00				
957	10/9	CLOTHES – NEED	30 00				
958	10/9	CLOTHES – WANT	45 00				
959	10/10	CAR PAYMENT	312 00				
960	10/11	GASOLINE	10 52				
961	10/12	PICTURE FRAMES	32 00				
962	10/14	DRUGS	26 00				
963	10/14	DRUGSTORE – MISC.	32 00				
964	10/15	PHONE – NEED	22 30				
965	10/15	PHONE – WANT	83 00				
966	10/16	CAMERA LENS	85 00				
967	10/17	BOOKS – NEED	12 00				
968	10/18	BOOKS – FUN	22 50				
969	10/19	FOOD – NEED	41 19				

REGISTER BEFORE WRITING CHEQUE

Figure 4.1

written for *everything*, including gasoline. Under food, clothes, telephone, and books, two checks were written—one for the items that were needed and another for the items that were simply wanted.

As you can see, we've hand drawn an additional column into the checkbook labeled "CAT" (Category). If you don't have room to draw this column, you can use the column which is titled "Date of Deposit" indicated by the arrow for your CAT column. We will come back to this CAT column in a moment, and you will see how it will make determining your present status a real breeze.

PERSONAL FINANCIAL CONTROL FORM

At the end of the month you will need to summarize the month's expenditures from the check register. You will place the summary on a sheet called the "Personal Financial Control Form." A sample of this is shown on the next page. (A supply of these is contained in *The Almighty and the Dollar Personal Planning Workbook.*)

If you will refer to Figure 4.2, you will see that this form has thirty-four lines numbered 1 to 34 and four columns labeled A, B, C, and D. Initially, you will work only in column C where you will enter your actual take-home pay and the actual expenses from your checkbook register. For example, you will probably have written several checks and entered them in your register under the category, *food–need.* You are going to need to total the amount of all those checks from that category and then put the total on line 13 under column C of the "Personal Financial Control Form."

I also suggest that you take the line numbers from the "Personal Financial Control Form" and enter them in your check register under your category column (CAT) as shown in Figure 4.3.

Entering the line numbers in this column makes it easy for you to go through the checkbook register and make decisions concerning which categories the various expenses fit into with-

PERSONAL FINANCIAL CONTROL – OPERATING PLAN-ACT			

Name _____ For Month Beginning _____

INCOME	(A) WANTS	(B) BUDGET	(C) ACTUAL	(D) OVER/UNDER
(1) Salary	/ / / / /	_____	_____	_____
(2) Spouse's Salary	/ / / / /	_____	_____	_____
(3) Other Income	/ / / / /	_____	_____	_____
(4) TOTAL INCOME	/ / / / /	_____	_____	_____
EXPENSES				
(5) Tithe	/ / / / /	_____	_____	_____
(6) Savings	/ / / / /	_____	_____	_____
(7) Rent/Mortgage	/ / / / /	_____	_____	_____
(8) Fuel	/ / / / /	_____	_____	_____
(9) Electricity	/ / / / /	_____	_____	_____
(10) Water	/ / / / /	_____	_____	_____
(11) Phone—Need	/ / / / /	_____	_____	_____
(12) Phone—Want		_____	_____	_____
(13) Food—Need	/ / / / /	_____	_____	_____
(14) Food—Want		_____	_____	_____
(15) Clothing—Need	/ / / / /	_____	_____	_____
(16) Clothing—Want		_____	_____	_____
(17) Household—Need	/ / / / /	_____	_____	_____
(18) Household—Want		_____	_____	_____
(19) Medical	/ / / / /	_____	_____	_____
(20) Drug Store—Wants		_____	_____	_____
(21) Auto Payment	/ / / / /	_____	_____	_____
(22) Auto Operation	/ / / / /	_____	_____	_____
(23) Recreation		_____	_____	_____
(24) Toys—Adult & Child		_____	_____	_____
(25) Food Production	/ / / / /	_____	_____	_____
(26) Gifts		_____	_____	_____
(27) Contributions		_____	_____	_____
(28) Books—Education		_____	_____	_____
(29) Loans Paid—Principal		_____	_____	_____
(30) Loans Paid—Interest		_____	_____	_____
(31) Miscellaneous		_____	_____	_____
(32)		_____	_____	_____
(33)		_____	_____	_____
(34) TOTAL EXPENSES	_____	_____	_____	_____

Figure 4.2

out worrying about totals or calculations. After you have done this, you will go back and total all checks that are in the same category, I would suggest two things when you do this. One is that you total only the dollars (ignoring the cents). The other is that you place a check mark by each item after you have added it into your total so that you know that it has been accounted for. In Figure 4.3 you can see that we've placed a check mark by the two items labeled *food-need* as we totaled them together and came up with a total of $84. These two checks were the only expenditures in the category of *food-need* for the month that we were looking at so we would enter this $84 on our "Personal Financial Control Form" as our total amount spent on necessary food for that month.

CHEQUE NO.	DATE	CHEQUE ISSUED TO	CAT	AMOUNT OF CHEQUE		DATE OF DEP.	AMOUNT OF DEPOSIT	BALANCE	
953	10/5	FOOD - NEED ✓	13	43	12				
954	10/5	FOOD - WANT	14	26	52				
955	10/5	RENT	7	620	00				
—	10/7	MY SALARY	1	→			300	00	
—	10/8	WIFE'S SALARY	2	→			200	00	
956	10/9	FILM	20	8	00				
957	10/9	CLOTHES - NEED	15	30	00				
958	10/9	CLOTHES - WANT	16	45	00				
959	10/10	CAR PAYMENT	21	312	00				
960	10/11	GASOLINE	22	10	52				
961	10/12	PICTURE FRAMES	18	32	00				
962	10/14	DRUGS	19	26	00				
963	10/14	DRUGSTORE - MISC.	20	32	00				
964	10/15	PHONE - NEED	11	22	30				
965	10/15	PHONE - WANT	12	83	00				
966	10/16	CAMARA LENS	24	85	00				
967	10/17	BOOKS - NEED	28	12	00				
968	10/18	BOOKS - FUN	23	22	50				
969	10/19	FOOD - NEED ✓	13	41	19				

REGISTER BEFORE WRITING CHEQUE

Figure 4.3

We can then total column A to find out how much we are spending in the "want" category and can clearly see the difference in the costs of our wants and our needs.

After doing this for a month (or possibly two months) a distressed couple, such as Mr. and Mrs. I. M. Sinking, could have their "Personal Financial Control Form" look something like

the one shown in Figure 4.4. At that point at least they would
know their realistic present status.

PERSONAL FINANCIAL CONTROL – OPERATING PLAN-ACT				
Name _____ For Month Beginning _____				
INCOME	(A) WANTS	(B) BUDGET	(C) ACTUAL	(D) OVER/UNDER
(1) Salary	/ / / / /		1200	
(2) Spouse's Salary	/ / / / /		900	
(3) Other Income	/ / / / /		0	
(4) TOTAL INCOME	/ / / / /		2100	
EXPENSES				
(5) Tithe	/ / / / /		0	
(6) Savings	/ / / / /		0	
(7) Rent/Mortgage	/ / / / /		620	
(8) Fuel	/ / / / /		150	
(9) Electricity	/ / / / /		60	
(10) Water	/ / / / /		10	
(11) Phone–Need	/ / / / /		22	
(12) Phone–Want	83		83	
(13) Food–Need	/ / / / /		300	
(14) Food–Want	250		250	
(15) Clothing–Need	/ / / / /		100	
(16) Clothing–Want	150		150	
(17) Household–Need	/ / / / /		0	
(18) Household–Want	0		0	
(19) Medical	/ / / / /		30	
(20) Drug Store–Wants	42		42	
(21) Auto Payment	/ / / / /		312	
(22) Auto Operation	/ / / / /		100	
(23) Recreation	0		0	
(24) Toys–Adult & Child	85		85	
(25) Food Production	/ / / / /		0	
(26) Gifts	0		0	
(27) Contributions	0		0	
(28) Books–Education	0		0	
(29) Loans Paid–Principal	0		0	
(30) Loans Paid–Interest	0		0	
(31) Miscellaneous	0		200	
(32)				
(33)				
(34) TOTAL EXPENSES	610		2514	

Figure 4.4

Another important step in using this "Personal Financial Control Form" concerns credit cards. For credit cards, such as Visa and Master Charge, when you make a payment, you will again write two checks. The amount of the check that will go to pay interest should be entered on line 30. The rest of the payment (the other check amount) should be entered on line 29, representing what actually goes to pay off the principal of that loan.

Under "Auto Operation" you should enter car washings, parking costs, auto repairs, and tires. For hobbies such as photography, stamp collecting, skiing, and so forth, the amounts can be entered either as "recreation" or "toys" depending on how you might view them. Some people will try to claim that their recreation is "essential." You can see that it is certainly not essential for life if you look at the people in any of the Third World nations who somehow survive with minimal food and shelter.

Now that we have determined our present status, this is the time to prayerfully get on our knees before the Lord and ask Him what changes He would have us to make in our personal finances.

START WITH YOUR INCOME

As we begin to think about making changes, there is a process that we need to go through, and it begins with our income figure.

The income that we will deal with is your "net income." I would define your net income as your remaining income after the minimum amount of taxes have been withheld. The reason I say *minimum* amount of taxes is that some people declare fewer dependents than they actually have so they will have excess withholding tax taken out of their pay. They do this so they can get a big tax refund in the following year.

Anyway you want to look at that, it is poor stewardship, and I definitely do not recommend it. The government has your money all year long, and they don't even pay you interest on it!

Thus, I feel that a Christian should have the minimum allowable amount of taxes deducted, and he should use the difference as the Lord leads him.

If you have hospitalization or any other deductions taken out of your pay check, I would, for planning purposes, add those amounts back into your salary and create a line on your financial control form to show those as expenditures.

A young married couple may want to consider showing the salary figure and establishing a budget based only on the husband's salary in the event that the wife becomes pregnant and is unable to work. This should be a matter of prayer in determining how to control your family finances.

To demonstrate how to use this approach to financial control and budgeting, we will take the I. M. Sinking family as an illustration (see Figure 4.5). Mr. Sinking had been having about $200 per month in extra withholding taxes taken out of his salary. This he has now corrected, which gives him $200 more net income per month for a total of $2300 per month.

After praying about it, they felt they should tithe the first 10 percent to the Lord and save the second 10 percent so these were the first two items entered into their budget.

After further prayer, they felt they should not change their place of residence (although they were willing to) so in the budget column B, they left their rent amount the same. However, they felt they could save money on fuel costs by keeping their house a little cooler and by tacking clear plastic over the outsides of their windows. They also felt that they could save about 30 percent on their electricity by turning off unnecessary lights at night. They knew what their costs for fuel and electricity had previously been since these amounts had been totaled from their checkbook and entered in column C. So they reduced these by 30 percent and entered their new cost projections as a budget figure in column B.

They felt they should eliminate many of the excess long distance telephone calls they usually made to relatives just to chat so they reduced their telephone bill drastically in their budget.

PERSONAL FINANCIAL CONTROL – OPERATING PLAN–ACT				
Name _____ For Month Beginning _____				
INCOME	(A) WANTS	(B) BUDGET	(C) ACTUAL	(D) OVER/UNDER
(1) Salary	/ / / / /	1400	_____	_____
(2) Spouse's Salary	/ / / / /	900	_____	_____
(3) Other Income	/ / / / /	0	_____	_____
(4) TOTAL INCOME	/ / / / /	2300	_____	_____
EXPENSES				
(5) Tithe	/ / / / /	200	_____	_____
(6) Savings	/ / / / /	200	_____	_____
(7) Rent/Mortgage	/ / / / /	620	_____	_____
(8) Fuel	/ / / / /	100	_____	_____
(9) Electricity	/ / / / /	40	_____	_____
(10) Water	/ / / / /	10	_____	_____
(11) Phone—Need	/ / / / /	22	_____	_____
(12) Phone—Want	_____	20	_____	_____
(13) Food—Need	/ / / / /	300	_____	_____
(14) Food—Want	_____	50	_____	_____
(15) Clothing—Need	/ / / / /	100	_____	_____
(16) Clothing—Want	_____	0	_____	_____
(17) Household—Need	/ / / / /	20	_____	_____
(18) Household—Want	_____	0	_____	_____
(19) Medical	/ / / / /	50	_____	_____
(20) Drug Store—Wants	_____	10	_____	_____
(21) Auto Payment	/ / / / /	312	_____	_____
(22) Auto Operation	/ / / / /	100	_____	_____
(23) Recreation	_____	20	_____	_____
(24) Toys—Adult & Child	_____	20	_____	_____
(25) Food Production	/ / / / /	20	_____	_____
(26) Gifts	_____	0	_____	_____
(27) Contributions	_____	0	_____	_____
(28) Books—Education	_____	20	_____	_____
(29) Loans Paid—Principal	_____	0	_____	_____
(30) Loans Paid—Interest	_____	0	_____	_____
(31) Miscellaneous	_____	100	_____	_____
(32)	_____	_____	_____	_____
(33)	_____	_____	_____	_____
(34) TOTAL EXPENSES	_____	2334	_____	_____

Figure 4.5

As they were praying about their food bill, the Lord really convicted them about all of the junk food and soft drinks they were consuming. They left their essential food budget figure the same as their actual cost figure since this could not really be reduced. But they reduced their *food–want* budget figure to $200 less than what their actual cost figure had been.

In the clothing category, they felt that they should eliminate all of the clothing costs in the *clothing-want* category but
that $100 per month would be a reasonable amount to replace
existing clothes as they wore out.

Since their apartment was really furnished and equipped,
they only budgeted $20 per month for replacement of critical
items; this they entered on line 17 as a *household-need* amount.
For recreation and toys they allocated $40 a month between
the two.

They thought the Lord wanted them to begin to produce
some of their own food, which hopefully would eventually reduce their food bill, so they entered $20 per month for garden
equipment, seeds, and so forth. After reducing some of their
recreational costs, they budgeted $20 a month for good books.

Under "miscellaneous" they included $100 per month to
allow for a life insurance payment that was due quarterly and
any other miscellaneous things that might come up. Now their
expenses were much more in keeping with their income, although they could see that things were going to be tight. They
told the Lord that they were willing to move to a smaller place
or to sell their new car and get an older one that they could
pay for completely. They were willing to do this in order to be
good stewards—to pay the Lord the tithe to begin with and
then to save ten percent.

Since we have mentioned the tithe several times, we should
deal with it before proceeding.

DON'T ROB GOD—PAY YOUR TITHE

Since so much has been written on the tithe I won't go
into it in depth. But regardless of what you think of the church
you are attending, your pastor, or any other considerations, the
Lord says that if you do not give 10 percent to His work, you
are robbing Him. This is found in Malachi 3:

> 8 "Will a man rob God? Yet you are robbing Me! But you say,
> 'How have we robbed Thee?' In tithes and offerings.
>
> 9 "You are cursed with a curse, for you are robbing Me. the
> whole nation *of you!*

10 "Bring the whole tithe into the storehouse, so that there may be food in My house, and test Me now in this," says the LORD of hosts, "if I will not open for you the windows of heaven, and pour out for you a blessing until it overflows.

11 "Then I will rebuke the devourer for you, so that it may not destroy the fruits of the ground; nor will your vine in the field cast *its grapes,"* says the LORD of hosts.

12 "And all the nations will call you blessed, for you shall be a delightful land," says the LORD of hosts. . . ."

Some Christians try to rationalize and think, "Oh, I'm spending so much time working for the Lord, I don't have to contribute 10 percent of my income." When you read the Bible, what it clearly says is that such an individual is "robbing God."

Other Christians say that the tithe was only for the Old Testament and that Christ did not teach that we should tithe. That is not true. Christ comments on this in Matthew 23:23.

23 "Woe to you, scribes and Pharisees, hypocrites! For you tithe mint and dill and cummin, and have neglected the weightier provisions of the law: justice and mercy and faithfulness; but these are the things you should have done without neglecting the others. . . ."

As is pointed out here, the scribes and the Pharisees were so meticulous in their tithing that if they gathered a hundred leaves of mint out of their gardens, they would take ten of those and contribute them to the priest in the temple. Christ says clearly that this tithing is something they should have done but without neglecting the more important things. As far as I am concerned, in this passage Christ clearly reinforces the fact that we should tithe.

A more difficult question concerns whether we should tithe our gross salary or our net salary. As far as I am concerned, every man must do what God tells him to do and what gives him a peace with God. For me, God has said that it is the "net salary," which I have defined as the gross salary with the minimum amount of taxes deducted.

It is true that the Lord is the owner of all that you possess, and all of your expenditures should ultimately be under His control. However, if you do not take the first 10 percent and give it to God, you are robbing God, and you will eventually have to give an account to Him for that.

THE I. M. SINKING FAMILY

You will recall that in Figure 4.5 the I. M. Sinking's developed a budget, which is now a target or goal for them.

As the month proceeds and they write checks, hopefully they keep the budget in mind. Then at the end of the month, they total all of the checks they have written just as they had done for the previous month. They enter these totals into column C on that same form so they can see how much they were over or under their budget. We have shown this in Figure 4.6. As can be seen, they missed their target (budget) in several categories. Now they must either revise their budget or their spending. At least they now have a picture of their finances and are making progress.

I have not tried to present an elaborate system or one that is all inclusive. For homeowners, there are other considerations such as real estate taxes. For others, there are union dues and other expenses to be considered. What I have tried to do is give you a direction so that you can adapt this to your own personal needs.

Keep in mind that this process is going to take time. Your finances may not be brought back into order within the first month, or two, or three. Your budget is going to need revising and continual prayer. However, in the end, if you become a good steward I believe God will bless you and prosper you.

SUMMARY AND CONCLUSION

I believe that each of us should give the first 10 percent of his net income to the Lord and then should save the second 10 percent for investments or a rainy day or an emergency. Out of these savings we can take funds to invest and thus be better stewards.

PERSONAL FINANCIAL CONTROL — OPERATING PLAN-ACT

Name _____ For Month Beginning _____

INCOME	(A) WANTS	(B) BUDGET	(C) ACTUAL	(D) OVER/UNDER
(1) Salary	/ / / / /	1400	1400	
(2) Spouse's Salary	/ / / / /	900	900	
(3) Other Income	/ / / / /	0	0	
(4) TOTAL INCOME	/ / / / /	2300	2300	
EXPENSES				
(5) Tithe	/ / / / /	200	200	
(6) Savings	/ / / / /	200	200	
(7) Rent/Mortgage	/ / / / /	620	620	
(8) Fuel	/ / / / /	100	120	
(9) Electricity	/ / / / /	40	50	
(10) Water	/ / / / /	10	10	
(11) Phone—Need	/ / / / /	22	22	
(12) Phone—Want		20	0	
(13) Food—Need	/ / / / /	300	340	
(14) Food—Want		50	50	
(15) Clothing—Need	/ / / / /	100	100	
(16) Clothing—Want		0	0	
(17) Household—Need	/ / / / /	20	25	
(18) Household—Want		0	0	
(19) Medical	/ / / / /	50	55	
(20) Drug Store—Wants		10	10	
(21) Auto Payment	/ / / / /	312	312	
(22) Auto Operation	/ / / / /	100	112	
(23) Recreation		20	15	
(24) Toys—Adult & Child		20	20	
(25) Food Production	/ / / / /	20	25	
(26) Gifts		0	0	
(27) Contributions		0	0	
(28) Books—Education		20	10	
(29) Loans Paid—Principal		0	0	
(30) Loans Paid—Interest		0	0	
(31) Miscellaneous		100	95	
(32)				
(33)				
(34) TOTAL EXPENSES		2,334	2,391	

Figure 4.6

We have examined the fact that in order to accomplish these two objectives, individuals may have to change their lifestyles. They might have to live in smaller residences, drive older cars, or cut out some of the items that fall into their "want" category.

In order to do this, the first place to start is to determine your present status. I outlined a way of writing more checks than usual in order to achieve this.

Once the present status is known, you can then develop a budget through prayer and seeking the Lord's wisdom. At the end of the month, you can then total your purchases to see how you have done in relation to your budget. You may then need to make some changes in either your budget goals or your expenditure habits.

I trust that this will help you to begin moving toward sound personal finance as you tithe, save, invest, then give extra offerings to the Lord.

5

DEVELOPING YOUR PLAN
OF ACTION

We have seen that there are significant economic problems on the horizon, from the third world debt to a banking crisis. However, I believe that eventually the worst problem will be inflation. At best, we could have serious inflation problems in the years ahead, and at worst, our currency could become worthless, which would cause major crises, particularly in the cities.

Before we discuss things you could do to help prepare for the future, you need to carefully examine your present status, and develop your view of the future and your personal goals.

When I used to consult with corporations, I would ask them what their goals were, other than to make money, and how they knew whether or not their day-to-day decisions were taking them toward their goals. I found that most corporations did not have any clearly-defined goals. Therefore, their day-to-day decisions tended to be somewhat random; some decisions moving them in one direction, others taking them in other directions.

I now consult only with individuals, and find that they too do not have clearly-defined goals or sometimes even a general plan. If you do not have goals, how can you be sure that your specific decisions take you in the direction you should be going? I believe that the good steward in the parable had a plan and a direction, and that we should too. Most individuals do not have what I call a contingency plan—a plan outlining what to do in the event of a disaster. What would you think of a group of people who started out in a ship on a thousand-mile ocean trip, and, instead of taking a life boat, they took some plywood, glue, and some oar locks in case they had to build one. You would probably think they were foolish. Yet if I were to ask you what your contingency plans are in case of a currency collapse, massive bank failure, or an economic crisis, you might find that you have the financial equivalents of plywood, glue, and oar locks. What we need is a financial life boat *already* put together, that we can utilize in times of crisis.

As part of our total plan we should have a contingency plan; we should look at the distribution of our assets; we should look at our income and expenses; we should even take a fresh look at possibly becoming involved with other countries.

Many people have very foggy ideas as to what their present financial status is. They don't know the present market value of their homes and consequently don't know how much their equity is worth. They don't know the cash value of their insurance policies. They don't know how much money they can borrow against their homes or against their insurance policies. Before we can do any planning at all, we must first determine our exact present financial status. In the parable of the talents, each steward knew exactly how much he had to begin with. If we are going to be good stewards over the assets God has given us, we too must find out how much we have at the present time.

STEPS IN DEVELOPING A
STEWARDSHIP PLAN–ACT

I like to think of planning and taking action together. It does us no good to plan if we don't act. So I call this not a "plan" but a PLAN–ACT. I have outlined below seven basic steps in developing a PLAN–ACT. You should initially use these to develop a STEWARDSHIP PLAN–ACT to see how your current assets are distributed. Even if you are a young person with just a small savings account, an automobile, and an apartment, you must know how much you are a steward over. This applies equally to the wealthy individual with several million dollars, as well as everyone in between. The seven steps are:

STEP NO.	ACTION TO BE TAKEN
1.	Determine your present status.
2.	Describe your view of the future.
3.	Develop your objectives.
4.	Write your goals.
5.	Write out your plan of action.
6.	Take action.
7.	Review periodically; revise your goals and go back to Step 5.

We will be going through each of these seven steps in detail. We will discuss the first three in this chapter and the last four in Chapter 15. I would strongly encourage you to take the time and effort necessary to do this planning, even if you feel that you have made adequate provisions for your financial and physical survival. Probably you realize that you have made very little preparation in these areas. Whatever your status, I believe you will find this planning to be, first, an eye opener and subsequently, very beneficial.

In this chapter, we will be using these seven steps in developing a PLAN–ACT in the financial area. These steps could also be applied to the physical area or even the spiritual side of a person's life. I think a Christian should put first things first, and certainly the spiritual is the most important. You may well want to go through these seven steps first in connection with your spiritual life to determine where you are with the Lord and where you would like to be. Then write down a plan for getting to where you feel you should be.

The second most important thing would be planning for the physical survival aspect of life. It does not do anyone any good to go through the time of turmoil ahead with his finances intact if he does not survive it. I would put physical preparations ahead of any investment decisions. We will have more to say about physical preparations later in this chapter.

The third most important area is the financial one because our lives are dependent upon financial transactions, and it is with the funds that the Lord gives us that we can provide for our family and help other people. In this book we are going to apply these seven steps primarily to the financial area. God loves you and does not want to see you struggling financially. Perhaps, He will use these steps to help you bring your finances into order.

STEP 1 – DETERMINE YOUR PRESENT STATUS

We have included a form called "Market Value Net Worth –Stewardship Plan-Act" in Figure 5.1 that you should use for determining your present status. This form is greatly reduced in size. A complete package of these forms in 8½ x 11 size and other forms that can be utilized in developing your Plan-Act are available. (For information, see Appendix B.)

You will notice that the form has been divided into five basic categories along the left side. Putting the most important aspects of our physical and financial matters first, we have placed physical survival and monetary survival at the top of our list. During initial consultations, I find that many of my consulting clients have almost nothing invested in stored food, survival supplies, or a place to go if the cities become violent. If this is the case with you, then zeroes should be entered in the column A of this area. Similarly, few individuals have made provisions for catastrophes such as the dollar becoming worthless or a banking crisis. If this is the case with you, put zeroes in column A in the monetary survival section.

Following "Monetary Survival" on the form are three categories of investments: (1) Liquid, (2) Illiquid, (3) Static. Before we begin to talk about investments, I would like to give my definition of an investment:

> An investment is something that you purchase, which you hope to sell later at a higher price and thus realize a profit as measured in gold, not currencies (paper money).

MARKET VALUE NET WORTH — STEWARDSHIP PLAN-ACT

NET WORTH OF _____ As of (Date) _____ Gold $/Oz. _____

NOTE: Amounts to be expressed in thousands of dollars. $10,518 should be written as $10.5.

	MARKET VALUE $ (A)	DEBT AMOUNT $ (B)	NET VALUE $ (C)	PCT NET WORTH (D)	GOAL VALUE $ (E)	PCT GOAL (F)	CHANGE VALUE (E) − (C) (G)
PHYSICAL SURVIVAL							
(1) Food Stored	$	$	$	%	$	%	$
(2) Retreat Property							
(3) Survival Vehicle & Equipment							
(4) Other _____							
(5) TOTAL PHYSICAL SURVIVAL							
MONETARY SURVIVAL							
(6) Gold Coins in Possession							
(7) Silver Coins in Possession							
(8) Cash (in currency)							
(9) TOTAL MONETARY SURVIVAL							
INVESTMENTS—LIQUID							
(10) Gold Coins or Bullion							
(11) Silver Coins or Bullion							
(12) Foreign Currency Accounts							
(13) Gold and Silver Mining Shares							
(14) Stock Shares—Publicly traded							
(15) Stock Options							
(16) Commodity Futures							
(17) Other _____							
(18) TOTAL INVESTMENT—LIQUID							
INVESTMENT—ILLIQUID							
(19) Real Estate (Vacant land)							
(20) Diamonds							
(21) Collectibles—Art, Antiques, etc.							
(22) Private Company shares							
(23) TOTAL INVESTMENTS—ILLIQUID							
STATIC (INCLUDE INCOME INVESTMENTS)							
(24) Bank Accounts							
(25) Bonds, T Bills, CD's, Savings							
(26) Whole Life Ins. (Cash Value)							
(27) Residence							
(28) Rental Property							
(29) Automobile(s)							
(30) Other (include personal loans)							
(31) TOTAL STATIC							
GRAND TOTAL AND NET WORTH	$	$	$ (Net Worth)	%	$	%	$

Gold $. _____ /ounce. Net Worth in ounces of Gold . _____ ounces.

Silver $ - ———— /ounce. Net Worth in ounces of Silver - ———— ounces.

Figure 5.1

For simplicity's sake, we will discuss profits as measured in currencies, specifically in U.S. dollars; however, this is a distorted way of looking at your real purchasing power.

If "profit" is a nasty word to you, we could use the word "gain." Christ, in the parable of the talents, praised the steward who "gained" 100 percent on his assets. Today we would say he made a profit of 100 percent. In order to be a good steward, we need to desire to make a gain or profit.

CALCULATE YOUR NET WORTH

Most calculations of net worth are confusing to the average person and are not useful as a planning tool. One reason for this is that the assets and liabilities are listed on top of each other, and the net worth of any one item is difficult to ascertain. Another confusion factor is that most people don't really know what their financial situation is, even if they have an accountant, because of the misleading accounting practices required by the U.S. Government.

The government requires that assets be shown at their purchase prices, and not at their market value. So, if a stock were purchased at a high price and is worth little today, it still shows its original value on the balance sheet. Similarly, something purchased for a song that has appreciated significantly adds no value to your balance sheet. If you purchased a twenty-story building from your rich uncle for $1.00, you could never show that building valued at more than $1.00 as an asset on your balance sheet. (But your property tax would be based on market value!)

To help you get a realistic picture of your financial situation, I am including the "Market Value Net Worth—Stewardship Plan-Act" form that I use in my consultations (see Figure 5.1). Once your true situation is determined, then and only then can planning for the redistribution of your investments be done intelligently. I think this form will throw a great deal of light on your finances, and I would encourage you to take the time to fill it out. Here again, this form is shown greatly reduced because of the size of this book. (Full size forms are available, see Appendix B.)

Before you begin work on the form, let me say a word or two about it. Under the "Physical Survival" category, you will find some things that could help you and your family during a time of famine or crisis in the city. You could place a camper, house trailer or motor home in this category. You could also include camping equipment such as tents, camp stoves, and so forth. Electrical generators or anything else that would help you survive physically during a time of crisis should be included here.

Under the category "Monetary Survival" we have listed only those things that can be considered true savings at this point in time. These are items that are 100 percent paid for and are in your possession or immediately accessible to you. I encourage you to separate any gold and silver coins you might have into two categories—*investments* and *insurance*. The insurance portion should be shown under "Monetary Survival." Insurance coins are ones you are going to keep regardless of price fluctuations. Investment coins are ones you intend to sell when the price goes up and buy back after the price drops.

"Liquid" investments—the third category—includes anything that you can convert to cash within twenty-four hours. It is with these investments that we are going to increase what the Lord has entrusted to us (be a good steward).

"Illiquid" investments are investments that cannot be converted into cash within twenty-four hours. My advice is to really pray about beginning to move out of any illiquid investments you already have. The day may come when there simply will not be any buyers for these investments. People will only be interested in buying food and other essential items. It is fine to have art works and antiques, but you should be realistic and realize that these are items that you own because you enjoy them. They may have been wise investments in the past, but time is beginning to run out on them. You may want to keep them simply because you enjoy them, or if you did buy them for an investment, perhaps God wants you to liquidate them and take your profit. Ask Him; He will tell you, but you should make a conscious decision as to why you are keeping them.

There is a fourth category—"Static Investments." These are investments that probably are not even keeping up with inflation. Here I have included all items that are in fixed dollar amounts, such as savings accounts, checking accounts, and bonds. I have also included rental property since frequently one is buying a cash flow (income), rather than an investment for resale. The value of one's residence may or may not be keeping up with inflation and may or may not be a wise investment, so we have placed it in this category. Frequently a residence is bought not because it is a good investment, but simply because one enjoys it and *wants* to live there. (Hopefully it is what God wants too!)

Again, the normal and misleading accounting practice in the U.S. is to list the purchase price of an item as its present value. On this form you should list the *present market value.* In order to determine this you may actually have to have your real estate and antiques appraised.

This form is not laid out in the traditional way with assets on top and liabilities on bottom. The present market value of each asset is shown in column A. To the right of that show any debt owed on the asset in column B. Then subtract column B from column A to get the present net value of the asset and enter it in column C. This way you can quickly see the net value of each of your assets. For example, if you own your residence, on line 27 you would enter its present market value in column A. The amount you still owe on it should be entered in column B. Then subtract column B from column A to calculate its present net value and enter that in column C. If for any item the present value is less than the amount owed on it, the entry in column C should be placed in parentheses to indicate that it is negative when adding up your net worth. Do the same thing for item 30 where you list any personal or unsecured loans which do not have an asset to go with them.

Step 1: The present market value for all of your assets should be entered in column A.

Step 2: In column B you should enter any debts against those items.

Step 3: Subtract column B from column A. This gives the net value of *each* item. Enter this in column C.

Step 4: Total column C. This will be your net worth. This is the amount over which you hold control as God's steward.

Step 5: After you have completed column C, the next

thing to do is compute column D. Column D is the percentage that each item is of the total net worth (the total of column C). This can be determined by the following simple calculation:

$$\% \text{ of item:} \quad \frac{\text{The net value of the item} \times 100}{\text{total net worth}}$$

The critical percentages that you will want to look at are the percentages of lines 5, 9, 18, 23, and 31. These five percentages give you the amount of your net assets you have allocated to the five basic categories.

After looking at these percentages, you might be in a state of shock. For example, at today's market prices most people have far more tied up in their residence than they realize.

When is the last time that any Christian you know got down on his knees before the Lord, with the distribution of his assets listed on a piece of paper, and asked the Lord what changes should be made in the way those assets were being used? When is the last time you personally had a session with the Lord like that?

How could a Christian possibly be a good steward, if he is not doing this? If we come before the Lord in this manner, He may say that everything is alright as it is. (But I doubt it.) He may tell us to sell our house and rent and give the proceeds to our church or to invest the proceeds. He may say to refinance our house and to give $5,000 of the proceeds to a good Christ-honoring organization and to use the other $25,000 as a down payment on a duplex. I don't know what God will tell you, and you will never know until you ask Him.

I have included a number of copies of this net worth form in the workbook that accompanies this book (see Appendix B) so that you can do this exercise at least once a year, or even better, every six months. If you calculate your net worth today, and calculate it one year from now, you can see if your net worth has grown at the rate of inflation plus, perhaps 10 percent, which would be about the minimum a good steward would want to produce. For example, if your net worth today were $10,000 and inflation was running at 20 percent, then your net worth one year from now should be at least $13,000 to have made 10 percent over the rate of inflation. How to manage money is something that is between every individual and the Lord. But unless you fill out some form like this at least yearly, how can you possibly know what kind of steward you are?

In the example of the parable of the talents where Christ taught on stewardship, the good stewards knew exactly what they had to start with and how much they had gained. Should we do less?

We want to honor and glorify the Lord in all that we do, and certainly this should carry over into the area of our finances.

DETAILS OF STEWARDSHIP PLAN–ACT METHOD

Now that we have looked at the form in general, let's take a couple of examples to show how it works in a practical sense. A middle-aged couple bought their home ten years ago for $32,000 and paid $10,000 down on it. They now have a camper, a bag of silver coins (this has a $1,000 face value), and an engagement ring they bought twenty years ago for $200. They also have some stocks they bought a long time ago, and they are not quite sure what they are worth today. They bought some land for investment that someone more or less talked them into, and today it is worth less than what they owe on it. They have a whole-life insurance policy on the husband that they have been paying on for about twenty years. They have about $5,000 in a savings account and own a couple of cars.

This family has no idea what its net worth is today. That is, they have no idea how much wealth the Lord has given them responsibility for. If they don't even know their present status, how could they possibly be making the right stewardship decisions? So let's walk through this form with this imaginary family. The results are shown in Figure 5.2, and in Figure 5.3.

As you can see from Figure 5.2, they went down to the bank and got the "blue book" price on their camper and two automobiles. They found out the value of their camper was now $8,000, but they still owed $7,000 on it. So they entered these

MARKET VALUE NET WORTH – STEWARDSHIP PLAN-ACT

NET WORTH OF _____ As of (Date) _____

NOTE: Amounts to be expressed in thousands of dollars. $10,518 should be written as $10.5.

	MARKET VALUE $ (A)	DEBT AMOUNT $ (B)	NET VALUE $ (C)
PHYSICAL SURVIVAL			
(1) Food Stored	$.	$.	$.
(2) Retreat Property			
(3) Survival Vehicle & Equipment	8.0	7.0	1.0
(4) Other _____	.	.	
(5) TOTAL PHYSICAL SURVIVAL	.	.	1.0
MONETARY SURVIVAL			
(6) Gold Coins in Possession	14.3	.0	14.3
(7) Silver Coins in Possession	.	.	.
(8) Cash (in currency)	.	.	.
(9) TOTAL MONETARY SURVIVAL	.	.	14.3
INVESTMENTS–LIQUID			
(10) Gold Coins or Builion	.	.	.
(11) Silver Coins or Bullion	.	.	.
(12) Foreign Currency Accounts	.	.	.
(13) Gold and Silver Mining Shares	.	.	.
(14) Stock Shares–Publicly traded	2.0	.0	2.0
(15) Stock Options	.	.	.
(16) Commodity Futures	.	.	.
(17) Other _____	.	.	.
(18) TOTAL INVESTMENT–LIQUID	.	.	2.0

Figure 5.2

two figures in columns A and B, under Survival Vehicle and Equipment; they subtracted column B from A and found the net value of the camper was $1,000. They called the coin store and learned that their bag of silver coins was worth $14,300, so they entered this. Since they didn't owe anything against these coins, they put a zero under column B and entered a net value of $14,300.

They called their broker and found out that the stock they

had purchased a number of years ago for $3,000 was worth only $2,000; they were quite disappointed when they found this out. They added that figure to their net worth form. If they had purchased the stock on margin, they would have put the margin amount that they had effectively borrowed from the stock brokerage firm under column B.

They had also bought some vacant land from a land company, so they phoned them and were given a song and dance about how valuable the lot still was. However, they called a real estate firm in that same town and found out what the lots on the land were going for on resale; they were disappointed to find out that the lot they bought out in the "wilderness" for $20,000 was worth less than the $10,000 owed on it. They had the diamond ring appraised and were delighted to find that it had increased in value substantially to $1,300. These items are shown added to the form in Figure 5.3.

As they checked into the husband's whole-life insurance policy ($50,000 face value), they were excited to find out that it had a cash value of $30,000 that they could borrow against.

Perhaps the biggest surprise of all was when they paid a real estate appraiser $150 to appraise their residence. They found it was worth $85,000, and they only owed $8,000 on it. They entered this on their net worth form, as shown in Figure 5.3. From their banker they got the "blue book" values on their automobiles. One of them was paid for, but they still owed $1,000 on the other one. They discovered they had a net worth of $4,000 in their automobiles. They had gotten into a fix once, and had taken out a personal loan of $2,000; they still owed $1,400 on this. So they entered this on line 30.

Now they were ready for the exciting step of totaling column C to find out what their net worth really was. For the first time, they were going to know how much the Lord had given them control over. They were surprised at how large the figure was. Their net worth was $126,000! Far more than they had expected.

This put them in the four talent category. (Remember, a talent of silver today is worth about $30,000.)

MARKET VALUE NET WORTH – STEWARDSHIP PLAN-ACT							
NET WORTH OF _____ As of (Date) _____ Gold $/Oz. _____							
NOTE: Amounts to be expressed in thousands of dollars. $10,518 should be written as $10.5.	MARKET VALUE $	DEBT AMOUNT $	NET VALUE $	PCT NET WORTH	GOAL VALUE $	PCT GOAL	CHANGE VALUE (E) – (C)
	(A)	(B)	(C)	(D)	(E)	(F)	(G)
PHYSICAL SURVIVAL							
(1) Food Stored	$.	$.	$.	. %	$.	. %	$.
(2) Retreat Property							
(3) Survival Vehicle & Equipment	8.0	7.0	1.0				
(4) Other _____							
(5) TOTAL PHYSICAL SURVIVAL			1.0				
MONETARY SURVIVAL							
(6) Gold Coins in Possession							
(7) Silver Coins in Possession	14.3	0	14.3				
(8) Cash (in currency)							
(9) TOTAL MONETARY SURVIVAL			14.3				
INVESTMENTS–LIQUID							
(10) Gold Coins or Bullion							
(11) Silver Coins or Bullion							
(12) Foreign Currency Accounts							
(13) Gold and Silver Mining Shares							
(14) Stock Shares- Publicly traded	2.0	0	2.0				
(15) Stock Options							
(16) Commodity Futures							
(17) Other							
(18) TOTAL INVESTMENT–LIQUID			2.0				
INVESTMENT–ILLIQUID							
(19) Real Estate (Vacant land)	8.0	10.0	(2.0)				
(20) Diamonds	1.3	0	1.3				
(21) Collectibles–Art, Antiques, etc.							
(22) Private Company shares							
(23) TOTAL INVESTMENTS–ILLIQUID			(.7)				
STATIC (INCLUDE INCOME INVESTMENTS)							
(24) Bank Accounts							
(25) Bonds, T Bills, CD's, Savings							
(26) Whole Life Ins. (Cash Value)	30.0	0	30.0				
(27) Residence	85.0	8.0	77.0				
(28) Rental Property							
(29) Automobile(s)	5.0	1.0	4.0				
(30) Other (include personal loans)	0	1.4	(1.4)				
(31) TOTAL STATIC			109.6				
GRAND TOTAL AND NET WORTH	$.	$.	$126.2 (Net Worth)	. %	$.	. %	$.

Gold $ _____ /ounce. Net Worth in ounces of Gold _____ ounces.
Silver $ _____ /ounce. Net Worth in ounces of Silver _____ ounces.

Figure 5.3

They then calculated what percentage of their net worth was tied up in each category. They calculated this percentage for lines 5, 9, 18, 23, and 31. The results were:

Physical Survival	.8 %
Monetary Survival	11.3 %
Liquid Investments	1.6 %
Illiquid Investments	(.6)%
Static Investments	86.9 %
TOTAL INVESTMENTS	100.0 %

These percentages were then entered in column D.

Now, at last, this family knew exactly what its present status was, and they were eager to begin to pray and ask God what changes, if any, he wanted to make in the way their assets were distributed.

They decided that they were going to do a new one of these forms every six months for a couple of years and then one annually.

YOUR PERSONAL NET WORTH AS MEASURED IN OUNCES OF GOLD

Now that you have a clear picture of how columns A, B, C, and D are used, we will move on to column E. At the bottom of the form is a place to enter the price of gold in dollars per ounce and the price of silver in dollars per ounce. This information can be obtained from your newspaper or from a local coin store. We will use this information to calculate column E, which will describe our net worth in ounces of gold. There is a very good reason for doing this.

To help you understand, let's take a simple example. What if the definition of an inch or a foot kept changing? Could we have an orderly society? If you went to the hardware store and bought some half-inch bolts based on one length of an inch, and then went to Sears and bought some half-inch wrenches which were made using a different sized inch, and then went to a third store and bought some half-inch nuts for the bolts made from still a different sized inch, what would you have? A *mess.* You can only have order where there are standards.

In fact, a department of our government is the Bureau of Standards, which maintains a precise yard, a precise pound, a precise gallon and so forth. All of the measures used in commerce must match these standards.

Going back to the U.S. dollar, its value as measured in ounces of gold or in other currencies fluctuates daily. Inflation makes the dollar worth continually less. If a man bought a house several years ago for $50,000 and sold it today for $80,000, did he really realize a gain? Will the $80,000 really purchase more than the $50,000 would have a few years ago?

In order to try to overcome this problem of no dollar standard, frequently financial reports will use "constant dollars." That is they will give the price of something like the stock market or gross national product based on 1970 dollars. Others use 1940 dollars or a dollar value from some other year. What they then try to do is to filter out by calculation all the inflation that has occurred in the interim. In fact, if you calculate the value of the stock market using constant 1968 dollars, the stock market is actually only about one-third as high as the present number would seem to indicate.

There is a simple solution for this dilemma. As far as I am concerned the only true money is gold. The price of gold does not go up and down as presented on our evening news broadcasts. The value of gold is constant, and the dollar goes up and down in relationship to it.

So that we can measure our net worth in an unchanging standard, I recommend that people calculate their net worth in terms of ounces of gold. To show you how this works, let's re-calculate the net worth of this same family, only this time we will calculate it in gold.

Assuming a gold worth of $600 per ounce, I have calculated their net worth to be 210 ounces of gold (see Figure 5.4). This was done by simply dividing their net worth, $126,200, by the current price of gold, $600. We can then calculate the ounces of gold for each category by multiplying the total number of ounces of gold times the percentage of our net worth in each category. However, in some ways this is unnecessary since

MARKET VALUE NET WORTH – STEWARDSHIP PLAN-ACT							

NET WORTH OF_____ As of (Date)_____ Gold $/Oz. _____

NOTE: Amounts to be expressed in thousands of dollars. $10,518 should be written as $10.5.	MARKET VALUE $ (A)	DEBT AMOUNT $ (B)	NET VALUE $ (C)	PCT NET WORTH (D)	GOAL VALUE $ (E)	PCT GOAL (F)	CHANGE VALUE (E) – (C) (G)
PHYSICAL SURVIVAL							
(1) Food Stored	$.	$.	$.	. %	$.	. %	$.
(2) Retreat Property	.	.	.	.	.	.	.
(3) Survival Vehicle & Equipment	8.0	7.0	1.0	.	.	.	.
(4) Other _____	.	.	.	.	.	.	.
(5) TOTAL PHYSICAL SURVIVAL	.	.	1.0	.	.	.	.
MONETARY SURVIVAL							
(6) Gold Coins in Possession	.	.	.	.	.	.	.
(7) Silver Coins in Possession	14.3	.0	14.3	.	.	.	.
(8) Cash (in currency)	.	.	.	.	.	.	.
(9) TOTAL MONETARY SURVIVAL	.	.	14.3	.	.	.	.
INVESTMENTS–LIQUID							
(10) Gold Coins or Bullion	.	.	.	.	.	.	.
(11) Silver Coins or Bullion	.	.	.	.	.	.	.
(12) Foreign Currency Accounts	.	.	.	.	.	.	.
(13) Gold and Silver Mining Shares	.	.	.	.	.	.	.
(14) Stock Shares- Publicly traded	2.0	.0	2.0	.	.	.	.
(15) Stock Options	.	.	.	.	.	.	.
(16) Commodity Futures	.	.	.	.	.	.	.
(17) Other _____	.	.	.	.	.	.	.
(18) TOTAL INVESTMENT–LIQUID	.	.	2.0	.	.	.	.
INVESTMENT– ILLIQUID							
(19) Real Estate (Vacant land)	8.0	10.0	(2.0)	.	.	.	.
(20) Diamonds	1.3	.0	1.3	.	.	.	.
(21) Collectibles–Art, Antiques, etc.	.	.	.	.	.	.	.
(22) Private Company shares	.	.	.	.	.	.	.
(23) TOTAL INVESTMENTS–ILLIQUID	.	.	.7	.	.	.	.
STATIC (INCLUDE INCOME INVESTMENTS)							
(24) Bank Accounts	.	.	.	.	.	.	.
(25) Bonds, T Bills, CD's, Savings	.	.	.	.	.	.	.
(26) Whole Life Ins. (Cash Value)	30.0	.0	30.0	.	.	.	.
(27) Residence	85.0	8.0	77.0	.	.	.	.
(28) Rental Property	.	.	.	.	.	.	.
(29) Automobile(s)	5.0	1.0	4.0	.	.	.	.
(30) Other (include personal loans)	.0	1.4	(1.4)	.	.	.	.
(31) TOTAL STATIC	.	.	109.6	.	.	.	.
GRAND TOTAL AND NET WORTH	$.	$.	$ 126.2 (Net Worth)	. %	$.	. %	$.

Gold $. **600** /ounce. Net Worth in ounces of Gold **210.33** ounces.

Silver $ - ———— /ounce. Net Worth in ounces of Silver - ---- --- ounces.

Figure 5.4

we will largely be looking at the total net worth in gold as a long-term standard. When we calculate our net worth six months or a year later, we can then see how much it has grown in ounces of gold.

Similarly, if a person buys and sells a piece of property, he can calculate its value in ounces of gold when he purchases it and can calculate its value in ounces of gold when he sells it to see if indeed he is making a profit on it. He may have made paper dollars on the sale but not actually increased his worth in terms of gold—the real money standard.

STEP 2 – DESCRIBE YOUR VIEW OF THE FUTURE

All of our decisions are based on our view of the future. You might buy IBM stock because you think it's going up, or you might buy gold because you think it is going to increase in price. You might sell an oil painting because you think it's going to decrease in value. You might buy a large house when you first get married because your view of the future is that you will have many children. All of the critical decisions that you will be making in the next few weeks and months will be based on your view of the future. You need, therefore, to sit down and figure out just what your expectations are.

One of the first questions you need to ask yourself is, "Will this time of monetary difficulty, shortages, and a tendency toward violence and chaos tend to increase over the next few years, or will it tend to decrease?" In order to make an intelligent evaluation of this you would have to look in depth at the underlying causes of each of these phenomena. There is not space to adequately do that here, but briefly we can conjecture concerning the basic causes. For example, will the government continue to print money without anything real behind it? Will the banks continue to make shaky loans? Will people continue to overuse their credit? The answer to these three questions, in your mind, is most likely yes. Look around you, and see if you can see anything that would cause these tendencies to reverse. If you don't, then I think it is safe to assume that our monetary problems will tend to remain with us.

One of the results of these monetary problems is the rapidly increasing cost of living, which is one of the key ingredients for potential violence. I recently read an interview with seven psychiatrists, who all felt that soaring prices are wrecking the lives of people. For example, Dr. Cancro, Professor of Psychology at the University of Connecticut, said that most Americans view inflation as a kind of personal thief, almost like being mugged. People feel frustrated and angry because they are left helpless to do anything about soaring prices. He went on to warn that inflation has fostered a mood among many Americans dangerously close to violence. He felt that we have a situation in which people are ready to fight—in which there is pressure to "get somebody" for all this inflation. The atmosphere is violent and potentially explosive.

Not only has price escalation created a mood of violence, but there are many other psychological factors, such as mistrust of government, disrespect for authority, bitterness of the working classes of all races, and a sense of hopelessness concerning the world situation. Are the causes for these feelings going to disappear, or will they continue to be with us? Unfortunately, it appears to me that they will be around for a while.

Since the underlying causes for our present economic problems are still very much with us, and possibly even increasing, we can project some possible "futures," based on actions the government might take. For example, the government could decide to stop printing money with nothing behind it. This would throw us into a severe deflationary depression. They could decide to continue to print this "funny money" and throw us into a full-blown runaway inflation, such as Germany experienced in the 1920's. Or, the government could continue to vacillate between these two postures, keeping things in chaos. If there is a severe monetary crisis, and a person's paper money will no longer purchase food, I think we will see people willing to steal and plunder for food and clothing. I see no possible repetition of the 1929 bread lines, where people patiently stood in line for hours for a few loaves of bread. If those who are more violently inclined begin to plunder, the average citizen will tend to join in to get some before everything is all gone, resulting in widespread violence. This could occur either after a runaway inflation or after a severe depression (or after both if we have an inflationary depression).

I would suggest that you write down five or six possible

"futures" as you see them. Listed below are some examples of the type of ingredients you would want to include in your future projections. From the five or six possible futures you write out, pick the two that seem the most likely. Then, if you can, come up with a single unified view of the future. If you cannot, don't worry. Use your two or three favorites in your planning:

FUTURE A

Present conditions
Small depression cured by more inflation
Money becomes worthless
Barter system
Gold and silver coins used as money
Restoration of society

FUTURE B

Present conditions
Severe depression with inflationary money printing
Money becomes worthless
Time of violence
Gold and silver coins used as money
Restoration of society

FUTURE C

Present conditions
Severe depression—no inflationary money printing
Mass unemployment
Times of violence
Paper currency still usable
Restoration of society

FUTURE D

Present conditions
Runaway inflation
Times of violence
Martial law
Dictator

FUTURE E

Present conditions
Global monetary crisis
World government
New world money

FUTURE F

Present conditions
Government balances budget
Inflation problems solved
Years of sluggish economy
Growth again

Obviously, each individual's view of the future must change continually. None of us viewed the future the same ten years ago as we do today. Therefore, whatever view of the future you develop, you must continually monitor the significant events and trends that are occurring in order to modify your planning. There will likely be combinations of several of the possibilities we've discussed. Any of these scenarios could lead to violence. Any of them could produce a time of barter. Any of them could include a time when gold and silver coins are used for money while a new solid currency is being created.

You should arrive at a view of the future you personally believe is most likely. Then you should develop a plan based on that view, but you should also plan for as many of the other futures as possible, so that you will be protected regardless of how the future actually unfolds.

THE BIBLICAL VIEW OF THE FUTURE

The Old Testament prophecies concerning the Messiah were fulfilled precisely by Jesus of Nazareth. This is why we as Christians accept Him as the promised Messiah.

The scores of other biblical prophecies that have all been fulfilled to the letter are too numerous to mention. The taking of the Israelites into captivity in Babylon was prophesied far before it happened. Even the name of the king who would allow them to return to their home land was prophesied 500 years before he was born.

Because of the accuracy of the biblical prophecies in the past, Christians today are looking for the fulfillment of the remaining prophecies, not yet fulfilled. I would like to examine two of these that give a clear description of what the Bible says the future *will* be.

THE END OF THIS AGE

I'm not a dispensationalist, but Christ clearly taught that history is divided into ages. The first great age ended when God personally intervened on planet Earth and gave Moses the Ten Commandments on Mt. Sinai. The second age ended when God again intervened on planet Earth with the birth, life, death, resurrection and ascension of Jesus Christ. At that time, a new age began. Christ taught that the age we are presently living in would end when God again intervenes on planet Earth bringing seven years of intense global turmoil (called "the Great Tribulation"). This age would climax with the return of Jesus Christ in power and glory to destroy his enemies. The next age would then be Christ ruling and reigning here on planet Earth for 1,000 years (called the millennium).

Christ taught His disciples so much about His return and the end of the age that near the end of His life they came to Him and asked Him a no-nonsense, straight-forward question about what things would be like at the end of the age and His coming back to the earth. (I might add that the word *age* is incorrectly translated *world* in the *King James Version* of the Bible.) I believe that Jesus gave them a straight-forward, no-nonsense answer to their question. This is recorded in Matthew 24:

> 3 And as He was sitting on the Mount of Olives, the disciples came to Him privately, saying, "Tell us, when will these things be, and what *will be* the sign of Your coming, and of the end of the age?"

4 And Jesus answered and said to them, "See to it that no one misleads you.

5 "For many will come in My name, saying, 'I am the Christ,' and will mislead many.

6 "And you will be hearing of wars and rumors of wars: see that you are not frightened, for *those things* must take place, but *that* is not yet the end.

7 "For nation will rise against nation, and kingdom against kingdom, and in various places there will be famines and earthquakes.

8 "But all these things are *merely* the beginning of birth pangs.

9 "Then they will deliver you to tribulation, and will kill you, and you will be hated by all nations on account of My name.

10 "And at that time many will fall away and will deliver up one another and hate one another.

11 "And many false prophets will arise, and will mislead many.

12 "And because lawlessness is increased, most people's love will grow cold.

13 "But the one who endures to the end, he shall be saved.

14 "And this gospel of the kingdom shall be preached in the whole world for a witness to all the nations, and then the end shall come.

15 "Therefore when you see the ABOMINATION OF DESOLATION which was spoken of through Daniel the prophet, standing in the holy place (let the reader understand),

16 then let those who are in Judea flee to the mountains;

17 let him who is on the housetop not go down to get the things out that are in his house;

18 and let him who is in the field not turn back to get his cloak.

19 "But woe to those who are with child and to those who nurse babes in those days!

20 "But pray that your flight may not be in the winter, or on a Sabbath;

21 for then there will be a great tribulation, such as has not occurred since the beginning of the world until now, nor ever shall. . . .

29 "But immediately after the tribulation of those days THE SUN WILL BE DARKENED, AND THE MOON WILL NOT GIVE ITS LIGHT, AND THE STARS WILL FALL from the sky, and the powers of the heavens will be shaken.

30 and then the sign of the Son of Man will appear in the sky, and then all the tribes of the earth will mourn, and they will see the SON OF MAN COMING ON THE CLOUDS OF THE SKY with power and great glory.

31 "And He will send forth His angels with A GREAT TRUMPET and THEY WILL GATHER TOGETHER His elect from the four winds, from one end of the sky to the other. . . ."

So we see that Christ said that preceding the Great Tribulation there would be a period of time which He called the time of "birth pangs." Other translations of the Bible call this the time of "birth pains" or "a time of sorrows." All of these terms were used in the Bible to describe a woman in labor, giving birth to a child.

What is being born here in Matthew 24 is the Great Tribulation. Christ clearly taught that the planet Earth was going to be in agony, pain and turmoil preceding the Great Tribulation.

Some Christians believe that all Christians will be taken from the earth immediately prior to the Great Tribulation. Others believe that this "catching-up" (rapture) of Christians will occur at the end of the Tribulation. Regardless of what a person believes about the time of the rapture, all Christians are going to go through this time of birth pains. In this time of birth pains, which Christ said would occur at the end of this age, we will see the following: (1) war, (2) famine, (3) earthquakes, (4) persecution of Christians, (5) the gospel taken to all nations.

Most Christians that I talk to today believe that we are living at the end of this current age and that the present generation is likely to see the return of Christ. Any Christian who believes that must also believe that he is going through this time of birth pains that precedes the Great Tribulation. So, as Christians, our view of the future must include war, famines, earth upheavels, persecution of Christians, and the spread of the gospel of Christ throughout the whole world. That is the future that God has told me clearly that I should prepare for, and that is the future that I would also encourage my fellow believers to prepare for.

THE BOOK OF REVELATION

The book of Revelation is the major prophetic work dealing with the end of this age and the return of Christ. Most Christians believe Revelation is simply not understandable. It is full of weird creatures and unfathomable symbols.

I believe that Satan will do everything he possibly can to keep a Christian from reading and studying the book of Revelation. Realizing this, God attached a special blessing to the book for those who read and heed the teachings. This is found in Revelation 1.

3 Blessed is he who reads and those who hear the words of the prophecy, and heed the things which are written in it; for the time is near.

This blessing is repeated in Revelation 22.

7 "And behold, I am coming quickly. Blessed is he who heeds the words of the prophecy of this book."

Did you notice that it says he who reads *and heeds* the prophecies of this book? This means there are many things contained in the book of Revelation that we need to be *doing* (heeding). God would not have asked us to do those things unless it were possible.

Before we can *heed* the things in the book of Revelation, we must *understand* them. I believe this is why the Lord led me to write the book, *Revelation for Laymen.* It is written for plain folks, and God has mightily used it in thousands of lives to help clear up the mystery of the book of Revelation. If you are interested in reading the book, information concerning how to get a copy is found in Appendix B.

Many of the things contained in the book of Revelation and discussed in my book on that subject should significantly influence your view of the future. So you might want to consider studying Revelation as a part of completing the second step in developing your personal survival plan. Now let's move on to Step 3.

STEP 3 – DEVELOP YOUR OBJECTIVES

After completing the first two steps, if two individuals found that they had the same amount and distribution of assets and the same view of the future, it is possible that they would nevertheless do very different things with their money, depending upon their objectives. For example, one client of mine is a Chinese widow in San Francisco. All she is interested in is security; she does not care if she makes another penny in her life. She simply does not want to lose any of the wealth that she has accumulated. Another client is a young medical doctor who is a "high roller." He wants to accumulate wealth during the coming chaos and is willing to take large risks. I would tell those two individuals to take almost opposite actions with their money.

We would all like to have an investment that does not risk our losing all or any part of our money yet which could make us wealthy over night. Such an investment does not exist; therefore, we have to decide how much of our money we are willing to lose—that is, how high a risk we are willing to take. Remember the higher the risk, usually the higher the potential reward *if* we invest correctly.

In developing your objectives you must also deal with what you and your family would do if there were massive violence and rioting. If you live in a city, would you try to remain where you are or flee from the city? What would you do if a form of government of which you did not approve, such as a dictatorship or communism, came to our country? Would you attempt to remain in the U.S., or would you flee to another country with a form of government more to your liking? All of these things need to be thought through and *written down*.

These objectives tell you where you are trying to go. They set down your aspirations and general directions. Then your objectives can be translated into specific goals.

SUMMARY AND CONCLUSION

We have looked at the significant economic problems that lie on the horizon. In previous chapters, we have called the greatest problem "hurricane inflation." There are other things that could happen such as a war, a dictatorship, wage/price controls, or a banking crisis which we need to prepare for. Of a more personal nature, an accident or illness could make the bread winner incapable of making a living. We have seen that a Christian should not be caught unaware in these things and should take them into account in his Stewardship Plan–Act.

We also looked at the seven steps that are necessary to develop a good survival plan, and we began to apply these, particularly in the area of our financial affairs.

We saw that the first thing we should do is to find out what our present status really is. We discussed using the net worth form to help in this. To assess your net worth you will probably need to get some assets appraised, find out the cash values of insurance policies, and so forth. Once you have compiled all this information, you can then see what your net worth really is and what percentage of your net worth is tied up in the various categories.

We then saw that the U.S. dollar is not an adequate standard measure for us to determine if we are gaining ground or losing ground so we recommended calculating your net worth in terms of ounces of gold.

After finding out the present status of your financial affairs, we said that the next step was to develop your view of the future. You can only commit yourself to *your* view of the coming years. If you took *my* view of the future, you could not really commit yourself to it. This is particularly important since all of your decisions are made based on your view of the future.

Then we looked at the third step which was to develop your objectives. These objectives are broad in nature but give a general direction to your financial and personal affairs. Later in the book, we will complete the remaining steps in developing the Plan–Act. We will talk about translating these broad objectives into specific goals and then developing a plan of action to get us from our present status to our desired status as defined by these specific goals.

One thing we must realize is that to be good stewards of

what the Lord has entrusted to us, our net worth should be increasing by a minimum of 5 to 10 percent per year over the inflation rate. So twelve months from now, your net worth should be greater by a percentage equal to the inflation rate plus about 5 to 10 percent. So if the inflation rate is 15 percent, your net worth one year from now should be about 25 percent greater than it is today if you are making wise use of the funds presently under your control.

It's wise to try to save 10 percent and add this to your net worth. In the next chapter we will be looking at savings and investing in such a way that our net worth can be increased.

6

SAVING VERSUS INVESTING

For years people in America were taught the virtues of saving. They were taught that it's wise to be thrifty and lay something aside for a rainy day. They learned to save in order to be able to pay cash for their purchases.

Today as I travel around America, I see that the inclination to save is gone. People tend to rush out and buy on credit before prices go up. They tell me, "Why save? Counting taxes and inflation, I lose money when I save."

So we find that inflation is a monster that has robbed people of the incentive to save, to pay cash, and to be thrifty.

There was a time when people were putting money in savings accounts at 5 percent, and inflation was running at 15 percent. They were losing 10 percent per year on their money. This means that in five years, they would have lost 50 percent of their purchasing power, simply because they saved. Maybe I should say because they "saved" by placing their funds in something denominated in U.S. dollars.

SAVING IS ESSENTIAL

I certainly believe it's essential to save by putting aside a portion of what you earn, but those funds should not be placed (for long) in something denominated in a fixed number of U.S. dollars. This means avoiding savings accounts, bonds, and whole-life insurance policies, which are the three traditional places to save.

Unfortunately, many Christians have simply stopped saving. They feel like they *should* be saving, but they see the futility of putting funds into a savings account. The message I would like to convey is that it is essential to save, but it should be done in a more creative way.

For example, consider Joseph in the Bible. God told him to save for a rainy day. That rainy day materialized as seven years of famine. Notice that Joseph did not save in the form of Egyptian money. He saved in grain—something that would retain its value regardless of what happened to the worth of the Egyptian money. We, too, should be saving, but probably in the form of gold coins, silver coins, or some other vehicle that will go up with inflation and keep ahead of it. Before we look briefly at some of these other investment possibilities, let's discuss the principle of saving.

THE RICHEST MAN IN BABYLON

I recently read a booklet entitled, *The Richest Man in Babylon Tells His Secret.* This is the story of a young boy in an Arab country who went to work for a rich merchant. He wanted to learn from the rich merchant. The merchant told him to always pay himself first when he got his wages before he paid anyone else. So he always paid himself 10 percent first. As the story goes, it was out of these savings that he was able to invest in businesses and merchandise, ultimately becoming the richest man in Babylon—all because he paid himself first.

As mentioned in the first chapter, I believe that when a person (or a family) gets paid, he should give the first 10 percent to the Lord and save the second 10 percent, keeping his living expenses within the remaining 80 percent. Again, I've had many Christians tell me that would be impossible for them. The fact is that anyone can do this if he really wants to. It might be necessary to live in a smaller house or apartment, drive a smaller or older car, or reduce your living standard in other ways. I will grant you that it may be impossible for many individuals to tithe, save 10 percent, and maintain their *existing* standard of living. Their debt payment schedules alone may be tremendous problems. However, unless they take corrective measures, they will always be living up against the wire, struggling to get by. My counsel to them would be to pay God first, and themselves second, and then to adjust their standard of living in order to be able to live on the other 80 percent.

You will recall that we discussed two tables in Chapter 3. One showed your expenses with the inflation rate factored in. The other was a form on which you could project both your income and expenses with inflation factored in. These two tables are being reproduced again on the next three pages for our use in discussing saving in light of inflation.

In Table 6.1, you can see that if someone had a savings of $50,000, which he was planning to use at some point in the future, and if inflation rates were averaging 20 percent, twenty years later he would find himself in an economy where it would cost $38,000 to buy what $1,000 would buy at the time he put his money in savings. As you can see, saving in the traditional way makes no sense whatsoever in light of the ravages of an inflationary economy.

To show you how destructive inflation can be for you over the long run, let's look at a couple of hypothetical individuals who are trying to plan their financial futures in an inflationary economy. To simplify the example we will select columns from the "INCOME AND EXPENSE PROJECTION WITH INFLATION" form found in Table 6.2. We will actually project hypothetical figures on this table to show you how this form can be used to forewarn you of significant problems that may be awaiting you in the coming years.

First, let's consider a forty-seven year old man whose present expenses are $3,000 per month. He estimates (very optimistically) that inflation will run at about a 6 percent per year average. He plans to retire at age sixty at 80 percent of the salary of his top income year. Table 6.3 shows that by age sixty his expenses will have doubled, while his monthly income will have stabilized at $4,000 per month. At that point, he will be going "in the hole" by $2,396 per month. If you follow this projection on out, you can see that his ever-increasing monthly expenses begin to dwarf his fixed monthly income, leading to financial disaster.

Table 6.1–Expenses with Inflation
AVERAGE INFLATION RATES 6%–18%

YEAR	YOUR AGE	6%	8%	10%	12%	14%	16%	18%
0.		$1,000	$1,000	$1,000	$1,000	$ 1,000	$ 1,000	$ 1,000
1.		1,060	1,080	1,100	1,120	1,140	1,160	1,180
2.		1,123	1,166	1,210	1,254	1,299	1,345	1,392
3.		1,191	1,259	1,331	1,404	1,481	1,560	1,643
4.		1,262	1,360	1,464	1,573	1,688	1,810	1,939
5.		1,338	1,469	1,610	1,762	1,925	2,100	2,288
6.		1,418	1,586	1,771	1,973	2,194	2,436	2,700
7.		1,503	1,713	1,948	2,210	2,502	2,826	3,185
8.		1,593	1,850	2,143	2,475	2,852	3,278	3,759
9.		1,689	1,999	2,357	2,773	3,251	3,802	4,435
10.		1,790	2,158	2,593	3,105	3,707	4,411	5,234
11.		1,898	2,331	2,853	3,478	4,226	5,117	6,176
12.		2,012	2,518	3,138	3,895	4,817	5,936	7,287
13.		2,132	2,719	3,452	4,363	5,492	6,885	8,599
14.		2,260	2,937	3,797	4,887	6,261	7,987	10,147
15.		2,396	3,172	4,177	5,473	7,137	9,265	11,974
16.		2,540	3,425	4,594	6,130	8,137	10,748	14,129
17.		2,692	3,700	5,054	6,866	9,276	12,467	16,672
18.		2,854	3,996	5,559	7,689	10,575	14,462	19,673
19.		3,025	4,315	6,115	8,612	12,055	16,776	23,214
20.		3,207	4,660	6,727	9,645	13,743	19,422	27,393

AVERAGE INFLATION RATES 20%–60%

YEAR	YOUR AGE	20%	25%	26%	30%	40%	60%
0.		$ 1,000	$ 1,000	$ 1,000	$ 1,000	$ 1,000	$ 1,000
1.		1,200	1,250	1,260	1,300	1,400	1,600
2.		1,440	1,562	1,587	1,690	1,960	2,560
3.		1,728	1,953	2,000	2,197	2,744	4,096
4.		2,073	2,441	2,520	2,856	3,841	6,553
5.		2,488	3,051	3,175	3,712	5,378	10,485
6.		2,985	3,814	4,002	4,826	7,529	16,777
7.		3,583	4,768	5,042	6,274	10,541	26,843
8.		4,299	5,960	6,352	8,157	14,757	42,949
9.		5,159	7,450	8,005	10,604	20,661	68,719
10.		6,191	9,313	10,085	13,785	28,925	109,951
11.		7,430	11,641	12,707	17,921	40,495	175,921
12.		8,916	14,551	16,012	23,298	56,693	281,474
13.		10,699	18,189	20,175	30,287	79,371	450,359
14.		12,839	22,737	25,420	39,373	111,120	720,575
15.		15,407	28,421	32,030	51,185	155,568	1,152,921
16.		18,488	35,527	40,357	66,541	217,795	1,844,674
17.		22,186	44,408	50,850	86,504	304,913	2,951,479
18.		26,623	55,511	64,072	112,455	426,878	4,722,366
19.		31,948	69,388	80,731	146,192	597,630	7,555,786
20.		38,338	86,735	101,721	190,050	836,682	12,089,258

Table 6.2–Income and Expense Projection with Inflation

For _____   Date _____

	(1) AGE	(2) EXPENSES BASIS NOW	(3) FROM INFL. TABLE	(4) EXPENSES ____ % INFL.	(5) INCOME FROM:	(6) INCOME FROM:	(7) INCOME FROM:	(8) TOTAL INCOME	(9) SURPLUS (DEFICIT)
YEAR									
0.									
1.									
2.									
3.									
4.									
5.									
6.									
7.									
8.									
9.									
10.									
11.									
12.									
13.									
14.									
15.									
16.									
17.									
18.									
19.									
20.									

Table 6.3

AGE	MONTHLY EXPENSES @ 6% INFLATION	MONTHLY INCOME	MONTHLY SURPLUS OR DEFICIT
47	$ 3,000	$3,500	$ 500
50	3,573	4,000	427
55	4,779	5,000	221
60	6,396	4,000	−2,396
65	8,562	4,000	−4,562
69	10,812	4,000	−6,812

Another example (shown in Table 6.4) describes a fifty-seven year old man who has a paid-for home, and his expenses are only $1,000 per month. He estimates that inflation will average 16 percent per year between now and the year 2000. He is presently living on the interest he gets from $200,000 that he has in a savings account at 6 percent interest per year. He has worked hard, saved this amount, has his house paid off, and plans to live comfortably for the rest of his life in his present house with his dividend income. As can be seen in the table, by the time he is sixty-five, he is going to need to remove $2,278 per month from his $200,000 principal just to make ends meet. This will begin to reduce his interest income and quickly erode his capital. By the time he is 79, there won't be $25,000 per month in capital left for him to take out, yet our projection shows that he will need more than $25,000 each month just to pay his bills.

Table 6.4

AGE	MONTHLY EXPENSES @ 16% INFLATION	MONTHLY INCOME	MONTHLY SURPLUS OR (DEFICIT)
57	$ 1,000	$1,000	$ −0−
60	1,560	1,000	(560)
65	3,278	1,000	(2,278)
70	6,885	1,000	(5,885)
75	14,462	1,000	(13,462)
79	26,186	1,000	(25,186)

In the example in Table 6.4, if this gentleman's $200,000 were invested in real estate, silver coins, and other investments not denominated in fixed dollar amounts, he probably would survive well. The problem is that these kinds of investments are not "easy." The savings account is simple; he can sit back and receive his checks, never having to do anything. In order to get an income out of these other types of investments, he has to at least occasionally buy and sell something. He might even lose money on an occasional investment. However, in the end, inflation will not eat him alive as it will if he places his money in a savings account.

As an aside, you can also see how much better off this man would be if he were self-sufficient, providing his own utilities and food. If a person is providing his own life necessities, he is simply not affected as much by price rises. I counsel everyone to become increasingly self-sufficient, moving as close as possible to total self-sufficiency.

THE GOVERNMENT SAYS YOU CANNOT SAVE

They may not have said this in so many words, but this is the position into which their actions have forced us. It's easy to see that if our savings account is paying 4 or 5 percent, and inflation is running at 6 to 10 percent, the money in our savings account is growing in number but is simply losing purchasing power each year. In fact, anything that is in a constant dollar form, such as bonds, a retirement policy, a savings account, or life insurance, will lose value as inflation progresses. In other words, if you save in anything denominated in a fixed amount of dollars, YOU LOSE!

It is unfortunate that the government, by creating inflation, has taken away the option of saving. Many people are motivated to work hard and put away savings for a rainy day; America was built on this principle. Now, since we can no longer save in the traditional manner, in reality the government has forced us to invest. This is problematic for people who may know their jobs, businesses, or professions very well, but who do not know anything about investments. Many such individuals have entered the investment field, lost money, and retreated back to savings accounts, bonds, and T-bills as a way to "get hurt less." This type of negative thinking will insure long-range disaster.

We should perceive entering the investment arena as a new challenge, with an opportunity to learn something new and increase our wealth in the process. This is one reason why we publish our investments-economics newsletter, the *McKeever Strategy Letter.* Our goal is to help our readers move intelligently, without too much risk, from the position of being a saver to that of an investor.

MOVE OUT OF DOLLARS

So for the long haul, we do not want our wealth stored in anything that is in a fixed amount of dollars, such as bonds, savings accounts, T-bills, cash, insurance, and annuity policies. Any of these types of investments are not going to serve us well over the next twenty years. Therefore, we should intelligently move out of them and into something not denominated in a fixed amount of dollars. This may mean moving into gold coins, silver coins, real estate, antiques, art, diamonds, stocks, commodities, or anything that could continue to increase in value at the same rate or better than the rate of inflation.

SAVING VERSUS INVESTING

We've pointed out, then, that saving is traditionally thought of in terms of savings accounts, bonds, and so forth. There was a time when you could place your funds in these types of vehicles, and they would gain real purchasing power for you. Unfortunately, if you save in this way now, you are guaranteeing a loss and possibly destruction for yourself. Another way to look at it is that the government, with its inflationary practices, has forced us to take some risks and invest.

Now that we've established a real need for investing rather than simply saving in the traditional ways, let's talk briefly about three ways that you could save regularly to avoid being locked into a fixed number of U.S. dollars. Here we are talking about ways to save as opposed to ways to invest.

SAVING IN FOREIGN CURRENCIES
IN A SWISS BANK ACCOUNT

Since I am recommending that people save 10 percent of their earnings, but that they save in a way to avoid the U.S. dollar, we must then look at other methods for saving. One way to save regularly in a form that is not based in U.S. dollars is to open a Swiss bank account. The very thought of opening a Swiss bank account might strike fear in your heart, but it's really a rather simple matter.

You can open a Swiss bank account quite easily through the mail. Your purpose for having this account would be to save funds in a currency that is growing stronger than the dollar. Each payday you could simply write a personal or cashier's check in U.S. dollars and send it to the Swiss bank with instructions to buy the foreign currency of your choice and put that currency in your account. The major currencies you would want to consider are the Swiss franc, the Deutsche mark, the British pound, and the Japanese yen.

Your purpose here would be not only to gain the interest on the savings account, but also to gain the appreciation of the currency or other investment you have purchased in your Swiss account.

SAVING WITH GOLD AND SILVER COINS

Some people would prefer to have their savings closer to home rather than over in Switzerland, and I agree with this, for 90 percent of your savings. Another alternative would be to save in the form of gold and silver coins. The simplest way to place your savings in gold and silver is to buy one-ounce gold coins, such as the South African Krugerrand or the Canadian Maple Leaf, or to buy the solid silver U.S. coins that were minted prior to 1965.

These coins can be bought from most coin stores or can be purchased through the mail from a number of reliable sources. I consider this an excellent means for saving and will cover this subject in detail in a later chapter.

Briefly, to show you the advantage of putting your money

into coins rather than into a bank account, consider that a real silver dollar is worth about $15.00 today. This means that you can now purchase a $100,000 home with 6,600 silver dollars. Think of the position you would be in now if you had put all of your savings into silver dollars back when you could buy one silver dollar for one paper dollar. I believe that this trend of strengthening silver values will continue and I will have more to say on this later.

SAVING IN THE STOCK MARKET

There are programs set up by most of the major brokerage firms and mutual funds whereby you can invest a fixed amount each month. Using a fixed amount, you may end up with an odd fraction of a share at times, but they will keep track of all this and give you your portion of the dividend if one is paid.

One advantage of doing this is that it lets you take advantage of "cost averaging." Since prices are moving upward with inflation, you are going to get fewer shares at higher and more shares at lower prices since you are putting in a fixed amount each month.

The disadvantage of saving in the stock market is that at times the market is very strong and your savings will increase greatly, but at other times it takes a nose dive and you can lose a great deal. In fact, this is one reason why we publish a newsletter. Omega's *Financial Guidance* keeps our subscribers up-to-date on when it is a good time to be entering the stock market and when it is not.

INVEST OUT OF YOUR SAVINGS

Once your savings increase considerably, you can take these surplus funds and invest them as the Lord leads you.

It is true that these three savings vehicles I have described are in themselves a form of investment. Even though you are putting aside a percentage of your earnings each month into something that is not denominated in a fixed number of U.S.

dollars, the value of the Swiss franc, gold coins, silver coins, or stocks could go up or down so there is a risk involved. Thus, they are a combination of savings and interim investments.

In Chapter 3 we gave three rules for investing; before concluding this chapter, let's discuss two more important rules.

McKEEVER'S RULE #4 FOR THE 1980's:

ANY INVESTMENT THAT IS NOT MAKING AT LEAST 5 PERCENT OVER THE INFLATION RATE SHOULD BE CONSIDERED FOR LIQUIDATION

If you have borrowed (and improved your lending/borrowing ratio), you now have cash in hand and must determine what to do with it so it will at least keep up with inflation, and, hopefully, make a profit above inflation. I have two suggestions:

1. Be as liquid as possible. I consider a liquid investment anything that you can sell within five minutes and have your money within twenty-four hours. Stocks, commodities, gold and silver coins are all very liquid. Moving down the liquidity ladder, we find stamps, diamonds and antiques. Real estate is low on the list, and equity in a private corporation is at the bottom, being most illiquid.

2. Choose the risk level carefully. With every investment there is a risk. If I buy an antique desk, it could burn up, it could get broken in moving, its value could simply go down, or I could find that it is a copy and not a true antique. You always want to weigh such risks against the potential rewards and when you have a risk/reward ratio that you are comfortable with, you have found a good investment. In something like the commodity market, the risk is very high, and the potential rewards are very high. With the sharp ups and downs in commodity prices, some people get too nervous and lose their personal peace.

It is essential though that you take some risks since this is the only way your investments can outpace inflation by at least 5 percent. Again, if your purchasing power is not gaining against inflation, it is relentlessly being destroyed.

The following table (Table 6.5) shows this graphically. This table shows how long it will take, at various inflation rates, for you to lose 50 percent of your purchasing power:

Table 6.5

INFLATION RATE	YEARS TO LOSE 50% OF PURCHASING POWER
7%	10.2
8%	9.0
9%	8.0
10%	7.3
12%	6.1
15%	5.0
20%	3.8
25%	3.1
30%	2.6

At a 15 percent inflation rate, this table says that *in just five years you will lose 50 percent of your purchasing power!* This means that if you have a life insurance policy, and you were to die five years from now, at this inflation rate the policy would buy only 50 percent of what it would buy if you were to die today. If you have bonds, in five years their value will purchase only half of what it will purchase today. Thus, we see that our store of wealth (no matter how small or large our wealth is, we all have some) *must* keep ahead of inflation, or we will quickly lose the war to our financial archenemy, *INFLATION.*

I have frequently stated, in times past, that I felt the average inflation rate for the next twenty years would be 15 percent. I am beginning to feel that this is low, and that it will probably average 20 percent or more. We will be using that as my estimate in the remainder of this book. This means that if you are not making 20 percent on an investment, you are not keeping up with inflation over the long run, and you are losing your assets. Assuming that your realistic goal is to make at least 5 percent above the inflation rate, this means that today you must be making 25 percent on an investment to be making any real profit at all. To help our newsletter subscribers evaluate their investments, in each issue of *Financial Guidance* we have a section called "Values–Indices–Prices (VIP)." We are reproducing a sample one here.

VALUES–INDICES–PRICES (VIP)

	Friday 9/5/80	Friday 8/29/80	Year Ago	% Chg	%* PAID
GOLD	$651.00	$631.25	$329.15	+97	+82
SILVER	17.20	16.15	11.82	+45	+30
DJIA	940.95	932.59	874.23	+7	−8
DJT (Transport)	325.43	320.11	258.57	+25	+10
DJSC (Spot Comm)	445.57	446.10	404.31	+10	−5
COINS					
AUS. 100 KORONA	633.50	618.00	341.00	+85	+70
KRUGERRAND	670.00	656.00	356.00	+88	+73
MEXICAN 50 PESO	802.50	785.50	432.00	+85	+70
SILVER COINS (bag)	12,750	12,300	8,740	+45	+30

*Profit After Inflation Deducted Using 15 Percent Inflation

As you can see from this VIP table, it gives the prices of these various items and indices for the last two Fridays, as well as for a year earlier. It shows the percent change of the current price as contrasted to the price a year ago. Looking at this VIP table, we can see that if one year ago you had put 100 percent of all of your wealth into gold, you would have made a 97 percent gross profit over the last year. With about a 15 percent inflation rate, this would leave a real profit of 82 percent.

PAID is our acronym for Profit After Inflation is Deducted, since this is the percentage you really get paid. If you had invested 100 percent in silver in September, 1979, you would have gotten PAID 30 percent since the percent change in price was 45 percent. If you had invested in the DJIA (stocks in the same mix as the Dow Jones Industrial Average) that change was +7 percent and you would actually have lost 8 percent. If you had invested in the stocks that compose the Dow Jones Transportation average (DJT), the percent increase in their value was 25 percent, and you would have been PAID +10 percent, and so forth.

In the VIP section we do a similar thing for the most popular gold and silver coins. Here you can see that these all fared quite nicely over that time span. However, this has not always been the case. Through most of 1975 and 1976, the percent change for gold, silver, gold shares and the coins themselves was negative. On the other hand, during those years, the percent changes for the DJIA and DJT were quite positive. You could set up a similar table for yourself on your investments, but it would require constant record keeping so that you would always have information on prices a year earlier. A subscription to our MSL newsletter would be of help if you're not able to keep such tables for yourself. This takes us to another one of McKeever's rules:

McKEEVER'S RULE #5 FOR THE 1980's:

> *YOU MUST SWITCH PERIODICALLY FROM ONE TYPE OF INVESTMENT TO ANOTHER TO WIN OVER INFLATION*

For years we advised people to buy gold; then at the beginning of 1975, in *The McKeever Strategy Letter* (the other newsletter I edit), we said to sell gold. About two years later, when gold was $115 an ounce, we said to move into the stock market. These are the types of moves from market to market that are required if one is going to be victorious over inflation. The reason for this is that almost all markets tend to move cyclically. That is, the price of something will tend to move upward for a period of months or years, then will move downward for a time. So it's necessary to periodically review and change your investments.

CHOOSING YOUR COUNSELORS

Before looking at other possible investments, we need to address one other important concern. There are some financial consultants who would not necessarily agree with the advice I've given up to this point, and there are Christians on radio and television who are teaching financial principles and strategies different from what you've been reading. Thus, we need to take a close look at choosing our "counselors"–those people to whom we listen for financial and economic advice.

WALK NOT IN THE COUNSEL OF THE UNGODLY

In Psalm 1 the Bible describes a righteous man as one who "walks not in the counsel of the ungodly." Therefore, I think it's extremely important that Christians choose for professional counsel and advice persons who also acknowledge Jesus Christ as their personal Savior. This means that you should try to determine whether or not those people whose advice you are taking have accepted Christ as their Savior. If you blindly accept the counsel of just anyone, you may find yourself inadvertently walking "in the counsel of the ungodly." If we're going to be good stewards over God's gifts to us, it's important that we follow His advice in the Bible, and this includes seeking and accepting only the counsel of the "godly."

Therefore, I believe a Christian should have:

- a Christian attorney
- a Christian CPA
- a Christian tax consultant
- a Christian financial consultant
- a Christian investment advisor.

If one felt he should go to a psychologist for counseling, he should try to locate a Christian who is a psychologist. Let me reemphasize what I'm saying. Any time a Christian needs professional advice, he should seek to "walk" in the counsel of the godly by finding a fellow Christian to advise him. Remember that Satan can try to use the well-meaning counsel of a non-Christian professional to play havoc with a believer.

Now let's apply this specifically to the financial investment world. I know many Christians who take a number of different financial investment newsletters, which frequently contradict each other. These investors often find themselves confused and immobilized when trying to take appropriate financial action because of these conflicting opinions. I believe this confusion is not of God, but comes from the enemy of all Christians. So my advice to you would be to immediately cancel all subscriptions to financial and investment newsletters not written by Christians. If you want to subscribe to financial and investment newsletters, I suggest that you switch to those that are written by Christians.

The financial investment newsletters that I know of that are written by Christians are as follows:

1. Jim McKeever, *Financial Guidance*, P.O. Box 4130, Medford, Oregon 97501. $89 per year.

2. Jim McKeever, *The McKeever Strategy Letter*, P.O. Box 4130, Medford, Oregon 97501. $195 per year.

3. R. E. McMaster, *The Reaper*, P.O. Box 39026, Phoenix, Arizona 85069. $195 per year.

4. Johnny Johnson, *Daily News Digest*, P.O. Box 39850, Phoenix, Arizona 85069. $97 per year.

5. Gary North, *Remnant Review*, P.O. Box 8204, Fort Worth, Texas 76112. $95 per year.

6. Don McAlvany, *McAlvany Intelligence Advisor*, P.O. Box 39810, Phoenix, Arizona 85069. $77 per year.

The annual subscription rates I have given were current as of the beginning of 1984.

YOUR FINANCIAL "HEAD COACH"

Concerning choosing counselors, all we have done to this point is to point out that the Bible says we should eliminate the "ungodly." We then need to choose carefully from among the Christian financial counselors because there are those of a very poor quality and those of top quality. As we mentioned in an earlier chapter there are many pastors and junior economists who have written books concerning Christians and their finances. There are preachers and TV speakers, who are indeed Christians, but who are giving advice on finances, which is a subject far outside of their field of expertise and spiritual gifts. I've seen Christian stockbrokers and real estate agents give very bad advice to fellow Christians. It's impossible to say whether the source of their poor advice was personal greed or ignorance; either way the result was the same—the people they counseled were hurt financially. So it's critically important that you choose not only a *Christian* financial advisor but also one who has a track record of winning advice.

I spoke at an international investment conference in New York in September, 1980, where I shared the platform with Louis Rukeyser, William Simon, Alan Greenspan, Arthur Laffer, Henry Kissinger and many other outstanding men. In my talk I compared investments to a football game. In both football and investments, there's a time for offense and a time for defense. There's a need to scout out one's opponent. There's a time to take three points, rather than gambling to get seven. The parallels between football and investments are really very close.

In that talk, I asked the people what they would think of the chances of a football team having a winning season if it had five strong-minded, co-equal head coaches. The audience laughed because it is highly unlikely the team would win even a single game. They realized that a football team needs one and only one head coach. He can have assistant coaches, but there must be only one head coach that the team looks to for direction and guidance. Similarly, I believe that Christians should pick one of the Christian financial advisors around for their "financial head coach." I would encourage a person to write the head coach's name down and possibly under that name, two or three assistant coaches. (In our *Almighty and the Dollar Personal Planning Workbook,* we provide a page for this.)

Once a person chooses someone to be his financial head coach, he should look to that coach for his primary financial advice.

Of course, the individual investor is like a quarterback who has the responsibility of calling his own plays. The coach can give him the best possible advice, but eventually the decision has to be the quarterback's.

Since there are innumerable investment advisors and newsletters being ricocheted about, and since our economy is in a chaotic state, the Christian needs to be much in prayer about whom to select as his financial head coach. If you take the time to do this now, you might simply write his name inside the front cover of this book. If later you decide to get a copy of our personal financial survival workbook, then you can subsequently transfer that name to the appropriate page. Now let's see what we have covered in this chapter.

SUMMARY AND CONCLUSION

First, I hope that I have sufficiently underscored the importance of saving. After you have paid your tithe, I encourage you to put at least 10 percent each month into savings. However, I do not think that it's best to put your money into savings accounts, bonds, whole life insurance, or anything denominated in a fixed number of U.S. dollars.

The secret then is to know how to wisely save this 10 percent. I recommend placing it in some other form, such as a foreign currency, gold coins, or silver coins, that will keep ahead of inflation. You could call things like silver coins that are half savings and half investments, "savements."

To know what is the best "savement" at a specific time, financial newsletters written by Christians can be very helpful. We looked at the different types of counselors, and I encouraged you not to use a non-Christian counselor in any area of your life, and that certainly would apply to the financial realm. I pointed out the need to rely on top quality professional advice from Christians, and I suggested you elect one person as your financial head coach.

A sound strategy is to build up your savings to a selected level, then to withdraw from this surplus for whatever purposes the Lord leads you in. You may find yourself making withdrawals for purchases, for donations to Christian ministries, for helping the poor, or for investing as a good steward.

In the next section, we will take the major investment areas, including the savement areas and deal with each of them in detail.

PART 2

INVESTMENTS

7

REAL ESTATE

As we now begin to look at the investment arena, I thought it best to start with the most familiar types of investments and work toward the least familiar. Almost everyone in America has owned his own home or at least lived in a home that his parents or grandparents owned. Usually, a home is the largest investment that a Christian family ever makes, so we will begin with a discussion of real estate.

We'll move from this familiar and comfortable type of investment through the various major investment vehicles of today in later chapters.

WHAT IS AN INVESTMENT?

Let's begin by redefining this term "investment"; otherwise we might have a communication problem.

As I said earlier, the definition of an investment is very plain and simple:

An investment is something that we buy in hopes that the price will go up, with every intention of selling it at the higher price.

To help you understand a distinction I'm making, I'll share an experience that I had once when consulting with a very "sophisticated" couple. The wife asked me "My *deah* Mr.

McKeever, are Persian rugs a good investment?" My reply to her was that if she was thinking of buying ten Persian rugs, storing them in a warehouse, and selling them five years later, she could evaluate that as an investment. But on the other hand, if she was thinking of buying a Persian rug and putting it on her floor to enjoy and to use, she should not try to convince herself that the rugs were an investment. I told her that she should view them simply as items to purchase for her own personal enjoyment. A purchase of this kind may or may not appreciate in value, but it really doesn't matter because there is no intent to sell it and "take profit." Thus, for something to be considered "an investment" there must be a commitment to eventually sell it for a profit.

OWNING YOUR OWN HOME

Most American couples dream of owning their own home. With prices rising and higher interest rates, this has become progressively more difficult for most families. So we have seen the tremendous increase in condominiums, where the property and common walls are shared, reducing the costs of a person owning his own place of residence.

Why do most people buy their own homes? Not usually for investment purposes. That is, most people don't buy a home with intentions of selling it for a profit within two to five years when the price rises. Most people buy a home because they plan to live in it for a long period of time. So buying your own home is similar to buying a Persian rug for your personal use. In fact, buying one's own home could be considered a poor investment, if there is a great deal of equity tied up in the home.

For example, let's suppose that someone had purchased a $25,000 home many years ago which has appreciated and is now worth $60,000. Let's also suppose that the principal loan has been paid down to $10,000. These people really have $50,000 tied up as equity in their house. The Lord may want them to continue just as they are or even to pay the house off. However, looking at the home purely as an investment, that may or may not be the wisest place to have $50,000 invested. But, again, most people really don't view their home as an investment but more as a Persian rug.

As another example, many doctors personally, or in separate corporations, purchase the building in which their practice is located. This usually has some tax advantages, but, again, this can't be considered an investment because there is no intention of selling it in two to five years when it increases in value.

While we're on the subject of owning your own home we should point out that there are a number of advantages to owning. Of course, you have a neighborhood where you can put down roots and have friends and your children have a yard to play in, and there are other obvious advantages. There is another advantage, however, that is not quite as apparent. If you are renting, as inflation continues upward, your rental might go from $300 per month to $800 per month to $1,000 per month to $5,000 per month. On the other hand, if you are purchasing your own home, and the payments are $300 per month, they will never increase and will always remain at that rate.

WHAT ABOUT RENTAL PROPERTY?

Rental property may or may not be an investment depending on the purchaser's goals and objectives.

One reason for buying a duplex, apartment house, or single-family dwelling to rent out would be that the purchaser wanted or needed the income. The value of the piece of property may indeed go up, but much like a person's home, there is no intent to sell it if the price rises since the income is the major consideration. What the purchaser is actually doing is buying a business, and it happens to be a rental business. When a person starts or buys a business, he is not doing it primarily as an investment, in most cases.

If he buys a restaurant and intends to run it and manage it, he's buying this business as a source of livelihood, usually with plans to retain it for many years regardless of how it appreciates in value. Similarly, if a person starts a business, say a hardware store, that business may indeed appreciate in value, but usually the purchaser has no intent or desire to sell it until he gets ready to retire, change geographic locations, or earn a living in some other way. It is the change of circumstances in his life that will cause him to sell it, not its increased value.

On the other hand, a rental property can be approached as an investment. If someone buys rental property in an area where he believes a major shopping center is going to be built, a free-way exit ramp is going to be placed, or city expansion is going to reach, he's buying the property basically for the increase in value. His plan would be to sell it after it had increased in value. The fact that there is rental income, which helps with the mort-gage and tax payments is a plus, but that's not his major reason for buying the property. In this case, the purchase of rental property would definitely be an investment.

Another reason for buying property would be to use it as insurance rather than as an investment. There is a little old lady in Germany who survived two world wars and a hyperinflation with a paid-for duplex. She lived in half of it, and the rental in-come from the other half paid her taxes and bought her food and clothing. In this case, a paid-for duplex was excellent insur-ance against economic chaos but was not necessarily a good investment.

So we find that there are at least four ways to view buying property: (1) for personal enjoyment and use, (2) for rental in-come, (3) for a kind of insurance, and (4) for investment pur-poses. In the remainder of this chapter we're going to be looking purely at *investing* in real estate.

A NEGATIVE SIDE TO INVESTING IN REAL ESTATE

Before we look at the positive side of investing in real es-tate, we should look at the big negative:

REAL ESTATE IS NOT LIQUID

Again, an investment is liquid when you can sell it within five minutes and have your money within twenty-four hours.

There are many investments such as stocks, commodities, gold, silver which are liquid. Any of these can be sold within minutes, and you can have a check the next day. Obviously, real estate does not fit into this category. Each piece is a specialized invest- ment, and it takes weeks or sometimes months to find the right buyer who is interested in the property. If the real estate mar- ket ever begins to crash, many people's *investments* in real estate could vanish very quickly before they could sell.

Another negative for real estate is that when you're ready to sell, you are at the mercy of the lending institutions. If the interest rates are too high for prospective buyers, it becomes im- possible to sell, or if the lending institutions are short of money or they do not like your particular type of real estate, again it could be very difficult to sell.

A third negative is that most real estate investments re- quire continuous monthly payments. If you are investing in raw land, the mortgage payments and taxes must be paid while you are holding it. If you invest in a recreational condominium, or a regular rental unit in a city, if the unit goes vacant for a few months, you still must put up the money for the mortgage pay- ments and taxes. Of course, for property on which there is a building, there are the usual maintenance costs of repairing broken pipes, windows, and so forth, as well as a need for peri- odic painting and grounds maintenance. Often what might in- deed be a good investment can eat an investor alive with such costs before he can sell the property at a profit.

CALCULATING YOUR PROFITS

Assuming that you want to get PAID at least 5 percent, this means that on any real estate you buy, you are going to have to double your money in four or five years. I did not say double the value of the real estate. I said double your money. For example, if you were able to buy a $50,000 house with $5,000 down, you would have to be able to sell the house with- in four or five years for $55,000 in order to give yourself a $5,000 profit, which would double your original investment of

$5,000. This is assuming that the rental received on the house would cover all closing costs, payments, interest and so forth. (A $5,000 profit after five years would be a 20 percent a year return on your money. If we subtract 15 percent inflation, we get PAID 5 percent.)

RAW LAND VERSUS RENTALS

When most people think of investing in real estate, they think of buying raw land out in the general direction of the growth of a city. This is fine for wealthy people, who can afford to make the mortgage payments and the tax payments out of their own pocket for many years. However, for most Christians this is unthinkable, so they are forced to invest in real estate that will provide at least enough income to pay all of their costs.

Even if an individual can afford to buy raw land, I do not recommend it. With the economy of our nation going up and down and many people, including myself, forecasting a depression, we could see city development and growth stopped. The value of raw land may continue to go up, but I doubt if it will keep up with the rate of inflation.

I think similar considerations apply to purchasing shopping centers, office buildings, and rentals geared for businesses. As the depression gets worse, businesses will fail, and one could find himself with a much higher than anticipated vacancy factor, jeopardizing the entire investment, including the initial capital invested.

So this narrows our investment choices to rental property geared for individuals. Before you begin looking for such rental property, there are two major decisions you must make:

1.   How many units per piece of property?
2.   Should the property be near you or in a small town?

First, let's consider how many living units we would want on the property. People with greater means might consider an eight-unit building or even one with one hundred or more apartments in it. There is some advantage to having all of your eggs in one basket (that is, all rental units on one property). There is less yard maintenance; you can have a live-in superintendent; and the economics are in general a little more feasible.

You should also keep in mind that often the government's answer to inflation is to impose wage and price controls. Even if the federal government doesn't, many cities and states have in the past put on rent controls. An interesting thing though is that buildings with four or fewer units are usually exempted. Thus, I would lean toward buying two buildings with four units each, or even four duplexes rather than a building with eight apartments. There is more traveling and time involved in overseeing multiple pieces of property, but they are easier to sell since the cost per piece of property would be less.

The second major consideration is whether to buy a property near you, which for most people means buying in a city, or to buy property more remote from you, perhaps in a small town. Here, I would suggest giving strong consideration to buying in a small town.

In the event that the cities become riot-torn, this would be a part of your assets that would likely not be affected. Also the people in a small town tend to be more stable and less transient; therefore, finding and keeping a good tenant should be much easier. Perhaps, the lower vacancy factor would compensate for the time and distance and possibly even the management fee that you might have to pay.

INVESTING IN DISTRESSED PROPERTY

By shopping around, you can usually find undervalued properties with eager sellers. For example, if someone has died and his heirs are anxious to dispose of a piece of real estate in order to settle the estate, you can frequently negotiate a small downpayment and good terms on paying it out (including an assignable mortgage). You can often get it for a price somewhat under its appraised value. This type of real estate investment is covered well in John Kamn's book, *How To Make Money Fast*

Speculating in Distressed Property (published by Pyramid Books). He deals with buying property at auctions from banks that have foreclosed, and so forth. One can often get good bargains and make substantial profits in this area.

INVESTING IN OPERATING FARMS

One of my favorite real estate investments is an operating farm. This can be either a small or a large operation, but regardless of size, it should have all of the outbuildings and necessary supplies. In southern Oregon, the value of this type of property is going up at about 25 percent per year, based on the total value. Comparing this to our earlier example, if you were able to pay $5,000 down on a $50,000 farm, and it went up in value 25 percent per year, this would mean that in four years the farm would be worth $100,000! If you broke even on all expenses, the $5,000 would have brought in an incredible $45,000 profit! This kind of investment will keep you well ahead of inflation.

SUMMARY AND CONCLUSION

There are many excellent books on the details of investing in real estate. They tell you what to look for in a property and in a neighborhood. They cover tenant relationships and point out inexpensive ways to fix up a piece of property. The intent here has not been to replace any of these books with a single chapter in this book, but rather to try to put real estate investments and owning your own home in their proper place in the overall picture of your financial planning.

We have seen that by making a small downpayment and letting the property appreciate, we can make a significant profit on our investment. Rental properties of four units or less, distressed properties, and operating farms appear to be some of the best bets for real estate *investment.* We would also be inclined to purchase these properties in smaller, more rural towns rather than in large cities. Who knows, you might need to go to one of those small towns and occupy one of your rental units in time of a social upheaval.

Most people who buy real estate are really not doing it for an investment although they might try to convince themselves of this. Most property is purchased to be lived in or to conduct a business in. Such purchases, for the average Christian, should not be classified as investments.

If God leads you to free up some of your assets and invest, then you should certainly do so. Real estate is one way in which you can invest if you truly do it for an investment. Now let's look at some other avenues of real investment for the Christian.

8

GOLD AND SILVER

If you are interested in an investment that you can purchase and simply set aside for five years—an investment that appears to have the best chance of keeping up with and beating
inflation—I would suggest silver. My second choice for an investment that will fare well against inflation would be gold.

There are four basic ways to invest in gold and silver:

1. Coins in your possession.

2. Bullion in a Swiss bank.

3. Stock in mining companies.

4. Futures contracts.

We will be discussing three of these in this chapter and will
save investing in gold and silver futures contracts for Chapter 11
where we discuss commodities.

GOLD AND SILVER COINS

The best way to invest in gold and silver is to invest in gold
and silver coins to keep in your possession.

To have coins "in your possession" means that they are
where you are. This could be a safe deposit box in a bank or
somewhere on your own property. Remember the adage that a
thief cannot steal what he cannot find. Many people hide coins
in their attics, in old paint cans, at the bottoms of potted plants,
or in other places where thieves will not likely find them.

A disadvantage to investing in coins, particularly in silver coins, is that they are heavy and bulky. It's by no means easy to invest in gold and silver coins. But if you would like to lay something aside for a rainy day that is going to keep its true value, I would place these coins at the top of the list.

There are two types of gold and silver coins that you can buy: (1) bullion coins, and (2) numismatic coins.

A gold bullion coin is a coin on which the value is determined strictly by the amount of its gold content. The most popular gold coins are given below:

Coin	Troy Ounces of Gold
Mexico 50 Peso	1.2056
Austrian 100 Korona	.9802
South African Kruggerand	1.00
Canadian Maple Leaf	1.00

As you can see, two of these coins contain an even one ounce. If you own coins that are exactly one ounce, and gold is at let's say $600 per ounce, you know that your coins should be worth $600 and slightly more. The "slightly more" is called the premium. Someone has to buy the gold bullion, melt it down, stamp it into coins, and distribute it. This premium is the money that you pay for all of this to happen. However, the premium can increase or decrease according to what the gold market is doing. If gold is in a strong bull market, owners of these coins will tend to demand a larger premium for their coins since so many buyers want to purchase them. During downward or sideways price movements buyers are more "choosy," and premiums fall back into their normal ranges.

On the other hand, you could invest in numismatic coins. This really means "rare" coins. Here, the value is partially determined by the amount of gold (or silver) the coin contains, but the greatest factor in its value is rarity.

Numismatic (rare) coins are fun to invest in, but one should always be aware that a significant part of their value lies in their rarity. It may be that in a time of crisis people will not place much value on rarity but rather will focus purely on bullion value.

I would not invest in any of the medallions or small bullion bars minted by private mints. These are difficult to sell and have other disadvantages. I would only invest in coins that are minted by an established government. If you want to invest in bullion bars, I would suggest you do it only through a Swiss bank.

The place that I recommend for the purchase of gold and silver coins is a company run by a Christian couple in Denver, Colorado. They sell gold and silver coins by mail all over the United States. Ask for Don or Molly McAlvany and tell them that you read about their service in a book by Jim McKeever. They will give you preferred treatment. You can contact them at:

International Collectors Associates   Phone: (303) 759-0308
Writer's Tower, Suite 309
1660 So. Albion St.
Denver, Colorado 80222

GOLD AND SILVER BULLION IN A SWISS BANK

One of the reasons that I do not recommend buying gold or silver bullion bars and taking them into your possession is that you have to have them reassayed before you can resell them. In the past, unscrupulous people have drilled out holes in the centers of silver bars, filled them with lead, and after coating the exterior holes with silver, sold the bars as pure silver. So most people who buy silver bars require that they be assayed before they will buy them.

There's also the disadvantage of size. If you had a one hundred ounce silver bar, and you wanted to sell a little of it, you could not just take a hacksaw and saw off some. With silver coins you could have the same amount of silver in smaller units that are more usable.

If you do want to invest in bullion bars, however, you can

avoid many problems by opening a Swiss bank account. You simply deposit money in the Swiss bank and have them buy the gold or silver for you. They will guarantee that it is good, deliverable bullion. They keep it in their possession, and when you get ready to sell it, they guarantee that it is good deliverable bullion so you do not have to go through the reassay process.

As you can see, a Swiss bank is not at all like a U.S. bank. A Swiss bank performs many versatile functions for its depositors. They can buy gold or silver coins (either bullion or numismatic), gold or silver bullion bars in various weights, and most of the major stocks on the various stock exchanges around the world. The bank that I recommend most is:

Foreign Commerce Bank
Bellariastrasse 82
8038 Zurich, Switzerland

We will cover this subject in greater detail in our chapter on Swiss banks. Also, we will repeat the address of this Swiss bank and others in Appendix B for your convenience.

STOCK IN MINING COMPANIES

Another way to invest in gold and silver would be to actually buy stock in companies that mine gold and silver, or you could invest in mutual funds or holding companies that invest solely in gold and silver mining companies.

Since the prosperity of the company is linked to the prosperity of the country in which it is located, you should view mining companies as being divided geographically. The divisions to consider are:

1. U.S. companies

2. Canadian companies

3. South African companies

4. Companies in other countries

Most of the gold and silver stocks that are purchased by U.S. investors are in the first three categories. Investing in these three categories is just about identical from an ease point of view. Any brokerage firm can easily buy the shares for you in U.S., Canadian, or South African companies.

There is another way to categorize stocks in mining companies which is even more significant. These categories are:

1. Holding companies
2. High quality producing mines
3. Low quality producing mines
4. Exploration companies

As you go down this list, the quality and safety decline progressively, which means the risks increase progressively. The last two categories must be classified "speculative," while the top two categories are generally considered "high quality."

The holding companies are much like mutual funds. They buy and sell stocks in mining companies. They have teams of experts that study the various mines and mining companies, and they try to invest in the ones that have the best potential and the best income. With a holding company, your risk is spread across a large number of mines, and it is unlikely that they would all go bad at once. Therefore, the risk here is low. The high-quality category would be mines with proven and defined ore bodies and an estimated ten-to-twenty-year life remaining. These usually also have prospects of other potential ore bodies that are not yet proven.

In the speculative category there are the older mines that initially had, perhaps, a twenty-year estimated life, but that was eighteen years ago. They are speculative since they may be nearly mined out. They are worth considering, though, since other ore bodies could be discovered. Or, if they contain large amounts of low grade ore, if the price of the precious metals rise, then they could mine the low grade ores at a profit.

The most speculative issues (those with the greatest risks and yet the greatest potential gains) are the exploration companies. Many of these companies have test holes that show there is some amount of ore available, but the ore body has not yet been defined nor has it been put into production. When an exploration company reaches the production stage, the stock usually skyrockets.

Since the status of the speculative mines and exploration companies changes with time, we will not include any recommendations on these in this book. However, as of this writing there are a number of stocks that are almost universally considered in the high-quality category. These are:

HIGH-QUALITY
HOLDING COMPANIES

ASA Limited
International Investors
Anglo American South African

HIGH-QUALITY
SOUTH AFRICAN COMPANIES

West Driefontein
West Vaalreeff
Kloof Gold Mines
Western Deep Levels
President Steyn
Amgold

HIGH-QUALITY
NORTH AMERICAN COMPANIES

Homestake
Campbell Redlake
Agnico–Eagle
Asarco
Sunshine
Callahan Mining
Day Mines
Dome Mines
Hecla

We will not take the time to discuss these stocks in this book; to do so would require a book all by itself. If you wish to pursue the subject, I would recommend a book by my friend Don Hoppe, entitled *How To Invest In Gold Stocks And Avoid The Pitfalls.*

RISK IN INVESTING IN GOLD AND SILVER MINING SHARES

If you choose to invest in the stocks of gold or silver mining companies rather than buying coins or bullion, you are assuming additional risk. These additional risks include:

1. The mine may not be operated profitably.

2. There could be a major labor strike.

3. There could be an accidental flooding or cave-in of the mine.

4. The management of the mine could do a poor job.

5. The mine's ore body could run out.

This list could go on and on. If you are going to take additional risks on an investment, there must also be additional potential for reward to compensate for the added risk. It has been my experience that gold stocks do not provide the additional reward. For example, if gold doubles in price, the stock in a good quality mine will generally only double. In order to compensate for the additional risks, it should go up at least triple. The only mines that tend to outperform the price of the bullion itself are the very low quality exploration mines that have even greater risks than what we have been discussing here. Therefore, in general, I am negative on investing in gold and silver mining shares and much more inclined toward investing in gold and silver coins or bullion bars through Swiss banks.

There is one exception to this, however. The South African shares (the *kaffirs)* tend to pay from about 10 or 20 percent in dividends each year. So if a person needed income but also wanted to protect his principal so that it would appreciate with inflation, *kaffirs* would tend to meet this need. However, these South African stocks carry additional special risks of which you should be aware.

About 80 percent of the free world's gold is mined in South Africa. Thus, the South African government, which controls all of the mines, is a major factor in the international gold market. The South African government can withhold gold, to a limited degree, from the world market and tend to cause gold prices to go up. Also, when the price of gold is high, the government often mandates that the mines mine lower quality ore which reduces their earnings. This is done in anticipation of the day when gold prices will be lower, and it will be economically necessary to come back and mine the higher grade ores. So the earnings of the stock can be affected by government regulations and decrees.

Another negative aspect of the South African companies is that they could be affected if the U.S. imposes foreign exchange controls again. The last time this occurred, buying and selling the South Africans was penalized by additional taxes on the U.S. investor. Another factor you must weigh is the future stability of the South African government. We have seen Rhodesia fall and become Zimbabwe, and we know that the Russians would love to control South Africa. So, as you can see, there are a number of risks you must assume when investing in these stocks. Yet with such high quality mines it's difficult to ignore the South Africans in the mining stock arena.

WHY SILVER AND GOLD?

Gold and silver are not valuable because some government or group of people has declared them valuable. Throughout history these metals are what the people themselves have chosen of their own free will for a measure of wealth, a store of value, and a medium of exchange.

Even in ancient history, gold and silver were the primary items of value. As we pointed out earlier, Genesis says that Abraham grew rich in "gold, silver, and cattle." We know from archeological excavations that a thousand years before Moses lived, taxes were paid in gold and silver in the ancient city of Elba.

This intrinsic value in gold and silver has continued into modern times and gives every indication of continuing. Recently, we saw a graphic example of the power of gold when South Viet Nam fell. For those who wanted to flee, an ounce of gold would buy a boat or plane ride out of South Viet Nam and nothing else would accomplish this. No amount of South Viet Nam's currency, piasters, diamonds, or anything else would suffice. An ounce of gold got an individual out, and if a person didn't have an ounce of gold he stayed behind no matter what he might have had of value. Thus, we can see from this example that even today gold is a refuge of last resort. It is the only store of value that is recognized in a time of total monetary and economic chaos.

GOLD IN WAR

An interesting thing happened during World War II. A friend of mine was in the underground in Europe. He was given orders to go to a certain German prison and free a high-ranking American officer. He told them that in order to do this he needed a two-ounce gold bar and a ten-ounce gold bar. Using a passport of a country that was in league with Germany, he took a train from France into Germany and then took a taxi to the prison. He spoke with a lieutenant who served as an orderly for the colonel who was in charge of the prison. When he asked to see the colonel, the lieutenant replied that it was impossible.

At this time my friend produced the two-ounce gold bar and said, "If you can get me in to see the colonel, this is yours." He said, "I'll be right back," and moments later ushered my friend into the colonel's office. My friend asked the colonel to release the high-ranking American officer to him. The colonel said that was totally impossible. He then produced the ten-ounce gold bar and told the colonel that if he would release the American prisoner to him, the ten-ounce gold bar would be his. The colonel replied, "Just one moment." He made a phone call, and within five minutes the American officer was escorted into the colonel's office. The colonel shook hands with both the

American officer and my friend, wished them well, and released them. The American officer was later returned to England via secret escape routes.

Again, from this World War II example we can see that gold seems to speak when everything else is silent. Incredible things can be done with gold because gold is the single universally recognized store of value and measure of wealth.

Silver is beginning to play this role and in some ways is becoming the "poor man's gold." However, holding several large silver coins in your hand still does not have the same impact as holding the dollar equivalent of a very small gold coin.

As insurance against a monetary or an economic collapse, I believe it is wise for a family to try to have at least a few gold coins or some silver coins. These should prove to be a good investment during inflationary times and will also serve as insurance in the event of a monetary collapse.

SUMMARY AND CONCLUSION

We have looked at investing in gold and silver and have suggested using gold and silver coins as insurance against a monetary or economic crisis. We discouraged the purchase of gold or silver bars or medallions, except through a Swiss bank. We recommended purchasing gold and silver coins actually minted by some recognized government.

We discussed bullion coins, which have their value basically because of their silver or gold content, and we discussed numismatic coins, which are valuable partially because of their precious metal content and partially because of their rarity. The numismatic coins generally prove to be good investments during normal times, but would not hold value as well as bullion coins during monetary crises because of the limited market. During monetary crises people are much less interested in buying something simply because of its rarity.

We also looked at investing in gold and silver by buying shares in gold and silver mining companies. We pointed out that there is greater risk in investing in mining stocks than there is in investing in gold and silver coins. In order for mining stocks to be a wise investment for a good steward, there would have to be additional potential for reward to compensate for the additional risk.

There is one additional way to invest in gold and silver, and this is through commodity futures contracts. These will be discussed in Chapter 11 when we discuss commodities.

In the interim, at the very top of our list would remain gold and silver coins as (1) a liquid investment, (2) a way to save regularly, (3) an investment that will keep up with inflation, and (4) an insurance for a time of economic or monetary chaos.

9

COLLECTIBLES—ART, ANTIQUES, STAMPS, NUMISMATIC COINS

With the exception of gold mining shares, the investments we have discussed so far—real estate, gold, and silver—are what you would call *tangibles*. These are things that you can touch and handle, not pieces of paper. Later we will be discussing *intangibles*, such as stocks, bonds, commodity futures, and currencies. These investments are pieces of paper. In some instances, pieces of paper represent tangibles, but they are not tangibles themselves.

In this chapter we would like to discuss "collectibles," which fall into this tangible category. Tangibles would be such things as oil paintings, antiques, diamonds, stamps, and other physical objects that people enjoy collecting.

INVESTING IN ANTIQUES

Here, it's important to make a distinction; we are talking about *investing* in antiques, not *buying* antiques. Among some investors, there is the familiar truism that you shouldn't buy new furniture; you should buy antiques to use because you can enjoy them while they appreciate in value. That is a nice theory, but in the vast majority of cases, it is purely a rationalization, making it emotionally easier to pay more for an antique dresser or armoire than we might pay for a contemporary one. The fallacy in this thinking is that usually when we buy antiques, there is never any real intention of selling them. In fact, quite the opposite. Once we buy an antique and use it for a few years, we tend to become attached to it, and to sell it would almost be an emotional trauma.

For example, I have a friend who bought a beautiful hand-carved buffet and china cabinet for his dining room. He got it at a "good price," and he and his wife delight in thinking that it is increasing in value. My personal opinion is that the chances of their ever selling that antique are close to zero. In their case, I would have to consider this beautiful antique buffet a purchase and not an *investment* in antiques.

Purchasers of antiques usually go through antique stores and look for a "bargain" or a "good deal." Those who *invest* in antiques go to auctions and visit rural areas where they can knock on doors and ask people if they have any old furniture in their attic. Investors also pick up antiques in disrepair and refinish them. The people who are really into investing in antiques are looking to buy something at the cheapest possible price and then to sell it at a profit as quickly as they can. These investors usually own antique stores or run ads in the newspaper, or have some other ready means of disposing of the antiques.

Doubtless, most readers of this book are not really interested in making the purchase and sale of antiques a profit-making business for themselves. Most of you are really buyers of antiques rather than investors in antiques. If you wish to buy an antique, and the Lord gives you peace about it, then buy it and don't worry about it, but do not try to fool yourself into thinking that it is an investment.

INVESTING IN STAMPS

Many of us have had stamp collections as children and enjoyed looking for unusual stamps on old envelopes or perhaps occasionally buying a packet of stamps at the local five-and-dime store. Few of us ever graduated from that level of collecting and actually began buying and selling rare stamps for significant amounts of money.

If you are going to invest in stamps, you must spend a great deal of time in studying stamps and the stamp market. You must be acquainted with current prices and must be able and willing to locate bargains and make purchases. As an investor in stamps you must also attend stamp auctions and stamp shows in order to gather information and get the best prices. In addition, you must also have a ready market for selling or auctioning your stamps after they have appreciated. This type of true investing in stamps is done by very few.

If a person is considering investing in stamps, not as a hobby but rather for the profit, he should first count the costs. In addition to studying stamps and the stamp market, he should be able to recognize forgeries and ascertain the quality of stamps as well as their authenticity. In that sense, he would almost have to become an appraiser of stamps to do a proper job of investing.

An advantage to investing in stamps is that one can carry much wealth in his coat pocket or in a small envelope. Of course, stamps are undetectable by metal detectors in airports so a great deal of wealth can be transported undetected. However, in turbulent times of economic upheaval when the average person is struggling to buy food, clothing, and shelter, there may be very little interest in purchasing rare stamps. Thus, a stamp could have value, but there might not be anyone interested in buying it.

INVESTING IN DIAMONDS

Like some of the other items we have discussed, it's possible to *invest* in diamonds and it's possible to *purchase* diamonds. These are two entirely different transactions. Again, we don't want to buy a diamond ring, a diamond brooch, or a diamond tie tack as an "investment" unless it really is. Any diamond already made into jewelry is really not an investment because it has already been marked up roughly 300 percent. This means that the value of the diamond would have to triple in price before one could even break even in trying to sell it for the worth of its contents.

Investing in diamonds is quite another thing. There are reputable companies where you can buy a diamond of investment grade. These come with an AGI (American Gemological Institute) certificate. AGI has strict standards for size, cut, clarity, color, and so forth. If there is an AGI certificate with your investment grade diamond and/or a photo print of the refractivity of the diamond, it can be considered an investment. These are usually contained in sealed, clear plastic envelopes, and most people maintain them in safe deposit boxes. The investor's goal, of course, is to subsequently sell these investment grade diamonds for a profit.

In my opinion, once that diamond is taken out of the plastic envelope and made into a piece of jewelry, it is no longer an investment because the intent to sell it no longer exists or, at best, is greatly diminished.

Investing in diamonds does have certain advantages. Diamonds have consistently kept up with inflation. This is due not only to the ever-decreasing value of the U.S. dollar, but also to the strong control of the diamond industry by the DeBeers Corporation. DeBeers has control over such a significant portion of the diamond industry that they can exercise considerable force in maintaining diamond prices. You can attend a DeBeers diamond sale, which they have four times each year, only by invitation. They will offer to you a box of diamonds, which you are not even permitted to see, with information concerning the number of carats and the price at which they are offering the diamonds. There is no negotiation permitted; you either take their offer or not. If you do not, you are not invited to another DeBeers sale. By setting prices in this manner, DeBeers has thus far been able to ensure that market prices have not declined.

Another advantage of owning diamonds is, as with owning rare stamps, that one can transport a great deal of wealth in a small space, undetected by metal detectors.

Investments in diamonds are basically for the very wealthy, who wish to have a diversification for some amount of their funds.

Since the average Christian is not going to invest in diamonds in keeping with our definition of an investment, I would question the stewardship of a Christian who tied up very much money in a diamond ring. Perhaps a ring containing a synthetic diamond or an artificial diamond (such as Zircon) would look as nice and would free up the Lord's money to do other things. Unless you are going to become a serious investor in diamonds, I would advise you to stay away from them.

If you do wish to *invest* in diamonds, I would suggest contacting:

Gemstone Trading Corporation   Phone: 1-800-223-0490
30 Rockefeller Plaza
New York, NY 10020

INVESTING IN ART

When we talk about investing in art, we are not just talking about investing in oil paintings. We could apply our investment criteria to watercolors, original prints, statues, pottery, and other *objets d'art*. For simplicity's sake, we will use oil paintings as an example for discussing all of these art media.

Again, we need to remind ourselves of the difference between investing and buying. It is certainly legitimate for Christians to own a home and want to have paintings on the walls. If under God's guidance He tells you to buy some, that's fine. There are a number of very inexpensive reproductions that can be purchased that are very beautiful. These can be framed with ready-made frames, and, with very little total cash expended, they can significantly beautify one's home. To buy an original oil painting, and to have a frame custom made, simply for the pride of having such an object hanging on one's wall seems to leave many unanswered questions about motives.

Perhaps, in the area of art works there are more people who do indeed invest rather than buy. I know people who buy oil paintings by well-known artists, enjoy them for a couple of years, then take them to an art auction or gallery and sell them. I don't know how much money they make as compared to their other investments, but, as with buying and selling anything, if it is done with sufficient research and skill, it can be profitable.

If someone were really interested in investing in art, with a view to making money, he would need to approach this arena just as the rare stamp investor approaches his field. He would have to attend art auctions in order to buy good quality paintings at bargain prices. He would have to attend estate liquidation sales where paintings and other household belongings are being liquidated to see if he could purchase an oil painting cheaply so he could turn around and sell it for more. He would run ads in newspapers to sell his paintings or might even have his own small gallery through which he could dispose of the paintings he purchased.

When an artist dies, the value of his paintings usually begins to move up appreciably, probably because of the newly-limited supply (there will never be anymore paintings by that particular artist). Therefore, many people who invest in art look beyond the painting to the artist. They try to find out his age, sometimes even the condition of his health, and how many paintings he's done. This is the kind of information that an investor needs to acquire if he is going to truly invest in oil paintings rather than just acquire them for his personal enjoyment.

INVESTING IN OTHER COLLECTIBLES

There are many other collectibles that we could discuss. Some people enjoy collecting antique dolls; others collect miniatures; others collect old horse-drawn farm equipment; and the list could go on and on. Probably almost everything in existence has been collected by someone at some time.

If you enjoy collecting something and want to do it as a hobby for fun and relaxation, that's wonderful, as long as it doesn't absorb you, taking your mind and energy away from the Lord. However, if you fully intend to invest and make money at collecting items, selling them, buying others, and selling those, then you need to view those collectibles purely as investments just as you would evaluate any other investment. You need to determine how much profit can be made and what the annual average increase in value is. Then you must determine where you will sell these collectibles, how big a market there is, how liquid this market is, what your selling costs will be, and so forth.

Please, don't misunderstand; I certainly do not want to sound derogatory toward collectibles. One simply needs to proceed with caution with this type of investment. I know one man who collects horse-drawn farm equipment. When he finds a good horse-drawn hay rake, for example, he tries to bargain, negotiate, or trade to get it at a good price. Then if he already has a horse-drawn hay rake which he has repaired or reconditioned, he runs an ad to sell it, hopefully at a profit. This man's view of the future is that some day, whether because of energy shortages, breakdowns in oil distribution, or whatever, he might have to actually farm with horse-drawn equipment. Thus, if such a breakdown ever occurred, he could get a good team of horses and actually use his collection. So he considers this an investment, both for making money and for insurance purposes if he ever needs to actually use the equipment.

10

STOCKS AND BONDS

Before we look at paper investments, we should touch upon the major, negative aspects of that type of investment. When you invest in the stock market, bond market, or commodity market, what you get for your money is a piece of paper that says that you own or have an interest in something. The piece of paper usually comes from a company; thus, it is only as good as the company is.

For instance, if you decided to buy gold coins on margin through a certain company, they would give you a piece of paper indicating that you had put up a deposit and, therefore, you owned a partial interest in so many actual gold coins. However, if that company were to go bankrupt, most of the people who purchased gold coins on margin would lose most, if not all, of their investment. So in making these financial (paper) investments, one of the immediate dangers you must take into consideration is the possibility that the company issuing the piece of paper could become unsound or even extinct.

Another major negative of investing in paper assets is that you must time those investments fairly accurately. Our economy goes in cycles, and there are periods when paper assets as a whole will increase significantly in value, and there are periods where they decrease greatly, wiping out the investment dollars of those people who purchased them. This is not to say that paper assets should be avoided, but simply that there are risks involved with timing.

Possibly the most all-encompassing negative of paper investments is that they either float or sink on the ocean of the world economy. That is, paper money, bonds, stocks, mortgage paper, and all other financial assets are, at the bottom line, only pieces of paper. They are only worth what other people are willing to pay for them. As long as the general confidence level of the mass of purchasers is high on a given currency, stock, or other paper asset, the value of that investment will remain high. But the minute the public loses confidence in that piece of paper, its value will fall quickly. This is the primary difference in *tangible* and *paper* assets. An ounce of gold will always be worth an ounce of gold. Food, land, a home, or any other physical item retains its value for its owner regardless of what happens to the worth of paper investments or currencies. A paper asset retains its worth only inasmuch as the public has confidence both in it and in the economy of which it is a part.

In recent years we have become painfully aware of how fragile the paper money system is. With disturbingly high inflation rates, bond market crashes, soaring energy prices, wildly gyrating interest rates, and other signs of an underlying chaos in the world monetary interplay, we have to question how stable the paper assets will be across long periods of time.

This is not to say that we should not involve ourselves in this kind of investment. It simply means that we must use paper investments and enjoy their benefits when the time is right, and we must be prepared to move quickly out of them and into tangibles if we begin to detect serious signs of our monetary system starting to crumble. We recently learned from Mt. St. Helens that even a volcano will give tremor signs before it erupts. Our strategy should be to use the paper assets to our advantage but to stay vigilantly sensitive to the world monetary system to detect any "evacuate" signs.

Now that I have given you the negative side of paper investments, I'll point out the many positives to investing in stocks, stock options, and commodities.

STOCKS AND BONDS

For many people, the phrase "stocks and bonds" conjures images of Wall Street wheeler dealers smoking big cigars, and stock market crashes with people jumping out of windows. If this is your image of investing in stocks and bonds, let's try to get a little more realistic picture.

WHAT ARE BONDS?

A bond is much like a special purpose savings account. Suppose that a bank had a special kind of savings account into which you could put $1,000, and they would pay you 12 percent interest a year, but you couldn't draw the $1,000 out until a specified year, let's say the year 1999. Basically, you have loaned the bank $1,000, and they are willing to pay you a higher than normal interest rate because you've committed yourself to leave your funds with them for a large number of years.

When you hear of General Motors bonds or U.S. Treasury bonds you're looking at a very similar thing. Bond purchasers are loaning that company, or the U.S. Government, a fixed amount of money at a fixed interest rate for a long number of years. Most bonds pay interest to the holder of the bond at regular intervals, such as annually or quarterly. However, a Series E savings bond, with which many people are familiar, postpones the interest payment until the bond is due and then pays it all in one sum. For example, if you pay $75 for a $100 bond (really it is a $75 bond), they simply pay you $25 interest at the time the bond comes due by redeeming the bond for $100.

Unlike the savings account, which is in your name only, the bond is simply a piece of paper (think of it as a passbook) that you could sell to someone else. Let's say, for example, that you bought a $1,000 bond that paid 9 percent interest and was due in the year 1999. Suppose you held it for one year and then wanted to sell it. If the interest rate on new bonds being issued at that time was 9 percent, you could probably get most of your $1,000 when you sold your bond to someone. On the other hand, if interest rates on new bonds being issued had risen to 20 percent during that year, whoever buys your bond would not be willing to pay you nearly as much for it because he could buy a new one at 20 percent and make more interest on his money. If he paid you only $800 or $900 for it, he would end up making about 20 percent on the money he had invested since he would be getting 9 percent interest plus the savings of having bought the bond at a nice discount. On the other hand, if by some miracle during that year interest rates had dropped to 5 percent on new bonds, and yours was paying 9 percent, it would be worth more than the $1,000 you paid for it. So the prices of bonds rise and fall depending on the interest rates at the current time.

STABILITY OF BONDS

When interest rates were fairly stable, with only slight fluctuations across many years, the value of bonds was also fairly stable, and people used these like long-term savings accounts. Then, in late 1979 and early 1980 interest rates skyrocketed, and the value of bonds crashed downward losing billions of dollars in value for bond holders.

During the last depression (which was a deflationary-depression, with prices and interest rates falling) bonds were a very good investment. Those people who had their money in bonds rather than in the stock market did very well. However, as we have already pointed out, the depression that I believe we are headed into is going to be an inflationary-depression (one with prices and interest rates skyrocketing). Thus, we could see bonds falling in price because of significantly higher interest rates. In addition to this, you have to consider the purchasing power erosion. If the $1,000 bond is paid back in 1999, it may purchase no more than what $10 or $100 will purchase today. Thus, bonds in an inflationary environment are guaranteed to lose you money and to make you a poor steward.

STOCKS

So we find that when we buy bonds we are actually loaning the company or the government our money. When we buy a stock in a company we are actually buying a *part ownership* in that company. For example, if a new company opened, and it was going to sell one thousand shares, and you bought five hundred of those shares, you would be a 50 percent owner of the company. Under U.S. law, you would have no liabilities as a stockholder, but if the company were ever liquidated, you would be entitled to 50 percent of the proceeds. If it made enough earnings to pay dividends to the stockholders, you would get 50 percent of the total amount of dividends paid out.

The risk in this particular investment is that the company could go bankrupt, and the value of your stock would be worth almost nothing, even though the stock would still exist. Another risk is that even if the company does very well, when you're ready to sell your stock, you may have a hard time finding a buyer for it. On the positive side, if the company does well, it could pay you dividends each year, which could be significant. I've seen situations where people received more in dividends each year than they initially put into the stock. At least owning stock in this company has the potential for keeping up with or ahead of inflation, whereas a bond, we know, will not likely keep ahead of inflation.

THE STOCK MARKETS

In the simple example we have been using, you have been 50 percent owner of a company. Now let's look at buying stock in larger companies with thousands and sometimes millions of stockholders. If a stock owner (stockholder) wanted to sell his stock and he lived in Arizona, and another person wanted to buy stock in that company, but he lived in Virginia, they would have a difficult time finding each other. The stock markets are meeting places so that the man from Arizona and the man from Virginia can make their transaction.

Forgive the analogy, but you can think of the stock market like a used car lot where you bring your car and leave it, and they sell it to someone, and you pay them a commission for doing this. The stock markets are really "used stock" markets. (New stock is usually sold directly by the brokerage firms to their clients and does not go through the stock markets). Let's say you've bought a stock and you've "used" it for awhile, and now you want to sell it. You take it to your broker, who is a member of a stock market. Let's say that someone else wants to buy that stock, and he tells his broker, who is also a member of the stock market, to buy it for him. Then the two brokerage firms meet at a central marketing place where the transaction actually occurs.

There are three major stock markets in the United States. The New York Stock Exchange, located in New York City, the American Stock Exchange, located in Chicago, and the Over The Counter (OTC) market, for smaller stocks with less volume. Almost all stocks are traded on one of these three exchanges.

If a stock is not traded on one of these major exchanges (or on one of the minor exchanges such as one of the Canadian markets or the Pacific Coast Exchange) it is considered a stock in a "non-trading" company. The difficulty with holding stock in a non-trading company is that the stock may indeed go up in value, but, again, it may be very difficult for you to locate a buyer. I would discourage the average Christian of modest means from investing in non-trading companies, simply because of the difficulty in selling if he needs to.

A MEASURE OF THE STOCK MARKET

When you hear on the evening news that the stock market was up six points or down five points, what does that mean? To answer that we must look at something called the Dow Jones Industrial Average. What the Dow Jones company does is to monitor thirty stocks of what they call "industrial" companies. The "industrials" would exclude companies involved with transportation, utilities, and so forth. Using a formula that takes into account stock splits and other considerations, they come up with an "average" value of those thirty industrial stocks, which represent some of the largest companies in the United States. Thus the Dow Jones Industrial Average, "DJIA," is a pseudo-average of those thirty stocks. Supposedly, this gives a general picture of what the market is doing. In recent years this has not been the case. These thirty industrial giants may be rocking along with sideways prices while the stock prices of bright new companies are zooming upward, and the stock values of broken-down old companies are falling out of bed. Thus, the DJIA gives people a general idea about the market, but it may say absolutely nothing about the trend of an individual stock.

What this means is that if a person is going to invest in stocks, he is going to have to look at the *individual stock* itself rather than the Dow Jones Industrial Average. I find that a picture is indeed worth a thousand words, so I would encourage anyone who is going to invest in stocks to subscribe to a charting service that sends you the charts of all the stocks you are interested in weekly. The charting service that I like best is:

DAILY GRAPHS   (213) 820-2583
P.O. Box 24933
Los Angeles, CA 90024

(This address is repeated in Appendix B.) Even though the fee for this charting service is fairly high, I believe it is worth it since you can review at least weekly in a pictorial way the exact direction the stock is going.

HOW DO I DECIDE IF I SHOULD INVEST IN STOCKS?

Now that we have the basics and mechanics out of the way, we come to the more difficult question of *should* you invest in stocks. Space will not permit me to cover this subject in such detail that I could adequately answer that question in the context of each reader's specific situation, but I can give a few broad thoughts on the subject. Rather than investing in individual stocks, there is a way that is far better for most Christians, and is by using mutual funds. I will mention more on this later.

Looking at the stock market, as measured by the DJIA, it really peaked out in 1968. If you take inflation into account, the DJIA today would have to go over 2000 for you to have more purchasing power in U.S. dollars than you would have had in 1968. This means that, in real value terms, the DJIA has gone no where. If you measure the stock market in ounces of gold, the stock market has actually crashed. If you had taken your money out of the stock market in 1968 and put it 100 percent in gold, you would have made about 2000 percent since 1968 on your gold. Had you left it in stocks, you would have lost significantly in purchasing power.

During the 1950's and 60's, one could buy good quality stocks such as IBM and almost be assured that if he held them, five years later he could sell them for significantly more than what he paid. I believe those days are gone forever. In the economic environment of the 1980's, there will be occasions when people can make money in the stock market, and there will be times where it would be disastrous to be in the stock market. Thus one must move with caution into and out of the market. In *Financial Guidance* we keep our readers posted on a regular basis as to the timing for moving into or out of the stock market. We also recommend industries with the best prospects and beyond that we give specific stock recommendations.

I would consider the average broker who works in the average brokerage firm to be one of the world's worst sources of advice on the stock market. Remember these brokers are "used stock" salesmen, and they must be approached with the same caution as one would approach most used car salesmen. Their livelihood depends on selling stocks to you. They also get up very early in the morning to go to work and take your orders. If they were so smart and wise they wouldn't be acting as an order taker for investors; they would be one of the investors instead.

I would far rather see a Christian go to an independent Christian newsletter publisher whose livelihood depends on people subscribing to his newsletter. People are only going to continue subscribing to such newsletters if they recommend the right investments at the right time. Thus, they are highly motivated to recommend to you the right and the best investments. (I wish that stock brokers were paid based on the profits that their clients made rather than on the amount of money that they bring in on each sale. This would weed out the bad brokers, and the few good ones would remain.)

HOW DO I KNOW WHICH SPECIFIC STOCK TO BUY?

Concerning which stocks to buy, studies have shown that it is far more important to be in the right industry. It matters much less which stock within that industry you are in as long as you are in the right industry. For example, during the 1980's I believe that stocks in energy companies and stocks in electronic and computer companies are going to do well. It will matter less which oil company, or oil well drilling company, or oil well equipment company you're in. As long as there is a high demand for energy and a high price for it, the earnings of these companies will continue to do well.

Similarly, if the electronic and computer industry does well, it will not matter as much whether one is in IBM or NCR or one of the smaller companies. The important thing will be to be in the electronic and computer industry.

Even though you might be in the right industry, the stocks within the industry tend to go upward in a sawtoothed fashion, and one would like to time his purchases as close to the bottom of one of these sawtoothed moves as he can.

HOW DO I KNOW WHEN TO BUY A SPECIFIC STOCK?

Not only do we need to know which stock to buy but also *when* to buy and eventually *when* to sell. It's obvious that I cannot tell you here exactly when to buy. However, let me point out a couple of basic factors.

One is that the stock market has a basic four-year cycle. It goes up for roughly two years and then down for about two years, as can be seen in Figure 10.1. The market also usually

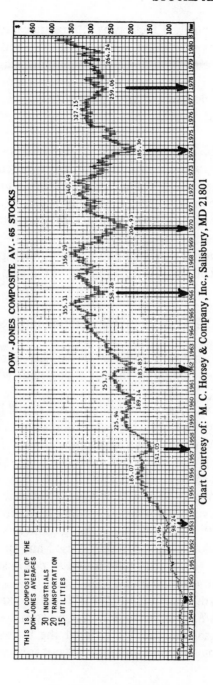

Chart Courtesy of: M. C. Horsey & Company, Inc., Salisbury, MD 21801

Figure 10.1

moves in the opposite direction of interest rates. If interest rates are rising, the stock market is usually falling, and after interest rates peak out and start down, the stock market usually starts up. In general it is better to be in the stock market during its two-year up cycle and out of it during its two-year down cycle, although certain stocks may move contrary to the general market.

Beyond this, you must look at the charts of the specific stocks to know when it is the best time to purchase a specific stock. The best time is frequently after the value of the stock has dropped down and then started up again. Do not take anyone's word for this, simply look at the charts for yourself to determine this.

The decision as to when to sell is a much harder one for most people. The use of stop loss orders makes this decision much easier.

THE USE OF STOP LOSS ORDERS

So we see that it is much easier to determine *which* stock to buy and *when* to buy it than it is to decide when to sell the stock.

The best way for the average person to sell his stocks is to use "stop loss orders." A stop loss order is an order such that if the stock comes down to a certain price level, it is automatically sold for you by the brokerage firm. For example, if you bought a stock at $20, and it moved up to $25, you could put a stop loss order in to sell it at $22. If the price of the stock ever did start declining, when it hit $22 it would automatically be sold out at that price. If one is going to invest in stocks, I believe that stop loss orders should be used and should be moved up weekly. The best place I have found to put in stop loss orders is right under an uptrend line.

To help you understand this, I'll use an example from an issue of *The McKeever Strategy Letter* written in October 1975. This example shows how we entered the Swiss franc futures market based on the chart and how we put in an initial stop loss order at the time we made the purchase. As the price moved up, we progressively moved up our stop loss orders. While we have used a commodity purchase for this illustration, the mechanics are the same for stocks, and you can duplicate the practice of using stop loss orders with any stock you buy. The following is a quote from *MSL* issue number 112.

"Use of Stop Loss Orders

"Because of the current volatility of the markets and because we want to be listening to what the markets are telling us, we must use stop loss orders, if we invest now. Figure [10.2], which is of Swiss Franc futures, shows how to successfully use stop loss orders. Here we bought (at Point A) after a double bottom (or the bottom was retested successfully). A more conservative move would have been to wait until it exceeded its previous high (Point B). At the time we buy we determine the maximum amount of money we want to lose and place a stop loss order. In this particular case a good number would be .3300 because it is reasonable to expect that it will not go below that point. After a short time has gone by and an uptrend line can be drawn (shown as a slanted line on the chart), we keep moving our stop loss order upward so that it remains slightly below the uptrend line. Assuming that we were conservative and bought at .3500, as soon as possible, we would like to have our stop loss sell order at slightly over our purchase price so that we can ensure that we will at least break even. Therefore, our first stop loss would probably be at .3550.

"As the Swiss Franc continues to move upward, we continue to move up our stop loss order (again keeping it slightly below the uptrend line). We move it to .3600, then to .3700, then to .3800. Later we move it to .3900 and finally to .4000. (In order to do this, you must either keep your own chart or subscribe to charting services. This is essential for properly using stop loss orders). Before we can move it up further the market comes back down through the uptrend line, and so the market has automatically sold us out at .4000. At this point we really do not know what the market is going to do. It may be a slight dip-down before a continued major move upward, or it may start to move down significantly. If it is only a slight dip-down before another move upward, we can buy again and start the same process all over again. Since the investment was made in October, 1974, and stopped out in February, 1975, a significant profit was realized across that seven month period. My experience has been that after a strong profit it is then best to leave that particular investment and

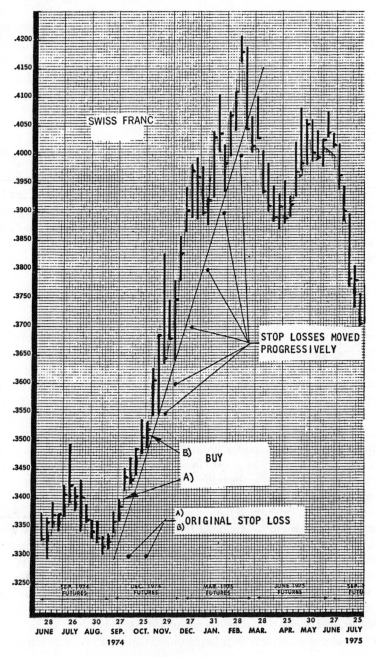

Figure 10.2

look for something else in which to invest. Remember, you only make money when you sell. Many people know when to buy; very few people know when to sell. Therefore, it is wisest to let the market tell you when to sell through the proper use of stop loss orders."

PARTICIPATING IN THE STOCK MARKET THROUGH OPTIONS

Even though the stock market has a great deal of potential reward, it also has much potential risk. One could lose all of his capital like many people did during the market crash in 1929. But the market doesn't have to crash for you to suffer losses; a company can simply go bankrupt or encounter significant problems for your individual stock to lose most or even all of its value.

Through the use of stock options you can participate in the future potential gain of a stock while limiting your potential loss. A stock option is much like an option to purchase a piece of property. It is a common practice to enter into an agreement with the owner of a piece of property to purchase it for a fixed amount within a certain period of time. That privilege—or "option to buy"—must be purchased for, perhaps, $500 or $1,000 or more. So there is the cost of buying the option, and it is only usable for a fixed amount of time.

Similarly, a stock option is an agreement whereby you can buy a stock (this is called a "call" option) at a fixed price at any time during a designated period of time. Or you can enter into an option to sell a stock (called a "put" option) at a fixed price for a fixed length of time. For this option there is a fee. Again, just like in the option to purchase land, you will lose the fee if you do not exercise the option. However, your total risk is limited to the amount of the option fee. For example, let's suppose that a stock is currently selling at $17 per share, and you get an option that would expire next December to purchase 100 shares of that stock for $20 per share. For that option you pay $100. If the stock value drops to $5, you only lose your $100. On the other hand, if the stock price moves up to $25 before the following December, you could sell your option for $500 or more and take your $400 profit, or you could actually use your option to purchase the stock at $20 per share and immediately sell it for its current market value—$25 a share. Now let's look at trading options in greater detail.

THE CALL OPTION

I would like to discuss a maximum way to take advantage of a move up in a stock. It should be emphasized here that I did not necessarily say *optimum*, I said *maximum*. By investing in the options market, you can potentially multiply your money by ten, twenty, or even forty times. This means that we are talking about turning $1,000 into $10,000–$40,000. While this has obvious appeal for those who want to multiply their funds quickly, it also has potential for the more conservative investor. I usually recommend that approximately 10 percent of one's investment portfolio be placed into highly speculative areas, such as the options market.

I should reemphasize though that investing in options is pure speculation. There is a good chance that you will lose, either partially or completely, anything that you put into the options market. Many people have lost significant amounts of money in the options market so there is a calculated risk involved here along with outstanding profit potential. Now let's learn the terms and mechanics of the options market so those of us who wish to can use this investment vehicle.

UNDERSTANDING THE TERMS

There are two types of stock options, *puts* and *calls*. In this book, we will only be discussing calls. Again, a call is the right to purchase a particular stock at a fixed price for a fixed amount of time. For this privilege, you pay a fee. For example, let's suppose that this is the month of August and MacDonalds is selling for about $55 per share. I could buy an option to purchase MacDonalds at $60 per share any time between now and the last Monday in January. In this illustration, the $60 is called the "strike price." The date the option runs out (the last Monday in January) is called the "expiration date." So you can describe any call by giving the following three items of information:

1. Name of stock
2. Expiration date (month)
3. Strike price

Thus, the option that we have described would be called "MacDonalds January 60."

OPTIONS PRICES IN THE WALL STREET JOURNAL

Once one understands the basic terminology, reading the prices out of the *Wall Street Journal* is a simple matter. The options prices are usually two pages from the back, on the page between the commodities and the over-the-counter markets. For Figure 10.3, I have reproduced a portion of these prices from an August 19th *Wall Street Journal.* As you can see, MacDonalds is the first option listed. At the far right you see the closing price of the stock (not the option) on August 18th. The first line shows the option for purchasing MacDonalds stock at $50 and across you have the price of the option for October, January and April. For each of these you are given the volume and the last price for August 18th. Thus, we see that for the privilege of purchasing MacDonalds at $50 before the last Monday in January, we would have to pay $8. For that same privilege for the last Monday in April, we would pay 9-3/8 ($9.37). However, if we go down to the MacDonalds 70, we can see that for January we would pay only $.75 (3/4). Each of these options contracts is sold in 100 share lots, so if we wanted a MacDonalds January 70, it would cost us $75.

If one is serious about options, I would recommend reading *Barrons,* in addition to the *Wall Street Journal.* Their statistical information is more complete, and their coverage is extensive.

Listed Options Quotations

Wednesday, August 18, 1976

Closing prices of all options. Sales unit usually is 100 shares. Security description includes exercise price. Stock close is New York Stock Exchange final price.

Option &	price	– Oct – Vol.	Last	– Jan – Vol.	Last	– Apr – Vol.	Last	N.Y. Close
Mc Don	. 50	85	6⅜	16	8	4	9⅜	55
Mc Don	. 60	296	1 1-16	107	2 13-16	11	4¼	55
Mc Don	. 70	50	⅛	164	¾	b	b	55
Merck	... 60	2	14	b	b	b	b	73¾
Merck	.. 70	93	5¼	11	7½	1	8¾	73¾
Merck	.. 80	65	⅝	89	2	a	a	73¾
M M M	..50	96	14⅛	10	14¾	b	b	63¾
M M M	. 60	486	4¾	180	6½	27	7⅜	63¾
M M M	. 70	259	½	130	1⅞	33	2⅞	63¾
Monsan	..80	72	10¼	a	a	1	13⅛	89
Monsan	..90	58	3⅛	12	5⅝	8	7½	89
Monsan	.100	16	7-16	15	1⅝	b	b	89
N C R	.. 25	5	10⅛	a	a	b	b	35
N C R	...30	52	5½	11	6½	3	7⅝	35
N C R	...35	352	1⅞	66	3	59	3⅞	35
Nw Air	.. 25	40	6½	a	a	b	b	31
Nw Air	.:30	197	2⅝	48	3¾	39	4¾	31
Nw Air	..35	249	⅝	131	1¾	61	2¼	31
Pennz	25	18	5⅞	a	a	b	b	30¾
Pennz	... 30	62	1 15-16	31	2⅞	48	3⅞	30¾
Pennz	... 35	58	⅜	12	1	1	1⅝	30¾

Figure 10.3

So if we buy a MacDonalds 70 option, and if MacDonalds stock goes up to $80 per share within the time prescribed, and the option is either executed (used to buy the stock) or sold, the gross profit will be $10 per share on 100 shares, which is $1,000. If we had purchased ten contracts for an investment of $750, we would have realized a gross profit of $10,000. To determine our net profit, of course, we would have to subtract our initial $750 investment as well as the commission charges.

OPTIONS VERSUS OWNING STOCK

In the same example of MacDonalds, if we had taken our $750 and actually purchased MacDonalds stock, we would have been able to buy about fourteen shares. If the stock then had gone from $55 up to $80, we would have realized a $25 per share profit for a total profit of $350. This profit of $350, compared to the gross profit of approximately $9,000 on the options basis, shows why people trade options. They trade them because of the tremendous leverage (multiplier) on profits. If a stock goes up 5 percent, the price on the option is liable to go up 100 percent.

In comparing purchasing stock to purchasing options, we must also look at the negative aspects of options. The primary negative is that you are likely to lose either a part or all of your money. For example, in our MacDonalds illustration, if you held the options until they expired, and if the stock had only gone up to $65 from $55, not reaching the $70 strike price, your options would have been worthless. You could also have sold your options at any time prior to the expiration date and taken a loss. The closer you get to the expiration date, the smaller the chance that the stock will move up to and beyond your strike price. Therefore, you can usually find speculators who are willing to buy your options, but as time passes and the expiration date grows nearer, they are willing to pay less and less for them.

On the other hand, if you had bought the stocks, you would have had a profit of $140; on the options you would have suffered a loss of $750. Similarly, suppose the stock had dropped to $50 and remained there through January. If you owned the stock, you would have lost $70. If you owned the options you would still have lost the full $750.

Placing this into a table, we see the following comparisons:

Table 10.1

Price of MacDonalds Stock On Date Of Sale	Profit or Loss From Purchasing Stock	Profit or Loss From Purchasing January 70 Option
$ 50	$ (70)	$ (750)
60	70	(750)
70	210	(750)
80	350	10,000
90	490	20,000
100	630	30,000
110	770	40,000

Looking again at Table 10.1, we find that by buying the stock itself you can lose a little or make a reasonable amount. By buying options, you either lose significantly or make it big.

Figure 10.4 shows the remarkable leverage option calls provide. For every $1 increase in the price of the stock above the strike price, the option provides an additional $100 profit, as opposed to only $10 for the stock.

WHICH OPTIONS TO BUY

There is a rule of thumb that I use in determining which options to buy after I have selected the proper stock. The basic rule of thumb is to buy the option where the strike price is barely above the current price of the stock and to buy the option with the latest expiration date. I would not buy an option where the current price of the stock is significantly above or below the strike price.

Take the MacDonalds example again, I would prefer the MacDonalds April 60 option based on this rule of thumb. I would like to compare two options, but since there is not a MacDonalds April 70, we will compare MacDonalds January 60 with MacDonalds January 70. This comparison is in Table 10.2.

THE ADVANTAGE OF BUYING CALLS INSTEAD OF STOCK
Results of Investing $1,000 in Calls
Compared to an Equal Investment in Stock.
*(Price of Stock When Purchased: $100
Premium of $100 Strike Price Calls: $10)*

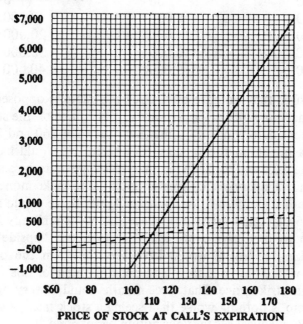

PROFIT OR LOSS

PRICE OF STOCK AT CALL'S EXPIRATION

———— *BUYING CALLS*   - - - - - - *BUYING STOCK*

Figure 10.4

To keep our dollar investment on the two options similar, we can only purchase three contracts for MacDonalds January 60 since it costs $2.81, whereas January 70 only costs $.75. The three contracts at $281 each gives us a purchase price of $843. One of the reasons that it goes up in value less rapidly than the

Table 10.2

Closing Price On Date of Sale	Profit or Loss from January 60	Profit or Loss from January 70
$ 50	$ (843)	$ (750)
60	(843)	(750)
70	3,000	(750)
80	6,000	10,000
90	9,000	20,000
100	12,000	30,000
110	15,000	40,000

January 70 is that we have only three contracts as opposed to ten contracts in January 70. However, if the price on the stock at settlement date winds up somewhere between $60 and $70, we have a profit on the January 60 whereas we would have a loss on the January 70. Thus, January 60 appears to be a safer option while January 70 has greater potential to make money.

If we had purchased MacDonalds April 60, we would have paid $4.25 per share for that privilege, and we would only have been able to buy two contracts. Therefore, our "upside" or profit-making potential would have been less. On the other hand, we would have had three additional months for this stock to reach its strike price. That three months could be very significant. There is nothing worse than seeing a stock make a spectacular rise two weeks after your option has expired.

LIQUIDATING YOUR INVESTMENT

Let's say that you have purchased an option, and you are now in a big profit position and you wish to sell it to take your gains. The question is: how do you do it? You could, of course, wait until you felt the stock was at a high point prior to the expiration date, take delivery of the stock, and immediately sell it, realizing your profit. In our example, let's say that you bought a MacDonalds 60, and the stock rose to $80. You could then buy the stock for $60 by exercising your option and turn around and immediately sell it for $80, taking your $20 per share profit.

There is actually an easier way to take your profits because of the liquidity provided by the options market. There is usually someone who is willing to buy your option. The people willing to buy your option fall into two categories:

1. People who initially sold and now need to buy to cover their position.

2. Traders, who will buy the option as you did, speculating that the price will go even higher.

Even the day before the option expires, if the stock is trading above your option's strike price, you will find buyers interested in purchasing your options.

USE WISE MONEY MANAGEMENT

You can also use stop loss orders for options. Let's say that you bought an option for $1, and it went up to $3. You could then put in a stop loss order at $2. If the price hit your stop, you would be sold out and still realize a profit. If the price keeps climbing, you would keep raising your stop loss order.

Another wise money management technique is to liquidate a part of your investment. After your money has doubled or tripled, you could sell half of your options, realize some profit, and keep the other half for even higher potential gain.

RISK–REWARD RATIO

The primary purpose for participating in stock options is to get a higher risk–reward ratio on your investment. In our comparison between purchasing the stock and purchasing a call option on the stock, we found that by purchasing the stock, we limited ourselves to relatively small losses and relatively small potential rewards. On the other hand, when we purchase an option, we are either going to lose a substantial amount of our money or make large rewards. Thus, the risk–reward ratio between the two is dramatically different.

Statistically, since the beginning of options trading on the exchanges, only 40 percent of the options have actually been exercised (used to purchase stocks). This means that approximately 60 percent of all options are allowed to expire and basic-ally become worthless at the time they expire. Thus, if you are planning to buy options to hold until near their expiration dates, you are speculating with the odds stacked against you six to four. Any money invested in stock options should be speculation funds that you are willing to lose completely.

THE BEST WAY . . . MUTUAL FUNDS

I believe the very best way for most people to invest in the stock market is through mutual funds. A mutual fund is a com-pany whose sole business is investing in the stock market. They may have several hundred professional people analyzing various stocks. Their professional management in almost every case makes them winners in the stock market. As you invest in their company and they make a profit in the stock market, then you make a profit. There are two basic types of mutual funds. These are:

1. Load mutual funds
2. No-load mutual funds

The mutual funds all started out by being loaded funds. That means that you had to pay about an 8 or 9 percent com-mission to the salesman in order to purchase them. Back in the 1960's, these tended to be a bit of a ripoff, since, if the stock market only went up 9 percent, the best you could do would be to break even. The load on most of the better mutual funds now has come down to where some of the load funds are actu-ally very attractive.

However, there are now no-load mutual funds, where there is no sales commission charged at all; hence the term "no-load." As far as the stock market goes, I believe, by and large, the no-load mutual funds are the very best way to invest in the stock market in the 1980's. There is no way you could compete with their huge professional management staff and these no-load funds have had a very good record up until now.

However, there are many different kinds of no-load mutual

funds and here is where guidance is necessary. Here are just a few of the various types of funds that exist:

1. Capital growth funds
2. Precious metals funds
3. Energy-related funds
4. Medical-related funds
5. Tax-exempt bond funds
6. High technology funds
7. Money market funds
8. Treasury bill funds

The funds that I like best are, in reality, a family of funds. That means that a single mutual fund may have sub-funds within it. A typical family of funds might have a money market fund from which you could actually write checks, a precious metals fund, a high technology fund, an energy-related fund, a treasury bond fund, a growth stock fund and so forth. The exciting thing is that you can switch from one fund to the other, usually without any charge, and do it over the telephone!

This is where our newsletter, *Financial Guidance*, comes in. It gives you the signals as to when to switch from one fund to another. When the stock market is going up, we may have you 50 percent in a growth stock fund and 50 percent in a high technology fund. When the stock market runs out of steam, we may switch you over into a treasury bond fund or a money market fund. Then, if gold and silver take off, we might advise that you move all or a portion of your funds into the precious metals fund. By judiciously moving from one fund to another, you can multiply the profit you will make on your investment and become an even better steward for the Lord.

When you initially enter one of these families of funds, we recommend that the first thing you do is to open a money market fund and establish your check-writing privileges. These checks are just as cashable as a check from your checking account. Then, move funds out of that money market fund into the various other funds at the appropriate time, according to the signals in *Financial Guidance*.

SUMMARY OF STOCKS AND BONDS

In this chapter we have said that bonds are denominated in a fixed number of U.S. dollars and therefore are guaranteed to lose against inflation. On the other hand, investing in stocks has the potential to at least keep up with inflation. Unfortunately, there are times when it is good to be in the stock market and times when it is very bad to be in the stock market.

We looked at the basic four-year cycle in the stock market, which in general has two years up and then two years down, with a peak coming usually somewhere in the presidential election year.

We examined the fact that it is more significant when investing in stocks to own a stock in the right industry. This is far more important than which specific stock you buy within that industry. We suggested that during the 1980's energy companies and companies involved in computers and electronics should, in general, do well.

For those who either want to limit their potential loss or who want to have the leverage (added profit-making power) to gain additional potential in the stock market, we looked at the use of options. One can buy *call* options if he anticipates the price of the stock is going to rise. Even though these options have advantages, we pointed out that only 40 percent of all options are ever executed so this investment would have a success probability of only 40 percent. Options, then, are high-risk investments that have the potential for making very large profits or substantial losses.

Keep in mind that stock certificates and bond certificates are pieces of paper. There are many people who feel that investing in anything that is paper is an increasingly dangerous investment. If you agree with this position, you will want to invest in tangible things such as gold coins, silver coins, real estate, and so forth.

11

COMMODITIES

We have found that for an investment to be profitable today, it must make at least 5 percent over the rate of inflation. With inflation running at around 15 percent, this means that the minimum we need to average on investments is 20 percent.

Continuing our overview of investments that have the potential to beat the inflation rate, we now come to the commodities market. Not everyone can afford to take on this kind of investment; it requires a considerable amount of money to open a commodity account, and, as with stock options, the risks are considerable.

About the minimum that I recommend you have available for investing in commodities would be $30,000. This $30,000 would have to be funds that you do not foresee needing in the immediate future and funds that you would consider "risk" capital. There is a great deal of money to be made in the commodity market, and this can be one avenue by which you expand significantly those funds over which God has given you control. However, because of the amounts required to become involved and because of the risks involved, this type of investment by its very nature is only for those individuals who are fairly well endowed.

If you do have considerable funds that you can afford to risk, this may be one of the most important chapters in this book for you. If you don't yet have sufficient funds for this type of investment you may want to skip forward to the next chapter, or you may want to read this chapter just to expand your understanding of the investment field.

INVESTING IN COMMODITIES

Many investors think in terms of *investing* in stocks and *gambling* in commodities. I have heard the commodities market referred to as "the biggest crap game in town." I attribute these comments basically to a fear of the unknown. Many individuals are already comfortable with stock investments, but commodity investments seem frightening to them. When I first learned about investing in commodities, I envisioned a big tractor pulling a boxcar full of frozen pork bellies up and parking it outside of my house. No amount of money in the world would have made me invest in frozen pork bellies!

I have drastically changed my mind and now view the commodity market as a primary market and the stock market as a secondary market. I will explain why. When I invest in wheat, the only variable I am dealing with is the price of wheat. This, by and large, will be governed by the fundamental laws of supply and demand. On the other hand, if I invest in the stock of a cereal producing company, let's say General Mills, I have many variables with which to deal, including the price of wheat. My stock investment is a bet that the price of wheat won't skyrocket, that the new cereal product that General Mills is bringing out will be accepted by the public, that the management of the company is competent, and so on. Therefore, I have a much more complex investment if I invest in General Mills than if I invest purely in the price of wheat. I believe that during the '80's the big money is going to be made in the commodity market rather than in the stock market. (However, there will always be periods of time when the stock market does well.) I would therefore encourage you to become familiar with commodities as an investment vehicle.

The basic difference between the stock market and the commodities market is that in the stock market you are actually buying a partial ownership in a company. If there are 100 million shares outstanding, and you buy 100 shares, you own one one-millionth of the company. If earnings are distributed among the stock owners, you get one one-millionth of the earnings. Theoretically, if the company goes out of business, after it has paid all its creditors and the liquidating lawyers and has sold all of its equipment, inventory, and other assets, you would be entitled to one one-millionth of what money remained. So when you own a stock, you are actually a part owner of the company.

On the other hand, when you deal in the commodities market, you are dealing with contracts rather than ownership. A contract is an agreement by which you agree to either buy or sell some commodity—gold, silver, corn, cattle, etc.—at a fixed price at some point in the future. Let's look at a simplistic example to show you why there is a need for the commodity market.

Let's say many years ago a farmer was preparing to plant his wheat crop. He needed to borrow some money for a tractor and other necessaries, and in order to plan accurately, he needed to be assured of how much money he was going to get for his crop. So he and the Giant Grain Company reached an agreement. The agreement was made early in the spring to sell wheat to the company the following October at 45¢ a bushel. The company agreed, in this contract, to buy the wheat at 45¢ the following October. This was beneficial to both parties since the Giant Grain Company knew what its costs would be and could plan ahead intelligently, and the farmer knew what his selling price would be so he could plan his financial affairs. So this agreement was reached, and each party put up some money as a guarantee that he would produce on his half of the contract.

Now let's move ahead to October of that year. It is very unlikely that the market price of wheat would be exactly 45¢. If the price of wheat was 50¢, the Giant Grain Company would have made money and, in a sense, the farmer would have lost money since if he had waited until October to sell his wheat he could have received 50¢ a bushel for it. Conversely, if the price of wheat in October was only 40¢ per bushel, the farmer would have gained and the company would have lost, since if they had waited until October to buy their wheat they could have bought it for 40¢ a bushel rather than paying 45¢ a bushel. So in making their agreement both parties were willing to forego the potential gain, as well as the risk of loss, in order to know ahead of time what their selling and buying price would be.

In today's world, a farmer who plans to have wheat to deliver in October would sell one or more futures contracts on one of the commodity exchanges for delivery next October. Let's take a specific example: suppose that on April 1 the farmer *sells* ten contracts at $3.60 a bushel. An investor who believes grain is going up *buys* ten contracts on that same day for $3.60 a bushel. A few days later on April 15, a grain company decides to *buy* ten contracts at $3.65 a bushel, and on that same day an investor who believes that grain prices are going to go down *sells* ten contracts for $3.65 a bushel. Let's then move ahead to a couple of weeks before the settlement date of the October contract. (The settlement date of a contract is the day it becomes due.) Let's assume that wheat has risen to $4.00 a bushel. On October 3 of that year, investor A, who initially bought ten contracts, sells ten contracts and makes his profit. On that same day investor B, who initially had sold "short" ten contracts, buys ten contracts and takes his loss. He has a loss because by selling initially, he was speculating that the price of wheat would go down. Had he bought initially, he would have been speculating that prices would go up.

Both of the investors have now obligated themselves to deliver ten contracts and also to accept delivery of ten contracts. So in effect they are delivering it to themselves and have no obligation to buy ten contracts worth of wheat and the farmer to deliver ten contracts worth of wheat. Their sales and purchases cancel each other out. The grain company still has an obligation to buy ten contracts worth of wheat and the farmer to deliver ten contracts of wheat. This delivery would actually take place. A diagram of this can be seen in Figure 11.1.

Following this figure through, you can see that investor A initially bought ten contracts at $3.60 a bushel and subsequently sold ten contracts for $4.00 a bushel. Therefore, he made a

	April 1	April 15	Oct. 3	Oct. 20
Farmer	Sells 10 contracts @ $3.60			Delivers wheat
Investor A	Buys 10 contracts @ $3.60		Sells 10 contracts @ $4.00	
Investor B		Sells 10 contracts @ $3.65	Buys 10 contracts @ $4.00	
Grain Co.		Buys 10 contracts @ $3.65		Receives wheat

Figure 11.1

profit of 40¢ per bushel. Meanwhile, investor B initially sold ten contracts at $3.65 per bushel and later in order to fulfill his obligation had to buy these at a higher price, $4.00 per bushel. Therefore, he lost 35¢ per bushel.

In today's market there are many investors buying and selling every day. The value of the investor in the commodities market is that a farmer can sell futures contracts at any time in order to insure his price, and at any time a grain company can buy futures contracts to guarantee itself a fixed cost. Thus, the investor serves a valuable function in the commodities market.

This brings us to one of the fundamental aspects of the commodity market. Only 2 percent of the contracts are actually delivered! The remainder are cancelled out by an investor "covering" or liquidating his position. An investor usually does not intend to either deliver a commodity or accept delivery. He intends to cover his position by taking the opposite position sometime before the settlement date of the contract. In other words, if he originally buys a contract, he "covers" or gets out of his position by selling a contract. If he originally sells, he must cover by buying.

The commodity market is somewhat like a lay-away plan. When I was a boy, I saw my mother go down to the store and make a down payment on a coat, and they "laid it away" for her. A month or two later, when she paid the remaining balance, she took the coat. The commodity markets are in some ways like this. We do have to make a down payment on the item that we have agreed to buy. And we are assuming an obligation to pay off the remainder of that contract at the settlement date. However, in the commodities market our intention is not to pay off the remainder but to take the opposite position, and thus cancel out our obligation. The down payments in the commodity markets range from about 5 percent to 10 percent of the value of the contracts. We must maintain a minimal amount of equity in that contract. If our equity gets too low we will get what is called a "margin call." (We will talk about margin calls later.) Now, let's look at the advantage of buying through the futures market as opposed to buying the commodities themselves.

LEVERAGE MEANS MULTIPLIED PROFITS
(OR LOSSES)

The advantage of the commodities market, as with the stock options market, is "leverage." Many of us have, at some time, used a pry bar to lift a large rock or other heavy object that we could not lift by ourselves. We placed the bar under this big rock, placed a piece of wood under the bar as a fulcrum, pushed down on the end of the bar and were easily able to lift a five hundred pound rock. The lever actually multiplied our force. Similarly, in the commodities market, paying a small down payment multiplies the amount of the commodity that you can control. For example, let us say that silver is selling at $20 an ounce, and you expect that it will rise to $40. With $90,000 you could buy 4,500 ounces of silver, and if it did indeed rise in value by $20 per ounce, your profit would be $90,000. Now, let's examine what would occur if you used the futures market. Each contract of silver controls 5,000 ounces, and the down payment on one contract is $9,000. Therefore, with $90,000 you could have purchased ten contracts. This means that you could have bought 10 x 5,000 ounces or 50,000 ounces of silver. If silver then went up to $40 per ounce, you would have made a profit of $1,000,000. This is the power that leverage gives you in the commodities market.

However, I should hasten to add that I do not recommend to most investors that they put down only the minimum down payment; there is considerable danger to this. A safer and more conservative way to approach investing in the commodities is to put down at least double the required down payment. This minimizes the possibility of a "margin call."

For example, in order to make the silver transaction described above, you should consider putting down a minimum of $18,000 per contract and buying only five contracts rather than ten. This means that you could control 25,000 ounces of silver (5 contracts times 5,000 ounces), and if silver went up to $40 per ounce, the profit would be $500,000. This is a more conservative way, and it minimizes the risk of getting a margin call.

MARGIN CALLS

Now let's take a look at this dreaded margin call. In the silver contracts that we were just discussing, investors are required, as of this writing, to keep a minimum balance of $9,000 per contract. Suppose you wanted to invest in five contracts of silver and only wanted to put down $9,500 per contract. This is permissible but not safe. Let's suppose that after you purchased some silver at $10 per ounce, the price of silver went down to $9.95. The value of the commodity would have decreased and you would have "lost" $250 (5 cents times 5,000 ounces) unless the price went back up. Therefore, your remaining equity would be only $9,250 per contract, but you would still be in an acceptable position. If silver dropped further to $9.90 per ounce, you would have lost another $250, and your equity would now be only $9,000 per contract. You would still be okay, but would definitely be on the borderline. If silver dropped again to $9.85 per ounce, you would have lost an additional $250, and your equity remaining would be only $8,750 per contract. Since you are required to maintain at least $9,000 per contract, you would then get a call from your friendly broker asking you to immediately (that same day) bring in an additional $250 per contract to bring your contract up to the $9,000 maintenance level. If you had invested all of your available money and had no additional cash reserves, you would be in trouble and would probably have to sell some of your contracts at a loss in order to meet the margin requirements of the contracts you wanted to continue to hold.

If, on the other hand, you had placed down $18,000 per contract, silver would have to drop to $8.20 per ounce before you would get a "margin call." If you felt that it was possible that silver could go that low or even lower, at the time you bought your contract you would want to put up four or five times the minimum down payment required or plan to liquidate your position at a smaller loss if it began going against you. Investing in this more conservative way requires that you buy fewer contracts, thereby limiting both your potential losses and gains.

You can gain *some* leverage by buying silver through a Swiss bank, but with disadvantages. If you wanted to buy silver "on margin" through a Swiss bank, they would require that you provide only 50 percent of the value of the silver, and they would loan you the other 50 percent. In other words, you can control twice as much silver with your money as you could if you were entering the bullion markets and buying the actual silver yourself.

Comparing this to the commodity futures contract we just described, with your $90,000 investment you could purchase 9,000 ounces of silver at $10 per ounce and have the Swiss bank purchase an additional 9,000 ounces for you. You could thereby control 18,000 ounces of silver. On the other hand, you would have a $90,000 loan from a Swiss bank on which to pay interest. In the commodity market, since you are dealing with a contract and not the actual purchase of the commodity, there is no loan and therefore no interest on the remaining balance.

THE PROFIT IS YOURS, AS YOU GO

One other major difference between the stock market and the commodity market is the mechanism in the commodity market which is the opposite side of the margin call. If I were inventing a name for it, I would call it the "profit give." Let's illustrate it with our same silver example. If you purchased silver, and the price went up in one week from $10 to $10.10 per ounce, you would have a profit of $500 per contract (10¢ times 5,000 ounces). That profit is immediately yours to do with as you choose. The brokerage firm will write you a check for that profit if you so desire.

If you had five contracts in silver and silver went up a dime, you would have made $2,500, and on that day you could have the brokerage firm write you a check for $2,500. If a week later silver went up another dime you could have them write you a check for another $2,500. If you did not wish to take that money in cash, you could use it to buy additional silver contracts. Let's say that silver went up by $3.60 per ounce, and you had an $18,000 profit. You could use the $18,000 as margin to buy one additional silver contract. This is called pyramiding your position and can be done to significant financial gain. You also have to be careful not to get too greedy in this pyramiding game. I would certainly utilize stop loss orders in order to minimize my downside risk.

LONG VS. SHORT

Another advantage of investing in the commodity market is that you can make money regardless of the direction commodity prices are moving. You can sell (short) the commodity if you think the price is going down, or you can buy (long) if you think the commodity price is going up. You can make just as much money if prices are going down as you can if prices are going up. You simply must speculate in the right direction. If you purchase silver through a Swiss bank, you cannot make money if the price is going down. In the futures market this is a very easy and routine thing to do. In our silver example, if you felt that silver was going down to $9.50 when it was at $10.00, you could have sold (short) ten contracts, still putting down the $18,000 per contract down payment. If silver dropped to your $9.50 per ounce target, you would have a profit of $2,500. If it dropped to $6.40, you would have an $18,000 profit which you could take out in cash or use to sell short an additional contract or use to invest in some other commodity. You could get a margin call if you shorted silver at $10.00 and it rose to $13.65. Therefore, you would want to protect yourself by using the opposite of a stop loss *sell* order, which is a *buy stop* order at a fixed price to cover your shorts. You would then automatically buy to cover your positions if silver rose to this price level.

After shorting silver, when silver got down to the point where you had the profit for which you were aiming, you would then buy five contracts to cancel out your position. When you liquidate your position you not only get your profits, but also you get back your initial down payment. Let's say that you withdraw nothing as your profits grow, and silver did go down to $9.50 and at that point you decided to liquidate. You would buy five contracts to cancel out your ten shorts. Your profit would be $12,500 (5 contracts times 5,000 ounces times 50¢ per ounce profit). Since you initially put in $90,000, you would now have $102,500 sitting in the balance of your account. You could either take out that $102,500 in cash, or let it sit there until the next good commodity investment came along.

DOWN LIMIT DAYS

The only time when stop loss orders do not work to protect your losses is when there are "down limit days" for the person who is long or "up limit days" for someone who is short. Each commodity has a different limit. There is a maximum amount that the exchange will allow any commodity to rise or fall in a single day. In silver this is 50¢ per ounce per day. It can only move 50¢ up or down in a single day. Suppose that silver was at $10.00 and closed there one day, and then the next day no one was willing to buy silver futures contracts for more than $8.00. The exchange would move the price down to $9.50, and no transactions would take place. If for some reason this condition lasted longer, on the third and fourth days the price could move one and one-half times the limit, or 75¢ a day, and then on the fifth day there is no limit whatsoever. These limit practices change from time to time, but this is normally the pattern the exchanges use. Total market forces are permitted to take over on the fifth day, moving the price to whatever level there are willing buyers and sellers.

Limiting price movements has the advantage of dampening out violent price swings, but it has the disadvantage of locking you in. For example, if for some reason you were long in silver and had purchased it at $10.00 an ounce, and you had a stop loss order in at $9.65 to limit your downside loss, if the price went down the limit, it would go to $9.50 and there would be no transactions—nobody buying or selling. A second down limit day would immediately drop the price to $9.00, and there would still be no transactions. Your stop loss order at $9.65 would have been passed. The next day if it dropped only 10¢ to $8.90, there would be transactions. At that point your stop loss order would be executed but you would have had a bigger loss than you anticipated.

Most of the commodities traded seldom have limit days. Others have a tendency to occasionally go up or down limit, but rarely do they lock up or down limit for a number of consecutive days. However, you should be aware of which commodities have a tendency toward limit days since your risks are even greater with these. Your broker can help you identify these markets, or you can study the price histories for yourself in back issues of the *Wall Street Journal* (almost any library will have these back issues).

This is not to say that you shouldn't invest in markets that have had up or down limit days in the past. It simply means that these markets require more reserve capital and closer monitoring.

There are ways to limit your losses in the event you get caught in one of these situations. For example, the nearest contract month in most commodities trades without any limits. Therefore, if you are long and get caught in a down limit market, you can short the nearby month of the same commodity, and if prices continue downward for several days, you will realize gains on your short position to offset the losses in your long position. There are other more esoteric ways to limit your losses which your broker should be able to help you understand.

CHOOSING THE MARKET AND STRATEGY

If you are going to invest in what I call the basic commodities, the grains, the meats, the timbers, and the foods, I believe you would want to begin by choosing only one market and studying it very carefully. You would want a market that is moving, regardless of its direction since you can make money either going up or going down. From this base you can expand, eventually reaching an awareness and expertise in many markets.

There are two basic ways to approach investing in commodities. One is based on *fundamentals*, the other is based on *technicals*. Of course you can use a combination of these. The fundamentalist is looking at seasonal cycles and the basic supply and demand factors. He researches agricultural reports, the political scene, and many other information sources to try to determine the future price of that product. On the other hand, the technician is only looking at charts and other technical indicators. He lets the charts tell him when to buy and when to sell, and he does not care what the fundamentals are saying. I believe that whichever approach you take you definitely should subscribe to a good commodity chart service. One that I would recommend is:

Commodity Research Bureau, Inc.
One Liberty Plaza
New York, NY 10006

There is another service which I have found to be excellent; it gives a wealth of information about each commodity. Their price is simply $1.00 per chart so if you are only interested in cattle, silver and gold, for $3.00 per week you can get the current month's charts. Their charts include moving averages, consensus opinions, and other helpful inputs. I am including a reproduction of one of their charts in Figure 11.2. You can contact them by writing to:

Hadady Publications
Bin 91
Pasadena, California 91109

Another thing you need is a good money management strategy. That is, you can't afford to just focus on commodity price movements; you must also have a strategy for managing your money. For example, one form of money management would be the pyramid—using profits to buy more contracts. Another one would be completely the opposite of pyramiding—taking profits in the form of cash. Another form of money management requires that when you have made enough profit to get back your initial investment, you take it and then you play with the "house" money. There are many strategies which I will not go into at this point in time but suggest that you think through your strategy *before* you invest.

YOUR OWN ACCOUNT OR A MANAGED ACCOUNT

Another fundamental decision you must make once you decide to invest in commodities is whether you want to have your own commodity account and give all of the buy and sell orders yourself, or whether you wish to have someone manage it for you. In either case the account belongs to you, and only you can take money out of it. The decision basically concerns who will give the buy and sell orders, and, if it is someone else, how much you are willing to pay him for providing this service for you.

Most of the major stock brokerage firms also deal in commodities. There are usually hundreds of commodity brokers in

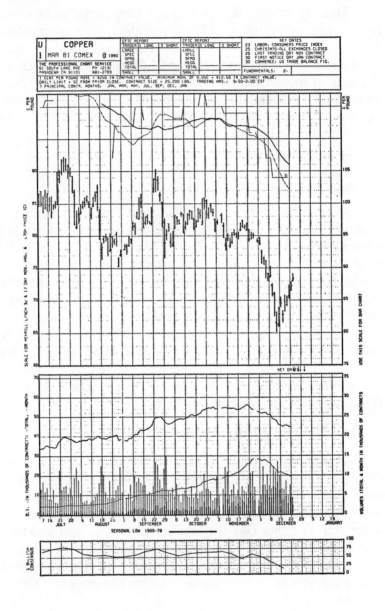

Figure 11.2

any major city. You need to find one with whom you feel a good rapport. Once you locate this individual and decide that he is the one, you will need to fill out the forms his company requires to open an account. Among other things, you will need to provide him with a statement of your net worth. They generally will not permit you to invest more than about 10 percent of your net worth in the commodities market.

After you choose a commodity broker and open a trading account, you should look to him only as a source of information on the mechanics of trading. I have found that most of these gentlemen are good order-takers but provide poor advice concerning what trades to make. If their advice were of a top quality, they would be taking it themselves and would be rich. They would not be getting up at the crack of dawn in order to take your orders. So my recommendation is that you look elsewhere for advice as to *what* and *when* to buy and sell—not to the broker himself. I believe that *The McKeever Strategy Letter* is one good source of this type of information.

One of the best men in the commodity field, who is also a Christian and for whom I have the utmost respect, is R. E. McMaster. He publishes a newsletter that deals purely with commodities and he also provides telephone consultations. His newsletter is:

The Reaper
P.O. Box 39026
Phoenix, Arizona 85069

Other commodity newsletters that I recommend are:

Hal Commodity Cycles by Walter J. Bressert
P.O. Box 223958
Dallas, Texas 75222

MBH Weekly Commodity Letter by Jake Bernstein
Box 353
Winnetka, IL 60093

On the other hand, you may determine that you prefer to have your account managed by a professional trader. There are many such firms around and we are happy to provide a recommended list to subscribers of either the *McKeever Strategy Letter* or *Financial Guidance.*

COMMODITIES SPREADS

While I don't have sufficient space here to go into this subject in detail, I want you to be aware of *commodities spreads.* One type of spread is where you buy the nearby month of a contract and sell a more distant month in the same commodity. The margin requirements are significantly lower for spreads than for non-spread investments. Instead of double for the two contracts, the total requirement is usually about one-third or less of the requirement for a single contract. For example, the margin requirement for a silver spread would be $1,000 as of this writing as opposed to $9,000 for a single position. There are some interesting uses of this as we get into taxes. For example, you could do a spread late in September for tax purposes. Let's just say you had a big capital gains and wanted to offset or roll this gain into the next year. By the middle of December, either the long half of your spread or the short half would be at a loss. You could liquidate the half that had lost for use as a capital loss in the current year. Early the next year you could liquidate the profitable half. What you accomplish here is a shift of your capital gains into a subsequent tax year.

You can also make money in spreads. For example, one type of spread is to use the same contract months but different (usually related) commodities. For example, during an oil embargo, glue becomes expensive because it contains petroleum. Therefore, plywood would likely rise in price against lumber. Therefore, you could short lumber and go long on plywood. As the two prices change in relation to each other, you can make money. I apologize for treating this spread so briefly here; I simply wanted to make you aware that spreads do exist. If you wish to pursue spreads, I would recommend two books: (1) *How To Make Money In Spreads* and (2) *How To Profit From The Coming Mideast War.*

WEIGHING THE RISKS

I always want to be as realistic as possible when examining an investment. You must be aware of the loss potential in investing in commodities. Just as the profits are leveraged (or multiplied) upward, the losses are also multiplied if the trade goes against you. If the settlement date in a commodities contract comes while the price is still lower than your purchase price, you will perforce suffer the loss. The wisest strategy for most investors is to calculate how much you are willing to lose and then place your stop loss orders accordingly.

Another aspect of the commodities market which is unlike the stock market is that you can lose more than you originally invested. If you invest $30,000 in selected commodities and they lock limit down for several days, you could lose two or three times what you initially put up. You are responsible to come up with the cash to cover such losses. Thus, the money management aspects of dealing in commodities become very important in order to manage this large potential liability.

SUMMARY AND CONCLUSION

We have looked at the difference between the stock market and the commodity market and have found that the commodity market gives us a great deal of leverage and multiplies our potential profits (and losses). If we invest more than the minimum down payment, we can minimize our margin-call risk. If we pick our commodity trades accurately there are significant profits to be realized.

We have said that you must decide whether you will make your own commodity investments or whether you will open an account with a professional manager. The advantage of having a managed account is that your funds are in the hands of a professional who studies the markets and monitors the price movements constantly. The disadvantage is that you must pay for this service.

206 CHAPTER 11 ...

For those who do decide to take the risks and enter the commodities world, either on your own or through a managed account, you will be involving yourself in an investment vehicle that can multiply your profits and help you significantly toward winning the war with inflation.

PART 3

VITAL CONSIDERATIONS

12

TAX CONSIDERATIONS

In looking at your stewardship and your financial situation in general, there are other things to consider than just income, expenses, saving, and investing. You could do well in these areas and yet pay an exorbitant amount in taxes and still end up a poor steward. Similarly, you could do well financially during your lifetime and not leave your estate will in good order, creating economic chaos for the loved ones that you leave behind. So let's look at some other vital considerations in our efforts to become good stewards.

CHRISTIANS AND THEIR TAXES

We know from Christ's teachings that He believed a person should pay all of the taxes that he owes. His teaching on this is found in Luke 20:

> **21** And they questioned Him, saying, "Teacher, we know that You speak and teach correctly, and You are not partial to any, but teach the way of God in truth.
> **22** "Is it lawful for us to pay taxes to Caesar, or not?"
> **23** But He detected their trickery and said to them,
> **24** "Show Me a denarius. Whose likeness and inscription does it have?" and they said, "Caesar's."
> **25** And He said to them, "Then render to Caesar the things that are Caesar's, and to God the things that are God's."

We see in this passage that Christ is really saying to render unto the government the things that belong to the government.

This means that any Christian or any Christian organization (including churches and fellowship groups) should be careful to pay to the government taxes which are due.

On the other hand, it is poor stewardship to give the government more in taxes than we should. Unfortunately, that is what many Christians do.

WHY DO PEOPLE PAY TOO MUCH IN TAXES?

Many people pay more in taxes than they should because of:

1. Poor tax planning

2. Poor tax counsel

3. Poor tax records

At the very beginning I should make clear that I am not a tax consultant or an accountant. I am simply passing on to you the results of my observations and research, and what I believe to be true concerning taxes. Any of these principles and practices should be discussed with competent tax counsel.

Tax planing, like any other planning, must be done before any action is taken. The best tax planning is done with a competent tax attorney, tax accountant, or tax consultant. For example, if one starts his own company with a goal of eventually selling it, the time to be concerned about capital gains taxes is not the point in time when the sale of the company's stock is being considered, but rather *before* any stock in that company is ever issued.

It is possible that your tax planning should include consideration of offshore options. This could involve establishing Swiss bank accounts, establishing trusts or companies in tax haven jursidictions, and/or having your affairs structured in a multinational fashion. I will have more to. say about this later in this chapter.

Another reason why people pay too much in taxes is because they are unknowledgeable about the various possible deductions. What most taxpayers do not realize is that their mental attitude or their "intent" at the time they take an action can determine whether or not an expenditure is deductible. For example, if you open a checking account for your convenience in paying bills, the service charges on that checking account are not deductible. However, if you open a checking account so that you will have records of your expenditures to help you in preparing your tax return, then the service charges are deductible.

Similarly, if you subscribe to a newspaper for your own pleasure, even though you may occasionally look at the stock prices, the cost of the newspaper is not deductible. On the other hand, if you subscribe to that newspaper so that you can check the stock market prices, even though you also read it for your own pleasure, the cost of the newspaper is tax deductible. The mere fact that something is also used for personal activities does not negate its tax deductibility. For example, I doubt if there is a business phone in the world on which personal calls are not also made. Similarly, personal letters are sometimes written on business typewriters and desks. Yet these phones, typewriters and desks are still 100 percent deductible as business items. On the same basis, if you put a telephone in your home so that you can be contacted by your office when you are needed, then the telephone is a deductible expense, even if you use it occasionally for personal use.

The items mentioned thus far have been small, but the matter of "intent" can be carried over into much bigger items. For example, if your wife wishes to give piano lessons, and you buy a piano for your own personal use on which she is also going to give piano lessons, it is not tax deductible. But if you buy a piano so that she can give lessons, the mere fact that she also uses it for her own personal pleasure does not negate it as a business expense. If she wishes to play records of outstanding piano artists for her students, then it is possible that a phonograph and record collection would be deductible. In this situation if your intent in attending operas, symphonies, and musicals is so that your wife can keep abreast of the current musical scene, then the cost of the tickets, transportation, parking, and other related expenses could be tax deductible. In a simple thing like giving piano lessons, the intent of these various purchases and activities is the significant and controlling factor.

There are other areas of tax deductibility that many people neglect. For example, the fair market value of all clothing, appliances, furniture, and books given to the Goodwill or Salvation Army is deductible. A diary is essential since you must keep track of anything you do that you think might be tax deductible. If you give a dinner party in your home for business associates, *all* of the expenses are deductible. This includes not only the food and beverages, but also the use of the house (electricity, heating, and so forth). If you have a client or a potential customer to your home for dinner, the same would apply. It may be that some of your recreational activities, if necessary for your health, are also deductible. Keep a log of all recreational trips.

The tax diary should also include a record of dinner parties —who attended and what was discussed. It should also include a record of trips—for investment advice, to have your tax return done, to doctors, and so forth. If you think that a deduction is legitimately yours, aggressive tax experts recommend that you put it down; if the government doesn't allow it, you can take it off, not having lost anything. However, if you never ask for it, you can be assured that you will never get it.

HOW TO REDUCE YOUR TAXES

History shows us that there is a limit to how much a government can tax its citizens before there is a tax revolt. This limit has generally been recognized by economists to be about 25 percent. At that rate, the government would be able to take one of every four chickens that you raise. Today in the United States, the tax rate is at least one of every three chickens, and probably closer to one of every two if we include all of the taxes we pay. Once taxes begin to get to the unbearable point, taxpayers start looking for ways to reduce them. This is a perfectly legitimate state of affairs as an English nobleman once pointed out:

No man in this country (UK) is under the smallest obligation, moral or other, so to arrange his legal relations to his
business or to his property as to enable the inland Revenue
to put the biggest possible shovel into his stores.

(Lord Clyde, President of the Court of Sessions, 1920)

There are some methods that many people use to reduce
their taxes, such as making heavy contributions in December to
a church or charity or any other work that God directs them
toward. On a larger scale, there are four major methods utilized
today to reduce taxes. These are to:

1. Keep better records (intent)

2. Invest in tax shelters

3. Have a Swiss bank account

4. Create a company or trust in a tax haven

I should point out that none of these methods will bear
the best fruit without proper tax planning. You should get a
good tax planner and do your planning well ahead of time.

BETTER TAX RECORDS

One of the best ways to keep better records is to set up
what I call a deduction file. You simply get some large envelopes and write across the top edge of each envelope the deduction category. The following are some basic deduction categories; a number of these are optional, and you should create only
the ones that fit your situation. Some deduction categories
might be:

* Auto Expenses
* Business Exchanges and Losses
* Business Profit or Loss
* Capital Gains
* Casualty and Theft Losses
* Contributions

* Investor Expenses
* Keogh and IRA Pension Plans
* Legal/Professional Services
* Literature Expenses
* Medical Expenses
* Miscellaneous

* Education Expenses
* Employee Business Expenses
* Farm Profit or Loss
* Gift Expenses
* Income
* Interest Expense

* Moving Expenses
* Partnerships
* Personal Residence
* Rental Property
* Taxes Paid Expenses

Into each of these envelopes you can put the paid bills or other documents that show you incurred the expense. On each bill write the check number of the check you used to pay it. This will help you to be sure that you don't miss anything. If you use cash for one of these things, such as putting a cash offering into the offering plate in church, then immediately write on a little slip of paper how much cash you expended, and when you get home place it in the "contributions" envelope.

REDUCING TAXES THROUGH TAX SHELTERS

The most common legal method for reducing taxes is the tax-sheltered investment. These are normally in the form of limited partnerships. The investor puts funds into the investment and thereby becomes a limited partner. Because of special tax considerations the entire indebtedness of the partnership can be added to the "tax basis" of the partnership. This allows for a very rapid depreciation of, let's say, a rental property owned by the partnership. Thus, an individual could place $2,000 into a tax shelter investment and deduct perhaps that much or more from his income tax because of loans to the partnership. Some of the more popular tax shelter investments today are: cattle feeding, real estate, farming operations, equipment leases, and movie productions. However, it should be noted that these investments simply delay the paying of the tax. Eventually, when the partnership is liquidated, the taxes will come due.

There is one company that specializes in tax sheltered investments that I would recommend. The company is Economic Research Analysts, Inc., and its president is Mr. Dick McIntyre. They have offices in thirty-seven states. Their telephone number is (800) 327-7826 and their address is:

Economic Research Analysts, Inc.
3050 Biscayne Blvd.
Miami, Florida 33137

NOW A WORD OF CAUTION. I have seen innumerable stupid investments made in tax shelter situations. One doctor, who is a client of mine, has a great deal of his wealth tied up in tax shelter investments, all of which are worthless. This brings us to one of McKeever's cardinal rules.

A TAX SHELTER INVESTMENT MUST FIRST OF ALL BE A GOOD, SOUND INVESTMENT, AND SECONDARILY IT SHOULD HAVE TAX ADVANTAGES.

Do not jump into these types of investments merely for the saving of taxes today. First, check the investment out to be sure that it is a sound investment that you would make even if there were no tax advantages. If this is true, double check the tax advantages, and check to make sure the investment is something that fits into your overall plan and objectives, then proceed.

SWISS BANK ACCOUNTS AND TAXES

I recently participated in a seminar in Amsterdam. At that seminar a friend of mine who is a Swiss banker said to me, "Jim, there is nothing that you can do with a tax haven that you can't do with a Swiss bank account, and establishing a tax haven entity is much more cumbersome and costly." My reply was that what he said was true, but utilizing a Swiss bank account to reduce taxes is illegal for U.S. citizens. Of course, many U.S. citizens are doing this in spite of its illegality.

In order to understand what I have just said, you have to understand how Swiss banks are different from banks in most other countries. A Swiss bank also acts as a stock broker, a broker of gold and silver bullion or gold and silver coins, and performs many other investment functions. For example, if a person with a Swiss bank account wanted to buy IBM stock, he could tell his Swiss bank to buy so many shares of IBM stock for him. The stock would be purchased for him and would belong to him; it would not be part of the assets of the bank, even though the name on the certificates would be the bank's name for the protection of the privacy of the individual depositor. Later, assuming the IBM stock rose in value, the depositor could have the Swiss bank sell the IBM stock. Since there are no capital gains in Switzerland, there is no special recording of the profit on that transaction. There is no U.S. capital gains tax, since capital gains by foreign purchasers are not taxed in the U.S. So the only way the IRS would have of knowing about the capital gains of this U.S. citizen would be if that citizen were honest enough to voluntarily declare the capital gains from his Swiss bank account.

Similarly, gold and silver bullion or gold and silver coins can be purchased by the bank for the depositor to be held in safekeeping. Here again, these do not become part of the assets of the bank but are held in a custodial account for the depositor.

Swiss bank accounts are sometimes illegally used to avoid estate taxes. By giving power of attorney on their Swiss bank accounts to the beneficiaries, people effectively "leave" the Swiss bank account to the beneficiaries at the time of their death. The beneficiaries (usually sons and daughters) can then continue to utilize the account. Of course the beneficiaries are supposed to report the Swiss bank account as part of the estate but frequently neglect to do so.

I think anyone with any substantial net worth should have a Swiss bank account, but not for illegal purposes. Such an account would be good insurance in the event that one had to someday flee the United States. The following are the two Swiss banks that I recommend most highly:

Foreign Commerce Bank
Hans C. Weber, Managing Director
Bellariastrasse 82, 8030 Zurich, Switzerland

Banque Indiana
Ms. Francine Misrahi, International Manager
50 Ave de la Gare, Lausanne, Switzerland

You can open an account at either bank by simply sending them a check. They will open the account and later send you the forms to fill out. The account will be opened faster if you send a cashier's check rather than a personal check.

I might add here that some individuals feel it's important to keep their financial affairs private. If you happen to prefer privacy concerning what you do with your funds, you may want to open your Swiss bank account by having a cashier's check made out to yourself and then endorsing the check on the back for deposit in your account in the Swiss bank. One of the reasons for this is that U.S. Government regulations require banks to microfilm the FRONT of each check, but not the back. Thus, all that would be photographed would be a cashier's check made out to yourself.

OFFSHORE TAX HAVENS

In short, a tax haven is a country where there are little or no taxes. One could form a company (corporation) in one of the tax haven jursidictions, and the company could then make investments in the U.S. and legally pay no capital gains tax in the U.S. (the U.S. gives a tax break to foreigners to try to attract foreign capital). The company could also legally pay no taxes in the tax haven jurisdiction. This is a very legal and legitimate way to function for most people in the world. However, it is illegal for U.S. citizens because if you establish such a company, you are the beneficial owner, and the company is a CFC (Controlled Foreign Corporation). The taxes on a CFC flow directly back to you.

Offshore corporations and trusts with a situs in tax haven jurisdictions can be legal and legitimate ways to reduce taxes if some of the principals involved are foreign citizens who are relatives or very long-term friends of the U.S. citizen involved. However, if all the principals involved are U.S. citizens, it is usually not a legitimate way to reduce one's taxes. One caution that I offer is that if a Christian visits one of these tax haven jurisdictions, he will receive every assurance there that everything is legal when in reality it is not.

The method that is usually used for these illegal maneuvers is that a foreign lawyer will buy stock shares or set up a company in his name (or his secretary's name) for you. However, legally you are still the beneficial owner, if not the legal owner, and you are liable for all of the taxes.

Stock shares can be purchased in the name of a foreign lawyer (or his secretary) who forms the company for you.

Some people go a step further and establish a trust which owns the company. However, if you are the primary beneficiary of this trust, again all the taxes are liable to you, whether distributed to you or not.

Many people use a Swiss bank account as a tax haven device. For example, they might send $100,000 over to Switzerland and invest it in silver. If the value rises by 50 percent, and they liquidate for $150,000, there is no tax to be paid in Switzerland and no reporting on that capital gains from the Swiss Government to the U.S. Government. The U.S. citizen is on his honor to report the $50,000 capital gains. Many people never do, and thus they have $50,000 overseas of what could be called "gray money." The problem comes with the repatriation of this money. The initial $100,000, of course, can be returned. The other $50,000 must then be spent overseas. It can never be returned to the U.S. without declaring the gains and paying the taxes. Unless one intends to do substantial business, travel, and investment overseas, this approach is shortsighted, as well as being illegal.

Under the present tax laws of the U.S., I have not been able to discover a legal method of tax avoidance by using offshore entities (companies, trusts, or bank accounts). It can be done illegally and is being done every day. But I believe that individuals should not listen to smooth-talking consultants who can give them the feeling that use of offshore entities is legal. The Lord will certainly not bless something that is illegal, so I suggest that you avoid this type of tax shelter unless you have a relative who is not a U.S. citizen and wants to include you in a business situation of some kind. Here you might have a legitimate tie to a foreign entity that would be worth exploring, but I suggest that you consult a reputable tax consultant before making such a decision.

I think that there are some advantages to having part of your assets overseas. I believe there are some advantages to structuring your affairs so that they are multinational in nature. However, I believe that it should all be done legally, and the appropriate taxes should be paid. I have had consulting clients who had "gray money" offshore, and I suggested to them that they simply file an amended return and pay the appropriate taxes. They later told me that they experienced a tremendous relief and new peace after paying their taxes. They felt they could quit looking over their shoulders in fear that they would be caught.

INFLATION IS A FORM OF TAX

Government seems to have an insatiable need to grow and to perform more and more functions for its citizens. This creates an ever-increasing need for more revenue, which is required in order to perform these functions and services. Once taxes get to a certain level (25 percent as mentioned earlier) governments find it very unpopular to raise taxes. How then do they go about satisfying the ever-increasing revenue needs? They must do something because the deficits are getting bigger and bigger. The solution they habitually have chosen is simply to increase the money supply—that is to create money out of thin air. The Federal Reserve is obligated to buy any of the government debt instruments that the private market does not purchase. The Federal Reserve does this by creating money. The government thus will never run out of money. They will continue to issue welfare checks, unemployment checks, checks for contracts, and other expenditures even if there is no money in the government bank. It is a very easy matter for the government to continue to print checks, and today, unlike Germany in the 1920's, there is no limit to the amount of zeroes that the computer can print on a check.

This creation of money, as we have seen, is the real reason why prices rise. This means that the purchasing power of people's savings and income is significantly lessened. This lessening of the purchasing power is the invisible and insidious tax of *"monetary inflation."* The real key in the future is going to be how to fight this tax of inflation. The best way to fight the effects of inflation is to purchase items which are essential to you now before the prices go up in the future. You should also try to pick a good time to convert many of your assets into a liquid form and place a certain amount of these in gold and silver, which will ultimately be the only true protection against inflation.

DO SOME GOOD WITH YOUR EX-TAXES

When you stop and look at the bottom line, taxes are the government's way of saying that, left to spend our money on our own, we would not spend it properly and therefore they must take some of it away from us and spend it like we should and would spend it if we were wise enough. They say that we would not spend enough on schools so they take it from us and spend it on education. They say we would not spend enough on charity and helping people so they take it away from us to support the poor and those unable to work. This list could go on and on.

I do not agree with this philosophy. I believe that if the government would get out of the charity business and allow the individual citizens to spend their money the way their hearts dictated, there would be adequate expenditures in all of these areas. One way to short-circuit this entire problem is to go ahead and spend your dollars on things that you think are important (and also tax deductible). You could donate funds to the college of your choice (they could use your financial help). This way you would be directly contributing to a specific educational institute of your choice, rather than having the government choose the recipients of your hard-earned dollars.

You could use some of your funds to help elect political candidates that would represent you and your point of view. Wouldn't you rather see these funds spent in this manner (according to *your choice*), rather than to see the government take your hard-earned money through taxes and spend it on political excursions overseas by various members of the legislative and executive branches?

Most important, however, are those things the Lord wants to accomplish by using you and your financial resources. There may be specific Christian organizations or charities that you feel God would have you support, or there may be missionary works that need your help. Again, contributions to these could likely do much more good than money poured into the bottomless well beside the Potomac.

From my point of view, one of the best uses for some of these funds is to make a contribution to your own church. In this way you are able to do some good for the spiritual and moral life of your own community. You have a more direct involvement and are able to see the results of your contributions.

Actually the tax laws of the U.S. Government encourage you to make these kinds of donations. Let's take a specific example. Let's say a couple's gross income was:

Wages	$ 60,000
Interest	20,000
Dividends	20,000
Rental Income	24,500
Total Gross Income	$124,700

Assuming an itemized deduction of $23,200, which produces a usable deduction of $20,000, and allowing for the $750 exemption per individual, this would leave taxable income of $103,200. The taxes on that amount would be $45,180. This would leave $79,520 ($124,700 − $45,180) for the couple to live on.

Individuals are allowed to donate up to 50 percent of their gross income. Thus, the same couple could make donations to various Christian works, churches, colleges, or political campaigns, of $62,350 (half of $124,700). This would leave a taxable income of $40,850. The taxes on that amount would be $11,082. Thus, of the $62,350 in donations, the government effectively would be contributing $34,098, or approximately 55 percent (the difference in the amount paid in taxes). In this latter case the couple would have $51,268 to live on. By reducing their net spendable income from $79,000 to $51,000, they would have $62,000 that they could spend (give) to the various educational, charitable, and religious organizations that they were interested in. This may not be as far out as you may think at first. If you were in this category, would you like to reduce your taxes from $45,000 to $11,000? Would you like to be able to give $62,000 where you think it would do the most good? Those are two very powerful incentives to reduce the amount spent on yourself by just a little.

The Lord has laid on my heart the necessity of ministering to the needs of Christians in the "end times." If the Lord has also convicted you of the need to help the body of Christ better understand and prepare for the end times, and you don't know how to go about it, please write to us for information on how you can be of help. (We also accept contributions, which are tax deductible.) Write to:

Omega Ministries
P.O. Box 1788
Medford, OR 97501

Omega Ministries publishes a newsletter entitled *End-Times News Digest*, which has a subscription rate of $20 per year.

SUMMARY AND CONCLUSION

We have seen that most Christians pay far more taxes than they really should pay. Christ tells us to pay our legitimate amount of taxes, but we need to be careful not to overpay. We looked at a number of ways to help us save on our taxes. One of these was keeping better records of expenses.

Another was to invest in tax-sheltered investments where we can write off roughly the amount of the investment as a tax deduction. This can defer taxes for a few years so that when the taxes eventually are paid, they can be paid with cheaper dollars.

We also looked at Swiss bank accounts and tax havens and saw that they had value but not for legally saving taxes.

We also mentioned inflation. That is the biggest problem ahead of us, particularly since it is an invisible tax. I believe that the most significant tax of all is yet to come and that it is the "inflation tax." This is the one that this book is primarily geared to help you fight against and protect yourself from. If you can survive the inflation tax, you can successfully survive the coming major confiscation by taxation.

Once we have legally reduced our taxes, it is incumbent upon us to seek the Lord's will concerning what to do with those dollars saved. We want to be good stewards of those funds, just as we want to be good stewards of all of our assets and income. The Lord will show us what He wants us to do with those funds in order to achieve good for our nation and our community, and especially for the kingdom of God.

13

INSURANCE, WILLS, AND YOUR ESTATE

To adequately cover this subject would require an entire book. In this chapter I will give you a broad overview, but I suggest that you read an outstanding book on the subject entitled, *Leave Your House In Order,* by John G. Watts (published by Tyndale House). I would encourage the head of every Christian home to get a copy of this and read it carefully. It deals with everything from planning, executing, and managing your will to dealing with trusts and taxes. I will give a few quotes from that book in this chapter to help you understand why you need it.

YOU HAVE A WILL WHETHER YOU HAVE WRITTEN ONE OR NOT

Most people do not realize that if they die without writing a will of their own, the state in which they live has a standard one that will be used instead. Would you rather make the decisions about what happens to your material goods, or would you rather have a stranger make those decisions? If both you and your spouse were to die in a common accident, would you prefer to determine who would raise your children, or would you rather have the government of the state in which you live determine who will raise your children?

Watts, on pages 21 and 22 of his book, gives the example of Catherine Marshall:

"Catherine Marshall, suddenly thrown into unfamiliar circumstances by the death of her husband, the late U.S. Senate Chaplain, tells of her anguish in *To Live Again.* Peter Marshall had left no will. She writes, 'It was necessary for me to appear in probate court to post an expensive bond and to be made administratrix of Peter's affairs. Everything thereafter came under the jurisdiction of the court. Not even funeral expenses, doctor, or hospital bills, nor ordinary household expenses could be paid until the court passed on them. . . . Then came the day when I had to reappear in probate court to be made Peter John's guardian. Since then I have been required to give a detailed financial accounting of my guardianship to the court each year. This will go on until my son becomes of age. Each year the account figures must be sworn before a notary public. Each year a fee must be paid to the Office of Register of Wills for the accounting.'

"Probably not every state would make the same stringent demands that Catherine Marshall's did. Requirements differ from state to state. However, there are certain basic laws which are common to many.

"Especially traumatic is what happens to the widow when a man dies without a will. Most states allow her from one-fifth to one-half of the estate, with the remainder going to the children. In some states one child may receive two-thirds of the estate and the widow one-third. In other states aged dependent parents may be unintentionally disinherited. In many states, when a man dies without surviving children the widow will have to share the estate with her husband's parents, brothers, sisters, nephews, and nieces.

"We usually assume that wives will automatically get the whole estate, and that they will take care of the children. But the state cannot assume that. The courts *usually* appoint the mother the guardian. However, in some states she must arrange permission to use funds from the children's share of the estate for their support. Each year an accounting will be required and she will have to explain this to the court. Since the court is not sure what the husband intended to be done, it safeguards the children against a possible careless and irresponsible mother. The state considers the possibility that there are dishonest, selfish, and greedy people associated with your family.

"Another problem encountered by the survivor of one who dies without a will is that taxes and expenses increase. One unscrupulous New England attorney recently said, 'I am delighted to discover one of my clients died without a will. It gives me that much more work to do.' The most expensive route to go home to be with the Lord is by way of intestacy (dying without a will)."

As you can see, one of the biggest problems of *not planning* for your death is the almost *total loss of control* your loved ones have because all of your finances and affairs are placed in the hands of unknown managers. By not having a will, you lose the right to dispose of your property and have your children raised in accordance with your wishes, and you leave those decisions to someone else.

Watts gives examples of reasons why people neglect to establish a will and an estate plan. These "reasons" are:

1. a reluctance to face death

2. procrastination

3. they think they have too little property

4. they feel a will is too expensive

5. they dislike legal documents

6. they lack the ability to plan for the future

7. there is a reluctance to place confidence in others

As far as I am concerned, these are all excuses and not valid reasons for neglecting proper planning for what happens to those that you leave behind after your death. Watts points this out beautifully on page 33 of his book:

"Whatever the reason people use to forfeit their privilege and obligation to plan the disposition of their resources for the benefit of loved ones, it is not adequate or scriptural. Granted, Hezekiah was sick unto death when Isaiah came to him and said, 'Thus saith the Lord, Set thine house in order; for thou shalt die and not live.' But no one can really be sure of the Lord's timing. No one knows when he or she might be 'sick unto death.' Therefore, we must take Isaiah's admonition to heart and set our own house in order, now."

Watts, in his excellent book, then takes us through the steps for planning a will, things that we need to consider, and forms that we can use. His book can be of tremendous help to you in prethinking your meeting with the attorney you select to make your will. The book will help you consider contingencies you might otherwise overlook. The important thing is to be sure that you have a will and that it meets all the legal requirements of your state. Otherwise, the state will use the will that they have already prepared for you.

WHAT ABOUT INSURANCE?

Some people feel that for a Christian to have insurance shows a lack of faith in God's provision. Other Christians are out busily selling insurance. What should a Christian's attitude be on this important matter?

I cannot answer that for you; only God can. He might lead some to live totally by faith and others to be heavily insured. So I am encouraging you to commit this to the Lord and ask Him for His guidance. I would like to give a few general thoughts on the subject which may help you in your considerations.

First, let me say that even though I feel that Christ is coming back in our generation, I believe that we should plan as though He's not going to come back for fifty years or more. He could indeed delay His coming, and if He does, we should certainly have planned our finances, our businesses, our children's education, and other long-range aspects of our lives. I don't believe He will be upset with us for having planned ahead.

As a part of our personal planning, I believe that insurance usually has a valid place. I realize that some Christians feel that we should "take no thought of tomorrow," but, as we discussed in the first chapter, when Christ said that, He was dealing primarily with worry, not planning. We know that He wants us to plan ahead as He taught in the parable of building a tower. On the other hand, a person can trust insurance rather than trusting God. Or, he can spend too much on insurance. This is not healthy spiritually, nor is it being a good steward. Our confidence must always be in God rather than in any other form of security. However, used properly, insurance can be a help to us in our planning.

There are many kinds of insurance. The strength of hospitalization insurance is that it protects a family against the huge catastrophic illnesses that can wipe out a family's financial base. When buying a home or automobile, a certain amount of fire insurance for the home, or collision insurance for the automobile is normally required so we don't have much choice there. If we own our own business, there is business liability and business continuation insurance that can be useful, if acquired under God's direction.

The largest insurance investment that most people make is for life insurance. There are two forms of life insurance:

1. term insurance

2. whole life insurance

These two forms of insurance are vastly different. One I feel fairly comfortable with, and the other I believe is a rip-off. Let me help you understand the difference between the two.

Term Insurance: If you buy a term insurance policy it usually covers you for a fixed number of years or until you reach a certain age. For instance, you might buy a $100,000 policy that would cover you for twenty years, or, perhaps, until you reach age sixty-five. In either case there would be a point in time when the insurance coverage would stop.

The rates for this kind of insurance are based on actuarial studies of mortality tables (the life expectancy of people of various ages). Statisticians determine that of all the people your age who take out the same insurance policy during the same year, some are going to die within a few months after taking out the policy, others will live past the end of the policy, and some will die during the term of the policy. The insurance company then calculates how much money it needs in monthly premiums in order to make a profit and cover the cost of paying all of the benefits.

There is a form of term insurance called declining term insurance which is used to pay off mortgages on homes. Let's say the mortgage on a home was $58,000 for twenty years. The declining term insurance policy begins with a face value of $58,000 and gradually decreases across the life of the mortgage to zero so that at any point if the breadwinner were to die, the mortgage on the house would be completely paid off.

For anyone, particularly a young married couple, some kind of term insurance can create a large estate very quickly and very inexpensively. Let's say there was a young couple and both the husband and the wife took out a $50,000 term life insurance policy. If one of them died, the other would have $50,000 in the estate. There is no other method in the world where one can create such a large estate by investing so few dollars.

Whole Life Insurance: On the other hand, whole life insurance is quite a different animal. The monthly premiums for whole life are much higher than the premiums for term insurance. The sales pitch that the insurance salesman usually give on this is that if you take out this $100,000 whole life insurance policy, you get the $100,000 if you die, and if you live to the end of the term of the policy, you get $100,000 in cash. They also rapidly point out that after the policy is in effect for a number of years, a cash residual is built up against which you can borrow money.

A whole life insurance policy really has two component parts. One part is a term insurance policy, and the other part is a forced savings account. Instead of buying $100,000 worth of whole life insurance, you would likely be better off buying a $100,000 term insurance policy and every month saving the difference between the monthly term premium and the whole life premium. If you were to die in the middle of the life of your term policy, you would still get $100,000, but you would also have all the money that you saved by not buying the more expensive whole life policy. Under a whole life policy, your beneficiaries get only $100,000 from the "term" portion of the policy; the insurance company gets to keep all of the "savings."

My recommendation to anyone who has a whole life insurance policy is to convert it to a term policy, take the cash value out, and do with that amount as the Lord leads you to. You can certainly be a better steward of it than the insurance company can; they are probably paying you a very small amount of interest on those funds.

Another absurdity of a whole life policy is that if you decide to borrow money against it, the insurance company loans you *your* money, and they charge you interest on it. That is absolutely audacious as far as I am concerned.

I am not against life insurance, but my analysis is that if one is going to have life insurance it should be of the "term" kind and should be utilized for a specific purpose, such as retiring a mortgage, providing transition funds for your family after a death, providing for your children's education, or building up an estate.

YOUR ESTATE

When many young couples think of their "estate," they think that they have none. However, as I have pointed out already, if they have an insurance policy, and either spouse should die, this could substantially increase their estate. Another thing not to be overlooked is that a relative of either spouse could die and leave them a substantial inheritance such as the homestead, insurance, proceeds, or other assets of which the young couple may not even be aware.

If a young couple has two children, and the couple and their parents were to die in a freak accident, the young couple should have their affairs in such an order that the funds from the grandparents will flow through to their children without being entangled in the courts or managed by strangers.

For those of more substantial means, I believe it is well worth it to find a Christian estate planner (not an insurance salesman), who can give you objective counsel concerning setting up trusts for your family, whether they be family trusts, unit trusts, living trusts, or offshore trusts.

Another thing to consider when buying insurance is the "hurricane inflation" that we talked about earlier. It is possible that even if you had a fixed amount of term insurance, let' say $100,000, you could have, in effect, a declining term policy.

The decline would not be in the face amount of the policy but in the purchasing power of the benefits.

SUMMARY AND CONCLUSION

We have seen that most Christians are negligent in that they have not had a will made out. If they die without one, the government of the state in which they live already has one ready for them. To insure that your material goods go where you want them to go—to members of your family, to your church, or to other Christian organizations—you must have a will made out. Also, to be assured that your children are raised by the individual of your choosing, you need a will.

No amount of rationalization or excuses will make up for a Christian not having a proper and a legal will executed.

We have looked at insurance (term insurance) as a way to build up an estate for a young couple and also as a way to insure the liquidation of a mortgage in the event of the death of a family's breadwinner.

None of us like to think about death. It is not a particularly pleasant subject, but on the other hand, God tells us to provide for our families. I believe that means to provide for them even after we are gone. Thus, we need to give some thought to what happens after we are gone. We should even consider leaving a letter or a memo to a trusted friend or relative to be opened in the event of our death, spelling out some of our explicit wishes.

I trust that each Christian reading this will pray about this matter and then do as the Lord leads him. The important thing is to realize that *now* is the time to get our house in order.

14

THE MULTINATIONAL
INDIVIDUAL

In this chapter we will discuss the advantages and methods of having some assets outside of the country. We will also discuss developing residency options in other countries as well as banking in Switzerland. You may find that these subjects don't apply to you if you feel your financial means are still too thin to spread out in this way. If so, I suggest you either read this chapter to expand your knowledge of the subject or simply skip it and go on to Chapter 15.

Before discussing becoming multinational, we should first realize that in some ways we have become spoiled. For example, early Christianity was founded and flourished under a dictatorship. It is possible to live a happy life in Christ under any form of government. The thing that is really important is what is inside a man. Yet if there were one country left in the world where democracy, civil liberties, individual rights, and free enterprise flourished, most of us would want to go to that country rather than to remain in a country with a form of government that we disliked intensely.

For many years corporations have found significant advantages to being "multinational." For example, what government can tell IBM that they cannot move $1 million from IBM Japan to IBM Mexico? In a sense, by being multinational, they tend to be "above governments."

To take a hypothetical example of the advantages of having multinational capability, let's say that a motorcycle manufacturer called "PONY of Japan" sells motorcycles manufactured in Japan at a price barely above cost to PONY of Cayman Islands. PONY of Cayman Islands could then sell to PONY of Germany the same motorcycles at a price barely below retail price. This means that the German corporation and the Japanese corporation would make very little profit and therefore pay minimal taxes, while the majority of the profit would be realized in PONY of Cayman Islands where there are no taxes. Thus, the entire operation could be carried on essentially tax free. Again, the question is: what government can tell the PONY family of corporations that they cannot do this?

I believe we are in the beginning of the era of the multinational individual. The multinational individual can enjoy freedoms today that multinational corporations have enjoyed for many years.

With proper planning, the multinational individual can establish his affairs such that he is independent of many of the acts of various governments. For example, I have had people ask me if I thought that the U.S. would eventually have a new currency. I think we *might* have one within the next ten to twenty years. However, the key is to not worry about what color it will be or whether it will be convertible to anything, but to have your affairs in such an order that they could change tomorrow to a pink and purple striped currency, and it would not affect your financial position significantly. Similarly, foreseeing that the government might impose foreign exchange restrictions, a person with wealth should have his affairs in such an order that this would have a minimal impact on his life and his investment strategy and position. The key way to achieve this is to become, to some degree, multinational.

This lesson was brought home to me vividly by a young lady who used to work for me. She was initially from a wealthy family in Cuba and had never had to cook meals or clean the house; her family had had many servants. After Castro took over Cuba and conditions became worse, her family applied for permission to leave. The Castro government came in and inventoried their home down to every tiny item. In fact, when they broke a vase they had to keep the pieces to prove to the government officials that they were not trying to steal that vase. They were allowed to leave Cuba, and this young lady left wearing a dress over which she wore two skirts and two blouses; she arrived in Florida with that and nothing else. In one hour she went from being wealthy to being very poor. I asked her, "Why didn't your family send some of their wealth to Switzerland, or the United States, or Canada so that when you arrived in Florida you would have had some wealth with which to begin life again?" Her reply was that they thought it could never happen in Cuba. The wise Cuban families had designed their affairs to be multinational years before so that when the time for them to leave Cuba came they could establish a new and comfortable life in a new country.

CHRISTIANS MAY NEED TO FLEE

Christians through the centuries have been forced to flee from their homes because of persecution or because of lack of religious freedom. We see this in the early church where the believers were scattered throughout the world because of the persecution in Jerusalem. They fled the city and took the good news of Jesus Christ with them.

Later in history the pilgrims fled from England to America so they could have religious freedom. In much more recent times we have seen Christians flee from Communist countries both to escape persecution and to obtain religious freedom. Judging from the Bible and church history, God tells some Christians to remain where they are and become martyrs. I am also equally convinced that God tells others to flee so they can live and perpetuate the gospel as the early church did.

We know that there is persecution ahead for Christians. Christ, in Matthew 24, talked about a "time of sorrows" or a "time of birth pains" which would precede the Great Tribulation. He said that during this period that preceded the Great Tribulation, there would be significant persecution of Christians.

If we are living in the period just before Christ returns, and I believe we are, then we Christians can expect to endure persecution *in our lifetime*. When we see persecution and people seeking to kill us, God will lead some Christians to accept martyrdom, and He will give to them the strength to do so. I believe He will give to others supernatural power to consume their enemies.

There are others that God might lead to flee from their home country or zone of persecution. Those whom God tells to flee are going to need four things:

1. a travel document to get across borders (passports and visas)

2. a means of transportation or something with which to buy transportation

3. a country or place to go to

4. a nest egg to start over once they get there.

When the time for fleeing comes, it will be very difficult to arrange for or to obtain any one of these four items. They must be planned for and obtained beforehand. Just like road flares, they are not available or easy to get when you need one.

We will take each of these vital areas one by one and examine them in detail.

GET PASSPORTS

I was in Saigon, Vietnam a few months before it fell. During its last days there was a desperate rush to get passports and visas; essentially, they were not available. I would strongly urge that you have a passport and a number of visas. The need for this was pointed out by a nurse that I know. She was invited to go on one of the planes to evacuate orphans from Vietnam and she could not go because she did not have a valid passport. There may be a time when you want to travel and travel quickly, and lack of a passport could prevent you from doing so. Be sure to get separate passports for every member of your family, including babies. You may get separated from each other or be forced to travel alone. Therefore a group or family passport would have severe disadvantages.

Once you get the passports, which are your basic travel documents, you need to get "visas" stamped on the pages. (A passport is a small booklet with basically blank pages.) You should go to the consulate offices of countries in which you think you might like to travel to get them to stamp their visa in your passport. This is their permission to visit their country. Normally they will give you a four-year visa, good for multiple entries. There is no cost, and your only investment will be a few hours of your time.

TRANSPORTATION

If you do flee your country, you are going to need transportation. If you live near the border of your country, it is possible to simply walk (or swim) across the border. If you live in the United States, and your home is near the Canadian or Mexican border, you could even walk across into those countries. Public transportation may not be available for various reasons, whether it be an oil shortage, a war, or government restrictions. Thus, a private vehicle, whether it be an automobile, a motorcycle, an airplane, or a boat may be the only way to leave a country.

In the event that you need to leave a country and do not have the transportation required, you will need something that people will accept in exchange for the transportation. People wanting to leave Vietnam just before South Vietnam fell encountered this dilemma. You will recall that earlier we talked about the fact that an ounce of gold could get one out of Vietnam when nothing else would. We believe that this is a valid reason for a family to try to have at least a few gold coins if at all possible.

RESIDENCY AND DOMICILE IN OTHER COUNTRIES

Once you get a passport and a visa you can visit the country that issued the visa, usually for six months. This is good for temporary "fleeing." However, if you wish to live there, you have to get "residency" permission from that country.

You can have more than one residence but only one domicile. For example, you could have residency in both Costa Rica and Canada; this is called a dual residency. However, you can only have one domicile which is the place you consider your primary place of residence. So you could be domiciled in Costa Rica but also a resident of Canada.

A valid visa from a country will allow you to visit that country but not to live there permanently. However, many countries, especially in time of emergency, will allow you to come in with a visitor's visa and then apply for a resident status after you arrive. If you intend to reside in a country other than the one where you have your citizenship, my advice is to begin to move in that direction before you have to, because *the world is shutting down.* It is becoming much more difficult to get permission to reside in another country.

The requirements for a *pensionado* status in Costa Rica have already increased. It is much more difficult to get permission to live in Canada than it used to be. A few years ago Australia would pay your passage if you would come and live in that country. Today they have tremendous unemployment problems and do not welcome new residents. You might ask, "What about wealthy people going to live in Australia?" This also presents a problem since their social institutions (hospitals, libraries, etc.) are full to capacity. If there were a larger influx of new people, they would have to build additional facilities.

The immigration policy of Australia is a good illustration of how rapidly and easily the world as a whole can shut down. In Australia the immigration policy does not require acts of their legislature, it is simply an administrative decision by a bureaucrat. This means that if this bureaucrat wanted to totally close the door to anyone coming to live in Australia he could do it in five minutes. It would not take the days and weeks necessary for the legislature to pass such a bill. The same is true for New Zealand. People are much less welcome there than they were at one time, and the immigration policy there also is simply an administrative decision that can be made very quickly.

I recently visited Australia and New Zealand to examine them as countries for potential residence. Their attitude toward immigrants was shown in this newspaper article I read while I was in New Zealand. The piece is by David Stenhouse.

"Disastrous overseas experience shows that 'gracious living' leads only to massive pollution; and more people means only more pollution. It seems, therefore, that we should try to avoid the mistakes of the oil countries, we should avoid polluting the good local environment, we should keep the population down and keep New Zealand green. 'But we cannot neglect the people from the overcrowded lands,' say the idealists. 'What will they do, if we prevent them escaping to join in our good life here?' This cry is a generous one, but it is based on misunderstanding of the relevant population biology.

"The basic point is that neither New Zealand nor Australia nor any other of the so-called empty lands can do anything worthwhile for their crowded neighbours merely by offering spill-over accommodation for surplus population. Anyone who is still thinking in terms of absorbing surplus population is about a century out of date. Even if we could accept a hundred million people here—and if we did, our present way of life would be utterly destroyed—how much breathing-time would that provide for the overcrowded countries of the Northern Hemisphere? The answer, alas, is pitiful; less than a single year. So there is no point whatever in continuing to think of our Pacific countries as offering an overflow spillway, a sort of sponge for absorbing other countries' excesses."

Some day people who decide they would like to live in another country will find that nobody wants them. Even though the world is in the process of shutting down, it has not shut down yet. It is still possible to get permission to live in any of these countries. It is simply more difficult than it used to be, and my projection is that it will get much more difficult in the future.

If you want to live in Canada, for example, you must go to your local Canadian consulate and apply for a "landed immigrant status." You will need to show that you have a job offer from a Canadian company or that you are self-supporting. Your application will be sent to Ottawa, and after it is returned to the local Canadian consulate you will contacted for an interview. If this interview is "passed" successfully, you will be asked to take a physical. If the physical proves you are healthy, you will be mailed permission to live in Canada. That permission normally must be exercised within approximately six months. The whole process takes from two to six months. This means that you should begin your application six to nine months before you plan to move to Canada.

When you arrive in Canada you "land" and establish a residence there. Then you have approximately five years in which to move all of your belongings to Canada. As you can see, moving to another country may not be as easy as it at first appears.

A COUNTRY FOR STORAGE OF WEALTH

If you have all of your wealth stored where you live and your citizenship is in that same country, then you are totally under the control of that government. If, for whatever reason, you are living in the same country in which you have your citizenship, the least you should do is to have some of your wealth outside that country. This can protect you from confiscation and foreign exchange controls and will allow you to flee if God tells you to. This will give you and your family something to start over with once you get into the new country.

In fact, if possible, it is wise to have some of your wealth stored in three different countries. Of course part of your wealth should be with you; another portion should be in Switzerland; and the last portion, in a country that is near the country in which you live.

It would be wise, if possible, to select countries that have strict banking secrecy laws in order to avoid the inquiring eyes of relatives, agents, or creditors. In addition to Switzerland there are two countries which fulfill this criteria that immediately come to my mind. One of them is Mexico. In Mexico you can have your account denominated in U.S. dollars rather than in *pesos*. Mexico has strict banking secrecy; if any bank or financial institution releases information that causes a depositor any financial loss whatsoever, that financial institution must repay the depositor for the loss.

The Cayman Islands, which is a popular tax haven, also has strict banking secrecy. Many of the major banks of the world, such as Barclays Bank, have branches there. These banks will be glad to open an account for you by mail. The address of Barclays is:

Barclays Bank International Ltd.   Tel: 9–4212
P.O. Box 68
Grand Cayman

For U.S. citizens, another option for storage of wealth is Canada, even though they do not have banking secrecy. If you live close to the Canadian border, it is handy. The banking system in Canada is, in my opinion, much safer than the U.S. banking system. In the U.S. there are over four thousand banks, while in Canada there are only fourteen. The U.S., in a banking crisis, could probably only "take care" of the top thirty or forty banks. I believe that in Canada, during a similar banking crisis, there would not be a single bank failure.

BANK CRISIS COMING

There is another very good reason to have some of your money outside of the country. I believe that at some point in the future, we will have a major banking crisis in America. Many banks, including savings and loan associations, are in a very illiquid position; they simply have run out of funds. Many banks have been "rolling over" bad loans for a long time, hoping that eventually the customer will be able to pay. Many banks also have made very large loans to big companies such as Lockheed and Pan American or to large city governments. In the eventuality that some of these entities go bankrupt, these large loans would go into default, putting the banks in an even worse predicament.

A further complication is that American banks show their assets (stocks, bonds, real estate, etc.) at purchased value, not at present market value. If these banks had to go into the market place and liquidate their assets, in many cases they would be worth only a fraction of what is shown on their financial statements. In addition, many banks have become vulnerable by making large unsecured loans or loans that are secured only by the signature, character, and reputation of the borrower rather than by tangible assets.

Another weakness is that banks are encouraged by the government to keep hanging on long after they are in heavy financial difficulty. In fact, Arthur F. Burns, while serving as Federal Reserve Chairman, told the American Bankers Association Convention in Honolulu, "The present regulatory system fosters what has sometimes been called 'competition in laxity'."

Here in the U.S., there will be a major attempt to keep rescuing banks, until eventually the entire system is in danger of going under. If this occurs, the government will try to rescue the bigger banks, allowing the smaller independent banks to declare bankruptcy.

It is imperative that you take the time to closely examine your bank's financial situation. Depositors in the San Diego U.S. National Bank or the Franklin National Bank did not realize that their bank was in trouble until they read about it in the newspaper. Do not be caught in this trap. Take a look at your bank's financial statement, and if necessary get someone to explain it to you.

Here are some important questions to ask:

1. What percent of the assets is in the largest loan?

2. What percent of the assets is in secure loans?

3. What percent of the assets is in mortgages?

4. What percent of the assets is in cash on hand?

5. What percent of the assets is immediately due from other banks?

6. What percent of the assets is in securities?

7. What percent of the secured loans is secured by gold and silver?

8. What is the loan to deposit ratio?

9. In general, how liquid is the bank?

242 CHAPTER 14 ...

SWISS BANK ACCOUNTS

For the last two hundred years, the best country in which to store wealth has been Switzerland. There are a number of reasons for this. One is that Swiss banking has been passed along from generation to generation as a tradition in Switzerland. During World War II no one bombed Switzerland because high officials on both sides of the conflict had their money there. Swiss banks are very conservative by nature and do not make the kinds of shaky loans that banks in other countries make. Also, Swiss banks provide complete secrecy unless a depositor has committed a crime that is also criminal in Switzerland. Even tax evasion is not a crime in Switzerland; therefore, if the authorities of any country suspect one of their citizens of using a Swiss bank account for tax evasion purposes, they can not have access to information concerning that account.

A third reason that Switzerland has proven to be a popular place for storing wealth is that a Swiss bank will perform many functions for an individual depositor that banks in other countries do not perform. As I pointed out earlier, a Swiss bank will buy and sell outright or on margin for its depositors, gold, silver, gold coins, silver coins, stocks, and other items.

Also, Swiss banks provide much more flexibility. For example, checks on most Swiss banks do not have a currency printed on them and can be written in any kind of currency. The conversion is made at the time the check clears the bank. Also funds can be freely transferred from currency to currency without worrying about foreign exchange controls. For example, you can move funds from Swiss francs to German marks and then to French francs and back to Swiss francs all within the same Swiss bank without having to worry about the foreign exchange controls that Germany and France may some day impose.

Most Swiss banks have three types of accounts. The first type is a "current account" which is very similar to our checking account and does not pay any interest. The second type of account is a "deposit account" which does pay a small amount of interest and is very similar to our regular savings account. The third type of account is a "custodial account" where you can have gold, silver, stocks, and other items that the Swiss bank stores for you. There is a small charge for this type of storage and for buying and selling items for a custodial account. It should be noted that items in custodial accounts are not part of he assets of the bank. The bank acts only as a custodian of hem. The assets legally belong to you. You can instruct a Swiss bank by a cable, telephone, or letter telling them what you would like to buy or sell and authorizing them to make withdrawals from either your current account or your deposit account to make the transactions.

I should say a word here about the renowned "numbered account" in Switzerland. This is a very awkward account, and I do not recommend it for citizens of North American countries. It is no more private than any other account. The only place where you have a little extra privacy is within the bank itself because all the records that the bank clerks deal with have a number rather than a name. However, in a vault in the bank there is a list of the numbers with the corresponding names, and there are usually two or three bank officers who have the combination to that vault. Therefore, in the event of a criminal act by a depositor, a numbered account would be exposed by the Swiss bank. This happened during the investigations involving the phony biography of Howard Hughes. That was a numbered account, but information concerning it was revealed because it involved criminal fraud in both the U.S. and Switzerland. In a numbered account you can make deposits only in person and preferably in cash. Moreover, you must make all withdrawals in person. This means that if you have a numbered account you have to actually make the transactions in Switzerland.

A good friend of mine, Otto Roethemund, Vice Chairman of the Foreign Commerce Bank in Switzerland, tells the story of a man who came in and wanted to make a deposit for a friend in his friend's numbered account. The Foreign Commerce Bank would not accept the deposit because in doing so they would be acknowledging that that friend had an account there. The only way that someone else could deposit money in your numbered account would be with a letter of authorization from you giving the number and authorizing the bank to accept the deposit. As far as I am concerned, a numbered account is more trouble than it is worth.

TYPES OF SWISS BANKS

There are basically two types of Swiss banks, the very large public banks and the smaller private banks. Three of the larger banks are:

1. Union Bank of Switzerland
    Bahnhofstrasse 45
    8021 Zurich, Switzerland

2. Swiss Bank Corporation
    Aesschenvorstadt 1
    4002 Basel, Switzerland

3. Swiss Credit Bank
    Paradeplatz
    8022 Zurich, Switzerland

These banks have the stability that comes with size but tend to be fairly impersonal. They are also not geared to correspond in English to the extent of some of the smaller banks. There are two smaller banks that I recommend. They are:

1. Banque Indiana (Suisse) S.A.   Telephone 20-47-41
    Francine Misrahi, International Manager
    50F Av. De La Gare
    Lausanne, Switzerland

2. Foreign Commerce Bank   Telephone 45-66-88
    Mr. Hans C. Weber, Managing Director
    Bellariastrasse 82AA
    8038 Zurich, Switzerland

I find that both of these banks are geared for opening accounts for North American citizens and can handle correspondence in English.

Foreign Commerce Bank is my favorite of all the banks in Switzerland. I also happen to feel it is one of the safest banks in the world. It is also a part of the Deak-Perrera complex. This means that after you have opened an account at Foreign Commerce Bank (FOCO), you can take funds into any Deak-Perrera office and they will transmit them to your account in Switzerland. You can check your telephone directory for the address of the nearest Deak and Company office or write to their president:

Dr. Nicholas Deak
Deak and Company
29 Broadway
New York, New York 10006

Banque Indiana (Suisse) S.A. in Lausanne is another excellent small, private bank. One advantage of this bank is that they will accept a very small minimum deposit. Many of the other banks have minimums of several thousand dollars, but Banque Indiana (Suisse) S.A. has a minimum deposit of 1,000 Swiss francs.

HOW TO OPEN A SWISS BANK ACCOUNT

If you wish to open a Swiss bank account directly, you can use either of two basic approaches. You can write to some banks for their financial statements and decide which one you would like to use. Or, if you have already decided which bank you would like to utilize, you can send them some money with a letter of instruction about what to do with that money. They will then send you the forms to fill out to "officially" open the account.

If privacy is important to you, you should use the same process I described in the tax chapter for opening a Swiss bank account. First, you get cash from your bank by cashing several smaller checks. Then you take this cash to a bank that you do not normally use. There you buy a cashier's check made out to yourself. Endorse the cashier's check on the back "for deposit only" to the bank where you would like to open an account.

246 CHAPTER 14 . . .

The reason for this process, again, is that the U.S. government requires banks to photograph the *fronts* of all checks (not the backs), and this will ensure a fair degree of secrecy for you since there is no permanent record of where your check was ultimately deposited. You should not send any check to Switzerland that is $5,000 or more. If you wish to send, let's say, $6,000, send two $3,000 cashier's checks.

If you would like this $6,000 utilized to buy Krugerrands on margin, then your letter of transmittal should say to them, "Please open a current account for me and buy as many Krugerrands on margin as is possible." The day they receive your letter and checks they will take these actions. If you send a personal check or something other than a cashier's check, there is about a two week delay before your personal check clears.

SUMMARY AND CONCLUSION

There are advantages to being multinational if one has any wealth at all. It could protect him in the event of a banking crisis or new currency in his home country. It allows one to take advantage of foreign markets and in some cases has tax advantages.

In the event of persecution of Christians, being a multinational individual has certain decided advantages. If God tells a person to leave the country, then all the elements are in place. He has a passport with a valid visa to another country, and transportation to that country, and some wealth stored there (or elsewhere) so he can start over when he gets there. God may well have something for him to do in that new country, as the pilgrims, the first century Christians, many missionaries, and other Christians have found in the past.

I'm not encouraging people to try to "save their life" at all costs. We should be willing to gladly lay down our lives for Christ. On the other hand, as our commander-in-chief, He may well want us to live so we can do a useful service for Him.

PART 4

GETTING STARTED

15

PRAYER, PLANNING, PRAYER, ACTION

In the preceding chapters we have discussed a great deal about proper budgeting to get money to invest. We have talked about investments, and we have talked about stewardship of all of our assets, which would include our investments. Now we need to begin to prayerfully apply these principles to our individual situations.

PRAY FOR WISDOM

Any planning and acting that we do in our own strength and in our own wisdom might be successful, but it also might take us further from the will of God. Thus, before we do any additional planning to determine how to apply the principles of this book to our own lives, we need to have a long session with God. First we need to confess our sins in a specific way asking for His forgiveness and cleansing. Then we need to ask Him to fill us with His Holy Spirit—to totally control our minds and our thoughts. A good verse to meditate on to help us do this is found in 2 Corinthians 10:

5 *We are* destroying speculations and every lofty thing raised up against the knowledge of God, and *we are* taking every thought captive to the obedience of Christ,

Here the Bible admonishes us to bring *every thought* into captivity, into obedience to Christ. This certainly must be possible or we wouldn't be admonished to do it. Remember, the Bible tells us that we often don't *have* because we don't *ask.* So I would encourage you to ask Christ daily to bring your every thought under His control.

Another verse good for meditation is found in Proverbs 3:

> 5 Trust in the LORD with all your heart,
>   And do not lean on your own understanding.
> 6 In all your ways acknowledge Him,
>   And He will make your paths straight.

In these verses it says that if we do three things, He will do something for us. These three things are:

1. trust in the Lord with all of our heart,

2. lean not to our own understanding,

3. in all our ways acknowledge Him.

It says that He will make our "paths straight" (or the King James says that He will direct our paths). However, the implication is that if we do the opposite of God's commandment and make our decisions based on our own understanding, God will not direct our paths. I believe that we need to rely, not on our own understanding and wisdom, but on God's directions to us. Speaking of wisdom, let's look at James 1:

> 5 But if any of you lacks wisdom, let him ask of God who gives to all men generously and without reproach, and it will be given to him.

Here it says that if we lack wisdom (and we all do) if we ask God He will give it to us generously and will not fuss at us. In fact He has promised that if we ask Him, He *will* give it to us. Praise the Lord! Another thing we can do daily is to ask for God's wisdom. As we begin to think in terms of our financial situation and even beyond it to our life in general, we need to have any planning that we do bathed in prayer and placed totally under God's control so that we are using God's wisdom rather than our own understanding and our own wisdom. This way we can be sure that we are in the center of God's will.

STEPS IN DEVELOPING A PERSONAL PLAN-ACT

You will recall that in Chapter 5 we outlined the seven basic steps in developing your PLAN-ACT. So far we have discussed two different PLAN-ACT's. First, we discussed developing a STEWARDSHIP PLAN-ACT. Then in Chapter 4 we talked about managing our income and expenses and developing a budget, which we will call our OPERATING PLAN-ACT.

We have discussed how developing these two PLAN-ACT's will be beneficial even to a young working person who lives in an apartment and has nothing more than a small savings account and an automobile. It will also be of help to the wealthy individual with several million dollars, or to anyone in any income bracket.

Hopefully, a person will also develop a SPIRITUAL PLAN-ACT. Eventually we will integrate all these together, but for now I would like to review the seven steps to developing any PLAN-ACT:

STEP NO.	ACTION TO BE TAKEN
1.	Determine your present status
2.	Describe your view of the future
3.	Develop your objectives
4.	Write out your goals
5.	Write out your plan of action
6.	Take action
7.	Review periodically and revise your goals and then go back to Step 5

In Chapter 4, where we discussed using your checkbook to find out your present income-expense status (Step 1), and then developing your objectives by forming a budget (Step 4), then beginning to make your expenditures according to your budget (Step 6), we actually went through these seven steps although we didn't discuss it from that perspective. We would encourage you to use these seven steps in your budget preparation and your income and expense considerations. Using these seven steps under the control of God's guidance can be very powerful in your total life direction and fulfillment.

In Chapter 5, we discussed your STEWARDSHIP PLAN–ACT, and we went through the first three steps in detail. I would like to review the form that we used in Chapter 5 and then discuss the last four steps.

Do you remember the I. M. Sinking family? In Figure 15.1 is their MARKET VALUE NET WORTH–STEWARDSHIP PLAN–ACT form on which they had completed columns A through D. They found out the market value and the amount owed against each of their assets and subtracted these to find out the net value of each one. They placed the difference in column C. Then they calculated the percentages each of those were of their total net worth. As a long-term measure of their true stewardship, they then converted their net worth to ounces of gold to see how many ounces of gold they were worth.

After spending time in prayer they felt before the Lord that they should convert their whole life insurance policy to term insurance. They decided to use the $30,000 they got from their whole life policy to buy some dehydrated food and some gold coins, to make a $3,000 donation to a Christian organization, to pay off their personal loan, to put $5,000 into a Swiss bank account, and to invest the remainder in good quality stocks. They are still praying about selling their "vacant land" and about refinancing their house. When God shows them what to do in these cases, they will make further revisions.

They then adjusted their "goal net dollars" in column E to reflect their new directions. The details of how this is done are found in the next part of this chapter.

STEP 4 – WRITE OUT GOALS

I guess you could call me a "goal bug." I believe that everyone should develop his goals and then develop a plan of action that will move him toward these goals. I have found that too many people behave like a log floating down the river without any direction and force of their own.

MARKET VALUE NET WORTH – STEWARDSHIP PLAN-ACT

NET WORTH OF _____   As of (Date) _____   Gold $/Oz. _____

NOTE: Amounts to be expressed in thousands of dollars. $10,518 should be written as $10.5.	MARKET VALUE $ (A)	DEBT AMOUNT $ (B)	NET VALUE $ (C)	PCT NET WORTH (D)	GOAL VALUE $ (E)	PCT GOAL (F)	CHANGE VALUE (E) – (C) (G)
PHYSICAL SURVIVAL							
(1) Food Stored	$.	$.	$.	. %	$.	. %	$.
(2) Retreat Property				.	.		.
(3) Survival Vehicle & Equipment	8.0	7.0	1.0	.	.		.
(4) Other _____				.	.		.
(5) TOTAL PHYSICAL SURVIVAL	.	.	1.0	.8	.		.
MONETARY SURVIVAL							
(6) Gold Coins in Possession				.	.		.
(7) Silver Coins in Possession	14.3	.0	14.3	.	.		.
(8) Cash (in currency)				.	.		.
(9) TOTAL MONETARY SURVIVAL	.	.	14.3	11.3	.		.
INVESTMENTS–LIQUID							
(10) Gold Coins or Bullion				.	.		.
(11) Silver Coins or Bullion				.	.		.
(12) Foreign Currency Accounts				.	.		.
(13) Gold and Silver Mining Shares				.	.		.
(14) Stock Shares–Publicly traded	2.0	.0	2.0	.	.		.
(15) Stock Options				.	.		.
(16) Commodity Futures				.	.		.
(17) Other _____				.	.		.
(18) TOTAL INVESTMENT–LIQUID	.	.	2.0	1.6	.		.
INVESTMENT–ILLIQUID							
(19) Real Estate (Vacant land)	8.0	10.0	(2.0)	.	.		.
(20) Diamonds	1.3	.0	1.3	.	.		.
(21) Collectibles–Art, Antiques, etc.				.	.		.
(22) Private Company shares				.	.		.
(23) TOTAL INVESTMENTS–ILLIQUID	.	.	(.7)	(.5)	.		.
STATIC (INCLUDE INCOME INVESTMENTS)							
(24) Bank Accounts				.	.		.
(25) Bonds, T Bills, CD's, Savings				.	.		.
(26) Whole Life Ins. (Cash Value)	30.0	.0	30.0	.	.		.
(27) Residence	85.0	8.0	77.0	.	.		.
(28) Rental Property				.	.		.
(29) Automobile(s)	5.0	1.0	4.0	.	.		.
(30) Other (include personal loans)	.0	1.4	(1.4)	.	.		.
(31) TOTAL STATIC	.	.	109.6	86.8	.		.
GRAND TOTAL AND NET WORTH	$.	$.	$ 126.2 (Net Worth)	100.0%	$.	. %	$.

Gold $ **600** /ounce. Net Worth in ounces of Gold **210.53** ounces.

Silver $ – _____ /ounce. Net Worth in ounces of Silver _____ ounces.

Figure 15.1

I would like to refer back to the form shown in Figure 15.1. We are now ready to develop columns E, F, and G. With what we know, we can now set down some approximate goals for our net worth, for lines 5, 9, 18, 23, and 31.

After we have made our goal entries, we will convert these dollar amounts to percentages by dividing them by our total net worth. Once we have filled in these subtotal lines, we can then redistribute these back up to the specific items within that category. This is shown in Figure 15.2.

MARKET VALUE NET WORTH — STEWARDSHIP PLAN-ACT

NET WORTH OF _____ As of (Date) _____ Gold $/Oz. _____

NOTE: Amounts to be expressed in thousands of dollars. $10,518 should be written as $10.5.

	MARKET VALUE $ (A)	DEBT AMOUNT $ (B)	NET VALUE $ (C)	PCT NET WORTH (D)	GOAL VALUE $ (E)	PCT GOAL (F)	CHANGE VALUE (E)–(C) (G)
PHYSICAL SURVIVAL							
(1) Food Stored	$.	$.	$.	. %	$.	. %	$.
(2) Retreat Property							
(3) Survival Vehicle & Equipment	8.0	7.0	1.0		1.0		
(4) Other _____							
(5) TOTAL PHYSICAL SURVIVAL			1.0	.8	1.0	.8	.0
MONETARY SURVIVAL							
(6) Gold Coins in Possession							
(7) Silver Coins in Possession	14.3	.0	14.3		14.3		
(8) Cash (in currency)							
(9) TOTAL MONETARY SURVIVAL			14.3	11.3	14.3	11.7	.0
INVESTMENTS–LIQUID							
(10) Gold Coins or Bullion					10.0		
(11) Silver Coins or Bullion							
(12) Foreign Currency Accounts							
(13) Gold and Silver Mining Shares							
(14) Stock Shares–Publicly traded	2.0	.0	2.0		12.0		
(15) Stock Options							
(16) Commodity Futures							
(17) Other _____							
(18) TOTAL INVESTMENT–LIQUID			2.0	1.6	22.0	17.9	20.0
INVESTMENT–ILLIQUID							
(19) Real Estate (Vacant land)	8.0	10.0	(2.0)		(2.0)		
(20) Diamonds	1.3	.0	1.3		1.3		
(21) Collectibles–Art, Antiques, etc.							
(22) Private Company shares							
(23) TOTAL INVESTMENTS–ILLIQUID			(.7)	(.5)	(.7)	(.5)	.0
STATIC (INCLUDE INCOME INVESTMENTS)							
(24) Bank Accounts					5.0		
(25) Bonds, T Bills, CD's, Savings							
(26) Whole Life Ins. (Cash Value)	30.0	.0	30.0		.0		
(27) Residence	85.0	8.0	77.0		77.0		
(28) Rental Property							
(29) Automobile(s)	5.0	1.0	4.0		4.0		
(30) Other (include personal loans)	.0	1.4	(1.4)				
(31) TOTAL STATIC			109.6	86.8	86.0	70.1	(23.6)
GRAND TOTAL AND NET WORTH	$.	$.	$ 126.2 (Net Worth)	100.0%	$128.6	100.0%	$ (3.6)

Gold $ _____ /ounce. Net Worth in ounces of Gold _____ ounces.

Silver $ _____ /ounce. Net Worth in ounces of Silver _____ ounces.

Figure 15.2

First, column E was completed by Mr. and Mrs. Sinking, reflecting the changes we mentioned that they wanted to make. They calculated the new percentages and placed them in column F. Then they calculated the change which is column E minus column C and recorded the difference in column G.

Let's take another example of a young professional couple whose view of the future includes the possibility of a monetary crisis with paper money becoming worthless, and social disorder and rioting becoming widespread. They are inclined to be fairly security-conscious, and they tend towards just a little speculation. Their analysis of their situation might go something like this:

INVESTMENTS	$ NOW	% NOW	$ GOAL	% GOAL
Physical Survival	0	0%	$ 2,000	20%
Monetary Survival	$ 1,000	10%	$ 5,000	50%
Liquid Investment	$ 5,000	50%	$ 3,000	30%
Static Investment	$ 4,000	40%	$ 0	0%
TOTAL	$10,000	100%	$10,000	100%

Here their "static investment" was the downpayment on a small house which, after planning, they decided to sell. Since they had no provision for physical emergencies, after praying about it they decided that they wanted to buy a trailer and load it with food, tents, and other survival items so they could hitch it up and move out of the city in a time of violence. Their uncle owns a farm about two hundred miles away where they could park the trailer and pitch their tent. The process they went through was to first analyze their net worth as it existed, then to calculate the present percentages. Next they developed a re-arrangement of their dollars to help them reach their goals, and lastly they calculated the percentages for their goals.

Then they developed a plan of action to move them toward the goals. This plan included putting their house up for sale. With the proceeds from the sale, they planned to purchase and stock the trailer. In the interim they planned to liquidate some of their common stocks and buy some gold and silver coins. The money that they were going to leave in the speculative category was to be used for a gold coin margin account, which would be a shift within the speculative category.

No matter how sophisticated an investor you might be, or how well ordered you think your affairs are, I challenge you to go through this calculation for yourself. You might be surprised by what you discover.

STEP 5 – WRITE OUT A PLAN OF ACTION

It does us no good to plan and develop our goals if we don't set forth a plan of action. Suppose I were in Los Angeles and wanted to drive to Chicago. What is the first thing I would do? I would get out a road map and lay down a plan for getting from one city to the other. Similarly, we determine our present status, describe our view of the future, state our objectives, and then translate these into our specific goals. For example, we may find that we have a $60,000 equity in our house when all we have to have is a $20,000 equity. We can either refinance the house or get a second mortgage giving us $40,000 in cash.

With this $40,000 we may buy some gold coins, some silver coins, a motor home, or something else. It may also be that we have some stocks and bonds that we would like to sell. Perhaps, we believe that the stock and bond markets will rise in the near future, enabling us to sell these for, let's say, about $20,000. We need to sit down and write out a step-by-step plan *with target dates* (due date) and an indication of the individual responsible for completing the action. One such plan might look like the one shown on the next page.

Basically, this family is making no major changes in its lifestyle. These people are still living in the same home, driving the same car, and living just as always. They are simply rearranging their affairs based on the goals that they have set forth by doing their self-analysis on the MARKET VALUE NET WORTH–STEWARDSHIP PLAN–ACT. Their actions of course will be changed slightly as the situation develops, but now the family at least has a general direction and a general schedule.

NO.	ACTION	APPROX. COST	INDIVIDUAL RESPONSIBLE	DATE DUE	DATE DONE
1.	Refinance house and acquire $40,000	—	John	9/1	
2.	Buy gold coins ($15,000), one and one-half bags of silver coins ($15,000), and pay down on motor home ($10,000)	$40,000	John	9/15	
3.	Sell stocks and bonds and realize $20,000	—	John.	1/15	
4.	Pay off motor home	$5,000	Mary	1/20	
5.	Buy five year's worth of dehydrated food	$5,000	Mary	2/1	
6.	Buy small piece of rural land on which to park motor home in time of emergency	$10,000	John	5/1	
7.	Receive inheritance from trust of $50,000	—	Mary	9/1	
8.	Invest in gold coins ($20,000) and invest the remainder in speculative investments ($30,000)	$50,000	John	9/15	

STEP 6 – TAKE ACTION

If we do a great job of planning and write out a sound plan of action, but we do not implement it, our effort will have done us no good whatsoever. If we want to build a house, the first thing we must do is draw a blueprint; then we must get busy and buy the materials; and then we can actually build the house. The planning we have done in this book so far represents a blueprint for your future. But remember, you cannot live inside a blueprint. A blueprint won't keep the rain off of your head or keep you warm in the winter. Good intentions are not enough. You must begin to actually implement your plan. More about this in the next chapter.

STEP 7 – MUST CHANGE TO SURVIVE

Now that we have made these plans and are preparing to take action, we must also be prepared to change our plans. The people who will survive the coming economic crisis are the ones who are willing and able to modify their strategy, their standard of living, their location, and their investment distribution.

In this changing world, the thing that will change least will be the preparations necessary for your actual physical survival. The second most stable preparation is the silver and gold coins, which we expect to utilize for money for monetary survival. The thing that will change most will be our investments.

With this in mind, let us take a look at our entire asset picture as it used to be, as it is now, and as it will be as we approach the economic crises we've been discussing in this book. Ultimately we will want to think through to beyond these crises.

In the 1960's and 1970's, illiquid investments were comfortable investments. Today, our investments should be more liquid. Some liquid investments, such as bonds and savings accounts, will not fare as well as inflation continues; they will lose capital. Therefore, these should be liquidated and moved into investments that we expect will float in the coming inflationary wave. Believe me, it is coming, and it will hit hard when it hits.

This necessity for changing and adapting in order to survive is true both in our STEWARDSHIP PLAN–ACT and in our OPERATING PLAN–ACT. In reviewing the STEWARDSHIP PLAN–ACT, I would suggest that every few months at first and eventually once per year, a person or family should review the plan, recalculate the net worth figure, and after prayer make any changes in the goals and plan of action that seem necessary.

To help you in this process, we have an ample supply of the STEWARDSHIP PLAN–ACT and the OPERATING PLAN–ACT forms, as well as forms for plans of action, in *The Almighty and the Dollar Personal Planning Workbook.*

SUMMARY AND CONCLUSION

Christ, in His parable about building a tower, told us to first count the cost and do some planning in order to reach our goals successfully. This also applies to our stewardship and our family or personal financial operations.

In order to do this there are seven steps that we need to go through. These take time and energy, but in the end they help bring our finances into a much better order—an order that will truly glorify the Lord and be under His control.

16

TYRANNY OF THE URGENT

Everywhere I go, as I travel all over the world, probably the most common complaint that I hear from Christians and Christian leaders concerns the "pressure" that they are under. This pressure comes from a variety of sources—the tense world situation, the "load" of the Lord's work, their personal financial problems, their business difficulties, their church financial problems, and many other areas.

Using their definition of "pressure," I believe it's going to get worse instead of better. There are going to be many people, including Christians, who are going to be laid off and become unemployed in the coming hard years. The peace in the Mideast is very tenuous. The Russian military superiority has been brought into vivid focus. "Pressures" are growing from every side.

Now there is an added "pressure" from this book—to be a good steward, to budget, to invest, and possibly even to become multinational. Before we look at the solutions, let's talk about pressure.

WHERE DOES PRESSURE COME FROM?

While I was employed with IBM, I took a year's leave of absence and went to live as caretaker at Intervarsity Christian Fellowship's camp on Catalina Island (twenty-nine miles off the coast of Los Angeles). At times I felt under incredible pressure;

for example, I felt that I just had to get a wall of the cabin that I was building completed on a particular day. The pressure that I felt was tremendous. I wondered where all of this pressure was coming from. I looked around in the cove where the camp was, and I was the only one there. The people responsible for the camp were over in Los Angeles, and they didn't even know that I was building a wall on that day. Then where was all of this pressure coming from? The conclusion that I unavoidably came to was that *I* was generating it.

Then I began to wonder if all pressure was self-generated. I thought that this was a ridiculous idea and that the way to disprove it was to find an exception to it. I tried to think of an example where pressure was not self-generated. I thought of two people contemplating the potential of a nuclear war occurring. One feels tremendous pressure. He feels that he can not do any planning for his future because of the unsettled world situation. The other man feels that nuclear war wouldn't bother him at all —that it would just be: BOOM, "Hello, Lord!"

I thought of two men out of work. One is about to commit suicide and the other one feels, "Oh, well—someone will take care of me . . . the Red Cross, the Salvation Army or someone. They won't let me starve to death." Or two people experiencing financial ruin. One person jumps out the window, while another tightens his belt and starts over. In every situation, *the circumstances create a need for a response.* The individual can then respond by creating pressure within himself or not. Thus, I concluded that all pressure is self-generated. To help you better understand, let's consider the following example.

PRESS AND SURE

Let's suppose that there are two men named "Mr. Press" and "Mr. Sure" who are both contemplating the potential for world war and the poor world situation in general. Let's compare their reactions.

Mr. Press gets nervous and wonders why our government doesn't do this or that before a nuclear war begins and we all get blown to atoms. How can a man make plans when he never knows what the next moment holds? He hears about the pressure from the world crises, and it ties him in knots. But Mr. Sure, reacting to the same situation, has inner peace. He feels that his tomorrows are all in God's hands and that he can only live one day at a time. If God would have him die in a nuclear blast, by a firing squad, or by any other means, it would only mean that he would immediately be in His presence.

These two men are both at the lower management level of the same company. Naturally, their superiors have given them specific projects with deadlines which are important to meet. If you could only hear Mr. Press talk to his wife about this! He comes in, drops in a chair, and after yelling at the children to be quiet he complains, "Honey, I don't see how they can expect anyone to endure such pressure. I get upset when one of my subordinates is late with his work or muffs it; I even get cross with my secretary when she is really trying. Yet, I must continually drive and push to meet the tremendous 'pressure' and deadlines my management places on me. If I don't complete this project on time I might even lose my job."

As we said before, Mr. Sure is in exactly the same position. His reaction, however, is different. He believes he should work heartily before the Lord. So he works with his whole heart. However, when there are setbacks (as there always are) his reaction is, "Lord, I'm doing the best I can, and I place my project and future in your hands." He comes home relaxed and ready to play with his children.

Each family has financial needs which somehow always appear to be greater than their present income level. Mr. Press is fighting and scheming and planning how to get to the next level in management. He spends much of his working day in this way and takes time to "visit" the boss's office in order to get to know him better. He has even been known to stab some of his peers in the back. This he does because of the "pressure" from his wife and children to get ahead. Meanwhile, on the other side of the building, Mr. Sure is working with his whole heart (as unto the Lord) on the present project, realizing that promotion comes from the Lord and that He knows the needs of his family.

The situation has created the need but who has created the pressures?

Unfortunately, even though Mr. Press missed his deadline while Mr. Sure met his and was therefore up for promotion, they both were laid off because of a merger of their company with a larger company. All of a sudden there was no job and no income.

IS THERE PRESSURE?

Yes, in Mr. Press's case he saw to it that there was. He organized the family, budgeted their savings out at so much per week, and found that their savings would only last them ten weeks! Then he spent most of his time at home worrying and complaining about the limited market for men of his managerial ability and income level. This ten-week deadline facing him was the worst one yet.

Mr. Sure, over on the other side of town, asked God what He was trying to teach him through this, and again he committed his future to his Owner. Since he was still working for God, he spent forty hours per week looking for a job, trusting God to provide him one. And there was no pressure.

Ten weeks later, the money was gone for both men and there was very little food left; the situation did not look very bright in either household. Mr. Press was at his rope's end and was even thinking about committing suicide. The "pressure"! You will never know.

Mr. Sure carried his problem to his Christian brothers. They of course shared with him out of the abundance the Lord had given them. Since they are one body, how can the arm be full and the leg hungry? The Lord also showed Mr. Sure that he had only been looking for high level jobs. The question emerged: was he willing to take a job as a laborer? After he had searched his heart and allowed God to show him his pride, he came to the state of mind where he was ready to take a job as a dishwasher in a local restaurant. Then a position higher than his previous managerial one was offered to him. He rejoiced in the lesson that God had taught him and in the fact that promotion truly comes from the Lord.

SELF-GENERATED

As you can see, in every instance in this little story, the situation only presented the challenge; the pressure was entirely self-generated. Simply recognizing this fact is half the battle. As long as Satan can convince us that the pressure is from without and that there is nothing we can do about it, we will remain the slaves of pressure. But once it is recognized that all pressure is self-generated, it can be controlled.

One simple example of such recognition and control would be a man driving home from work. Mr. Press and Mr. Sure both used to rush home from work (with nothing to do but wait thirty minutes for dinner). They got upset when someone tried to cut in front of them and usually sped up in order to prevent it. They whipped around slow drivers, shouting in their inner thoughts that such drivers should not be allowed to drive in a high speed era.

But once Mr. Sure recognized that the pressure was entirely of his own making, he relaxed and enjoyed the drive home. He sometimes prayed, sometimes paid special attention to the sunset or changing seasons, and sometimes just thought of home or work. Do you realize that it made less than 10 percent difference in his travel time? It took him thirty-two minutes instead of thirty. Simply recognizing that pressure was his own created Frankenstein really was his solution. Mr. Press? He didn't change and contracted his ulcer right on schedule.

BEING ANXIOUS

If pressure is of our own creation then it becomes sin, doesn't it? The Lord Jesus must have had us in mind when He said (Matt. 6:25, 26):

25 "For this reason I say to you, do not be anxious for your life, *as to* what you shall eat, or what you shall drink; nor for your body, *as to* what you shall put on. Is not life more than food, and the body than clothing?

26 "Look at the birds of the air, that they do not sow, neither do they reap, nor gather into barns, and *yet* your heavenly Father feeds them. Are you not worth much more than they? . . ."

Here Jesus Himself commands us not to be anxious (or to generate self pressure). To disobey this command is actually sin. He realized that we were the ones who generated anxiety within ourselves and told us not to do it. He also says that anxiety is not of faith, and we all know that what is not of faith is sin. Paul in writing about self-generated pressure says, "Have no anxiety about anything, but in everything by prayer and supplication with thanksgiving let your requests be made known to God. And the peace of God, which passes all understanding, will keep your hearts and your minds in Christ Jesus" (Phil. 4: 6-7). What Paul is saying here is that peace is the opposite of pressure or anxiety. When we generate pressure we automatically give up the peace of Jesus in our hearts. There can be no co-existence between the two.

WHAT TO DO ABOUT PRESSURE

We all know that Satan is a great thief. One of the things that he likes to steal most from Christians is their peace, which he replaces with a knot in the stomach (pressure or anxiety). I occasionally (not often) find myself in that situation. I *immediately* do something about it because Jesus gave me my peace, and it is rightfully mine. I will not tolerate Satan stealing it from me.

A friend of mine asked me, when we were talking about Satan stealing our peace, what caused the peace to go away. Was it temptation, was it demonic activity, was it this or that? I told him that I really didn't care *what* caused it and that I didn't stop to analyze it or become introspective about it; when this happened, I simply wanted my peace back.

The way to regain your peace is by first asking God for the

covering of the blood of Christ over yourself, and then you must bind Satan in the name of Jesus Christ. Once we have bound the "strong man," we can loose the things in his house that he has stolen from us (Matt. 12:29). We can then loose our peace to return to us in the name of our Lord Jesus Christ. My experience has been that every time, without exception, my peace does return. If Jesus Christ gave us this peace, should we tolerate Satan stealing it from us? I believe the answer is an emphatic NO! Satan would love to have you and me living with anxiety, and Jesus wants us to live in peace. Our hearts and our prayers are the determining factors as to which it will be.

TYRANNY OF THE URGENT

Even if we live with peace in our hearts, there seem to be demands on our time coming from every side. Most of us have much more to do than we can possibly achieve in twenty-four hours per day. Many of us have wished for a thirty or forty hour day to help us get everything done. In fact, this is one of the reasons that people subscribe to newsletters such as *Financial Guidance*; it saves them the time that it would take to attend investment conferences or to read numerous books, magazines, newsletters, newspapers, and so forth. Newsletters digest all of this information and present it in a compact way that saves the reader a great deal of time.

All of us have a long list of things which we are neglecting to do. There are unanswered letters; books that we have bought but never read; visits with friends, neighbors, and relatives; daily exercising; unfinished projects; educational courses that we would like to take; and so on. Sometimes we feel guilty because we are not doing many of these important things. One reason that we are not doing them is that these important things get crowded out by more urgent things.

CREATING VERSUS REACTING

At one time in my career I taught management courses to the executives of such companies as Blue Cross, Computer Science Corporation, and IBM. Once, I asked a group of executives to determine which of two functions they spent more time in, creating or reacting. Every one of them said that he spent more time reacting. I then asked them which they felt they *should* spend more time doing. All of them said creating. They were actually doing the opposite of what they felt they should be doing. The reason for this is:

THE URGENT THINGS IN LIFE ABSORB ALL OF OUR TIME AND KEEP US FROM DOING THE IMPORTANT THINGS.

The urgent things in life always have a deadline while the important things never do. The urgent things might include a report to get out, a sale to make, a dinner party, or a problem to solve. All of these have strict deadlines as to when they have to be done. Important things in life, such as spending time with our children, reading the Bible, taking a self-improvement course, or developing a new skill, do not have deadlines, and therefore get crowded out.

When I was teaching one of these courses to a group of Blue Cross executives, one man came up to me at the coffee break after our discussing this and said to me, "Jim, I have just learned an extremely valuable lesson. I could go home now and the course would have been well worth it to me. I'm going to go back and set aside time each day to create." I believe this man was very wise. We have to actually schedule in the important things and let some of the "urgent" things wait their turn. It is interesting that many things we consider urgent will tend to disappear of their own accord.

BE DOERS, NOT JUST READERS (HEARERS)

There was a young preacher once, fresh out of seminary, who went to pastor his first church. The first Sunday he preached a very good sermon. The next Sunday he preached the identical sermon. Some of the church fathers felt that he must have forgotten that he had preached it the previous Sunday. However, on the third Sunday he preached the same sermon again. After the service, one of the church fathers came up to him and said, "Young man, I don't want to be critical, but do you realize that you have preached the same sermon three Sundays in a row?" The young preacher said, "Well, the people in the church haven't done that yet; why should I go on and preach about something else?"

There was a great deal of truth in what that young preacher said. We all know that we should do many things. The problem is that we are simply not doing them. We know that we should:

- spend time reading the Bible

- spend time in prayer

- write to our Senators and Congressmen

- read some of the books that we have bought

- follow up new Christians

- be physically prepared for emergencies

The list could go on and on. We are aware of all of these good, important things to do. Why don't we do them then? Probably for two basic reasons. The first we just discussed. The urgent things tend to crowd out these important things. The second reason is that we twiddle away a great deal of time (T.V. being the big, single culprit). To me, the place to start would be to spend some time with the Lord, finding out which of the important things He really wants you to do. Once you have heard a word from the Lord, it is time to take the next step.

TAKE TIME TO PLAN, AND THEN ACT

Jesus commended and commanded planning. In the parable of the man building the tower, Christ says that before starting to build, the man should have first counted the cost to be sure that he had enough to finish. Christ is telling us both to plan and to budget.

As part of the planning process, it would be good to translate some of these important things into specific, achievable projects and then to assign a due date so that they too can become urgent. For example, instead of generally saying I should spend time reading the Bible, it would be better to say, "I want to read the book of John by the end of September," or "I want to read four chapters a day." These then become specific goals with time deadlines.

Similarly, after reading my book, *Christians Will Go Through The Tribulation—and how to prepare for it,* many people possibly felt in their hearts that they should do some of the things in the physical preparation area. However, it is likely that they have actually done nothing in that area. As I pointed out in the last chapter, it helps to write down these projects with a due date and the approximate cost for each.

For example, you may want to buy three water barrels (55 gallons each) and have these filled with water by September 15. Similarly, there could be an activity and a due date for such things as buying a flashlight to keep by the bed, having food stored, purchasing a first aid kit, and so forth. Some of the things that you may want to consider on the physical side might be:

1. *Water storage*—There should be approximately 30–55 gallons for each member of the family.

2. *Food stored*—You should store some amount of food, depending on how God is leading you. If God lays nothing specifically on your heart, a good target would be a year's supply of food for each member of your family.

3. *Emergency supplies*—This, as with all of these items, depends on how the Lord is leading you. You may want to store a first aid kit, candles, kerosene lamps, a propane camp stove and flashlights.

4. *Protection*—This means where you live. It could include a watchdog, smoke detectors, fire extinguishers, burglar alarms and whatever else the Lord lays on your heart as necessary for you to protect from adversaries that which He has given to you. (To be a good steward of something implies that you must retain it.)

5. *Nuclear fallout protection*—This could mean anything from storing some sandbags or bags of cement in your basement, to having a complete fallout shelter.

6. *Self-supporting house*—Have your house as self-sufficient as possible. Make it as independent as possible of utility systems and possible energy shortages.

7. *Raise your own food*—Obtain the skills, equipment, seeds and whatever else is necessary to be able to provide food for your own family.

I am not saying that every family should do all of these things, or even any of them. These are things to hold before the Lord. If He tells you to do one of them, write it down on your list of actions with a due date. Similarly, in the other areas of life, such as spending time with your family, you can schedule in a weekend trip or various other family activities. I do not think that it glorifies God for a man to be so involved in "God's work" that he neglects his family and doesn't spend quality time with his wife and children.

One should take care of any physical preparation that God lays on his heart, without neglecting the financial (stewardship) or spiritual sides of life. To help you do these things (and not be hearers only) you need a written plan of action.

YOUR PLAN OF ACTION

In the last chapter we discussed a plan of action for your STEWARDSHIP PLAN–ACT and for your OPERATING PLAN–ACT. You might wish to combine those with other actions the Lord is laying on your heart. I would encourage you to write these down as your total plan of action, rather than just having it in your head. This may be a plan of action for the entire family, or it may be just for yourself. If it is for the family, then someone should be designated as the individual responsible for each action to be taken. By outlining the actions that you feel God wants you to take, and setting an approximate date by which you feel He wants them completed, you could probably

NO.	ACTION	APPROX. COST	INDIVIDUAL RESPONSIBLE	DATE DUE	DATE DONE
1.	Buy water barrels	$50	John	10/1	
2.	Buy flashlights (2)	6	Billy	9/15	
3.	Read book of John	—	John	9/20	
4.	Take family to zoo	10	Family	10/5	
5.	Checkbook – analysis	—	John & Mary	11/1	
6.	Create budget	—	John	11/10	
7.	Start tithing and saving	100	John	12/1	
8.	Invest	200	John	2/1	

be more assured of achieving them. A total plan of action, using our plan of action forms might look like the one above.

However, let me hasten to add that this form should not become an item of "pressure" for you. This is simply recording a plan that God has laid on your heart. If God subsequently wants to change your plan, that is fine. What it will help you to do is to not let the little crises that come up crowd out some of the *important* things. It will also be an encouragement not to waste time on meaningless activities and neglect the important things.

REVIEW

So far we have said that all of us tend to feel a little guilty over some of the important things that we are letting go. As this builds up, we feel under tremendous "pressure." In trying to unravel this seemingly entangled mess of guilt (over neglecting important things) and pressure, we need to first realize that the pressure that we feel is *generated internally* and *not externally.* If Satan can convince us that the pressure is from outside ourselves, and that we can do nothing about it, he can continually rob us of our peace. *Jesus wants us to experience His peace, rather than pressure and anxiety.*

Once we have realized this and have peace, then how do we get some of these important things done? We first have to attack the two culprits. One is the wasting of time, and the other is letting the little crises and "urgent" things come in and crowd out the *important* things. One of the best ways to be sure that the important things get done is to make them specific and achievable with a due date. It is even good to write them down in a plan of action.

This total plan of action in no way should generate any "pressure" on you. It is simply a recording of what God has told you to do. Remember, *God will not ask you to do anything that He will not give you the time and the ability to do.* The important thing is to listen for a word from the Lord as to what He wants you to do. Then you must wholeheartedly, with joy and peace in your heart, set about doing your Master's business.

THINKING THROUGH THE BOOK

As we approach the end of the book, I thought it might be good to pause and look back over the ground we have covered. We began by discussing the biblical teaching on stewardship. Stewardship deals with your assets, whereas tithing deals with your income. In order to be a good steward we need to find out what our net worth is so we know how much God has entrusted to our stewardship. Once we determine this, we then need to go to God for His guidance as to adjustments and changes that He would have us to make concerning those assets (investments).

We then examined three of the trends in the U.S. economy and saw that they all pointed towards much worse inflation ahead. In fact we called this a hurricane that could destroy many people's financial situations. We described how you could examine the effects of "hurricane inflation" and some of the things that you could do to protect yourself against it.

We looked at individual income and expense situations and recommended that each person give the first 10 percent of his income to the Lord, save the second 10 percent (ultimately in something other than the U.S. dollars), and then give additional offerings to the Lord. We should then learn to live on the remaining 80 percent. From the 10 percent savings, as well as other savings that we are able to achieve out of the 80 percent, we get the funds to invest. It is through wise investments that we will be good stewards.

We then looked at various investments. One thing we concluded is that we wanted to be out of anything that was in a fixed amount of U.S. dollars, such as bonds, large savings accounts, or whole life insurance. We suggested moving into investments that would keep ahead of inflation. Some of the investments that could potentially keep ahead of inflation are real estate, stocks, gold coins, silver coins, commodities, antiques, and other rare items. We know that during some years some of these investments will do well and others will do poorly. Conversely, in the following years the ones that did poorly might do very well, and the ones that were booming might come

sliding down. Thus, one must be willing to move from one investment vehicle to another. To help people in the timing of
these moves, we publish the investment newsletter, *The
McKeever Strategy Letter.* (See Appendix B for information.)

We discussed many other vital considerations such as tax
planning, making a will, insurance, and becoming multinational.
Some of these things are critically important to people with a
substantial net worth, and to at least some degree these considerations are important for all people. This is particularly true of
making a will and estate planning.

We then concluded with emphasizing the seven steps for
developing a PLAN–ACT. This was a plan which we developed
with objectives and goals after determining our present status.
Once we established our goals, we created a plan of action to
move us from where we were to where we wanted to be. This
plan of action established target dates and listed the individual
responsible for completing each action. Forms to help you in
determining your present status in various areas and to help you
establish a plan of action are included along with additional information in *The Almighty and the Dollar Personal Planning
Workbook* (see Appendix B).

This PLAN–ACT technique is valuable for use not only in
the financial area of your life, but also in your spiritual growth
or in any physical preparations that the Lord may be having
you to make. It is best to create a TOTAL PLAN–ACT which
would include the financial, physical, educational, and spiritual
areas of your life.

We then discussed the "tyranny of the urgent." The urgent
things in life frequently crowd out the important things because
the important things in life never have deadlines. It does no
good for us to do our planning and design a plan of action if we
don't actually take those actions (you can't live in a blueprint).
So I strongly encourage each individual to pray diligently for
God's leading, then to take specific actions to carry out God's
will for his life.

WISE AS SERPENTS?

Some people will criticize this book and will say that I am encouraging people to be "money mad" or that I am overemphasizing material things to the neglect of spiritual things. I do not believe that this is true, and those who have read some of my other books, such as *Revelation for Laymen, You Can Overcome, The Coming Climax of History,* or *Christians Will Go Through the Tribulation—and how to prepare for it,* will realize that the material aspect of life is of infinitely less concern to me than is the spiritual side. Also in the monthly newsletter I edit, *End-Times News Digest,* the emphasis is totally on the spiritual side of life.

I believe that Christians should be sharp in every area of their lives. They should not be slothful in business. This includes their own personal financial business affairs. Unfortunately, some Christians are not sharp; they have been poor stewards and have their financial affairs in such a state that they do not glorify the Lord.

We Christians are a funny lot. We tend to latch onto a good truth or pattern of behavior and then do ourselves spiritual harm by overemphasizing this truth or behavioral pattern. Christ, in instructing his disciples on how to go out into the world, told them this (Matthew 10):

> 16 "Behold, I send you out as sheep in the midst of wolves; therefore be shrewd as serpents, and innocent as doves."

In the King James, it says be "wise as serpents and harmless as doves." By looking at both translations, you get a good feeling for what Christ was really saying.

We have a few sheep on the ranch where we live, and occasionally we have a coyote problem. Through the sheep the Lord has shown us some things about what this verse means. The sheep can't fight. They can't bite or claw or even kick. The most they can do is butt a little. This would be no defense or offense against a wolf or coyote attacking them. Just as they can do no harm to anyone, neither should a Christian. However, one can be as innocent and as harmless as a dove (or sheep) and yet get eaten alive. Therefore, something has to balance this characteristic.

I believe that today most Christians have emphasized (overemphasized?) being innocent and harmless. We have been told how good it is to be tolerant of everyone. This is a true statement in the same way that it is good to be innocent and harmless as a dove. However, without a balance, it can also be disastrous. I believe that the vast majority of Christians today are far *too* "loving," tolerant, and open for their own good. During the days of deception and persecution ahead, an overemphasis of these characteristics can be tragic.

To point out how much we have overemphasized this, just ask yourself how many Christians you know whom you would classify as innocent and harmless doves. You can probably think of many Christians who would fit that description. How many Christians do you know that you could say are as wise and shrewd as serpents? Probably not very many, if any at all. The ideal would be that people would say about each Christian that he or she is "as harmless as a dove *and* as shrewd as a serpent." Does this dual description fit you?

Since the sheep here on the ranch are defenseless (harmless), they must run to a place of safety when danger comes. Once they have run into the sheepfold (through the door), they are relatively safe. They run to the fold when anything startles them. It could be a coyote or a deer. Whatever it is—whether there is a danger or not—they run to the fold (through the door) to assure their safety.

In a similar way, when things come up in our Christian life, we need to be wise and shrewd enough to run for the fold (through the door) to check it out with the great Shepherd, to see if there is a danger or not. Otherwise, we can allow a wolf in sheep's clothing to come among us and do spiritual harm. We can be too trusting and too tolerant for our own good.

I would certainly encourage people to be as harmless as sheep or doves and to run to Jesus for protection. But I believe in our financial affairs we also need to be shrewd and sharp. My prayer is that this book will help you to bring this balance into your life.

FINAL WORD FROM THE AUTHOR

With my whole heart I want to glorify Jesus Christ and to lift Him up. I want to love those that He loves, and I know that He especially loves Christians. The Bible says that Christians are His own body.

Because of my love and concern for the body of Christ, I yearn for each one individually to be a good steward so that when he stands before the judgment seat of Christ, Jesus can say concerning his material stewardship, as well as his spiritual development, "Well done, my good and faithful servant."

I realize that the Lord would have some people give away everything they own and live in poverty. There are others that the Lord may want to make a great deal of wealth so that they can share it in needy places within the Kingdom of God. We must do God's will—whatever He tells us to do. However, as long as we have material and financial possessions, God expects us to be good stewards of them until He tells us to give them away. Once we give money to a church, a Christian organization, or a needy person, then whoever receives it takes up the baton and is then responsible for being a good steward of it from that point forward.

We should certainly be willing to lose all of our material possessions and even to lay down our lives for our beloved Savior, Jesus Christ. As the Tribulation nears and times get worse and worse, it may become progressively more important to have made preparations in various areas of our lives. If we are spending all of our income, and possibly even going progressively deeper into debt because of our high standard of living, we may find ourselves unable to buy food for storage or other things the Lord might want us to buy as preparations for the future. It would be a shame to see a Christian starving to death during the time of sorrows (time of birth pangs) that precedes the Tribulation simply because he had lives so luxuriously in the past. Things are getting serious in this world, and an economic crisis is getting nearer. I believe that *now* is the appointed time to get our house in order, become good stewards, and make preparations that God is leading us to make.

My prayer is that God would use this book to help each individual who reads it in these difficult days to come closer to Christ and to better glorify the Lord. I hope that each Christian who reads and does the things in this book will receive praise rather than disapproval when he stands before Jesus. May God bless you and keep you. Always love the Lord with all of your heart, and may all that you do glorify the Father and His precious Son, Jesus Christ, our Savior.

Our economy and the world financial situation are changing so rapidly that my thinking on some of the topics in this book may have changed by the time you read it. If you wish to get my current thinking, I would encourage you to subscribe to *Financial Guidance*, so you can get my latest thoughts every month.

In *Financial Guidance*, I also give the timing signals as to when to get out of one investment area and into another. The last page in this book has a form you can use to get my regular *Financial Guidance*. It could be a tremendous help to you.

APPENDICES

TABLE OF CONTENTS

APPENDIX A

HOW TO BECOME A CHRISTIAN

If you are reading this I am assuming that you are not sure that you have received Jesus Christ as your personal Savior. Not only is it possible to know this for sure, but God *wants* you to know. This is what 1 John 5:11-13 has to say:

11 And the witness is this, that God has given us eternal life, and this life is in His Son.

12 He who has the Son has the life; he who does not have the Son does not have the life.

13 These things I have written to you who believe in the name of the Son of God, in order that you may know that you have eternal life.

These things are written to us who believe in the name of the Son of God, so that we can *know* that we have eternal life. It is not a "guess so," or "hope so" or 'maybe so" situation. It is so that we can *know* for certain that we have eternal life. If you do not have this confidence, please read on.

In order to get to the point of knowing that we have eternal life, we need to first go back and review some basic principles. First, it is important to note that all things that God created (the stars, trees, animals, and so on) are doing exactly what they were created to do, except man. Isaiah 43 indicates why God created us·

7 Every one who is called by My name,
And whom I have created for My glory,
Whom I have formed even whom I have made.

Here it says that humans were created to glorify God. I am sure that neither you nor I have glorified God all of our lives in everything that we have done. This gives us our first clue as to what "sin" is. We find more about it in Romans 3:

23   for all have sinned and fall short of the glory of God.

This says that we have all sinned and that we all fall short of the purpose for which we were created—that of glorifying God. I have an even simpler definition of sin. I believe that sin is "living independent of God." A young person out of high school can choose which college to attend. If he makes this decision apart from God, it is "sin." This was the basic problem in the garden of Eden. Satan tempted Eve to eat the fruit of the tree of "the knowledge of good and evil." He said that if she would do this, she would know good from evil and would be wise like God. This would mean that she could make her own decisions and would not have to rely on God's wisdom and guidance. Since you and I fit in the category of living independent of God and not glorifying Him in everything we do, we need to look at what the results of this sin are.

First let me ask you what "wages" are. After thinking about it, because you probably receive wages from your job, you will probably come up with a definition something like "wages are what you get paid for what you do." That is a good answer. Now let's see what the Bible has to say concerning this, in Romans 6:

23   For the wages of sin is death, but the free gift of God is eternal life in Christ Jesus our Lord.

Here we see that the wages of sin is death—spiritual, eternal death. Death is what we get paid for the sin that we do. Yet this passage also gives us the other side of the coin: that is, that through Jesus Christ we can freely have eternal life, instead of eternal death. Isn't that wonderful?!

But let's return for a moment to this death penalty that the people without Christ have hanging over their heads, because of the sin that they live in. In the Old Testament God made a rule: "The soul who sins will die" (Ezekiel 18:4). If we were able to live a perfect, sinless life, we could make it to heaven on our own. If we live anything less than a perfect life, according to God's rule, we will not make it to heaven, but instead will be sentenced to death. All through the Bible we find no one living a good enough life to make it to heaven.

This brings us to the place where Jesus Christ fits into this whole picture. His place was beautifully illustrated to me when I was considering receiving Christ as my Savior, by a story about a judge in a small town.

In this small town, the newspapermen were against the judge and wanted to get him out of office. A case was coming up before the judge, concerning a vagrant—a drunken bum—who happened to have been a fraternity brother of the judge when they were at college. The newspapermen thought that this was their chance. If the judge let the vagrant off easy, the headlines would read, "Judge Shows Favoritism to Old Fraternity Brother." If the judge gave the vagrant the maximum penalty, the headlines would read, "Hardhearted Judge Shows No Mercy to Old Fraternity Brother." Either way they had him. The judge heard the case and gave the vagrant the maximum penalty of thirty days or $300 fine.

The judge then stood up, took off his robe, laid it down on his chair, walked down in front of the bench and put his arm around the shoulders of his old fraternity brother. He told him that as judge, in order to uphold the law, he had to give him the maximum penalty, because he was guilty. But because he cared about him, he wanted to pay the fine for him. So the judge took out his wallet and handed his old fraternity brother $300.

For God to be "just," He has to uphold the law that says 'the soul who sins will die." On the other hand, because He loves us He wants to pay that death penalty for us. I cannot pay the death penalty for you because I have a death penalty of my own that I have to worry about, since I, too, have sinned. If I were sinless, I could die in your place. I guess God could have sent down millions of sinless beings to die for us. But what

God chose to do was to send down *one* Person, who was equal in value, in God's eyes, to all of the people who will ever live, and yet who would remain sinless. Jesus Christ died physically and spiritually in order to pay the death penalty for you and me. The blood of Christ washes away all of our sins, and with it the death penalty that resulted from our sin.

The judge's old fraternity brother could have taken the $300 and said thank you, or he could have told the judge to keep his money and that he would do it on his own. Similarly, each person can thank God for allowing Christ to die in his place and receive Christ as his own Savior, or he can tell God to keep His payment and that he will make it on his own. What you do with that question determines where you will spend eternity.

Referring to Christ, John 1:12 says:

> **12 But as many as received Him, to them He gave the right to become children of God,** *even* **to those who believe in His name,**

John 3:16 says:

> **16 "For God so loved the world, that He gave His only begotten Son, that whoever believes in Him should not perish but have eternal life.**

Here we see that if we believe in Christ we won't perish, but we will have everlasting life and the right to become children of God. Right now you can tell God that you believe in Christ as the Son of God, that you are sorry for your sins and that you want to turn from them. You can tell Him that you want to accept Christ's payment for your sins, and yield your life to be controlled by Christ and the Holy Spirit. (You must accept Christ as your Savior *and your MASTER.)*

If you pray such a prayer, Christ will come and dwell within your heart and you will *know for sure* that you have *eternal life.*

If you have any questions about what you have just read, I would encourage you to go to someone that you know, who really knows Jesus Christ as his Savior, and ask him for help and guidance. After you receive Christ, I would encourage you to become part of a group of believers in Christ who study the scriptures together, worship God together and have a real love relationship with each other. This group (body of believers) can help nurture you and build you up in your new faith in Jesus Christ.

If you have received Christ, as a result of reading these pages, I would love to hear from you. My address is at the end of this book.

Welcome to the family of God.

Jim McKeever

APPENDIX B

WHO TO CONTACT
(Newsletters, Books, Money Management)

Throughout this book I've mentioned various services I feel would be helpful to you in becoming a better steward over your assets. For your convenience, I've listed those below along with a few others.

A. <u>MATERIALS BY JIM McKEEVER</u>:

1. *Financial Guidance.* For information, write to:

   Omega Financial Services
   P.O. Box 4130
   Medford, Oregon 97501

2. Books. Send check or money order to (see last page):

   Omega Publications
   P.O. Box 4130
   Medford, Oregon 97501

   Christians Will Go Through The Tribulation and How To Prepare For It . . .   softback — $5.95

   Revelation for Laymen . . .   softback — $5.95

   You Can Overcome . . .   softback — $6.95

   The Coming Climax of History . . .   softback $6.95

B.   WORKBOOK, for use with this book:

Personal Planning Workbook. This is a three-ring binder containing enlarged copies of all the forms you need to do goal planning and regular assessments of your stewardship progress. For each copy send $23.95 to:

Omega Publications
P.O. Box 4130
Medford, Oregon 97501

C.   FOOD AND SURVIVAL SUPPLIES:

For a complete catalog showing a wide variety of survival and homesteading equipment and foods for storage, send $2.00 to:

Omega Food and Supplies
P.O. Box 4636
Medford, Oregon 97501

D.   GOLD, SILVER, AND NUMISMATIC COINS:

Write to:

International Collectors Associates
Writer's Tower, Suite 309
1660 Albion Street
Denver, Colorado 80222
(303) 759-0308

This is a top-notch, reputable organization owned and operated by a wonderful Christian couple, Don and Molly McAlvany. We recommend them highly.

E.   SWISS BANKS:

Foreign Commerce Bank
Hans C. Weber
Managing Director
Bellariastrasse 82
8038 Zurich, Switzerland

Banque of Indiana
Ms. Francine Misrahi
International Manager
50 Ave de la Gare
Lausanne, Switzerland

Union Bank of Switzerland
Bahnhofstrasse 45
8021 Zurich, Switzerland

Swiss Bank Corporation
Aeschenvorstadt 1
4002 Basel, Switzerland

Swiss Credit Bank
Paradeplatz
8022 Zurich, Switzerland

F. COMMODITY CHARTS:

Each of the following services publishes updated charts
weekly.

1. *Commodity Perspective.* For information, write to:

> Commodity Perspective
> 327 South LaSalle Street
> Chicago, Illinois 60604

2. *Commodity Chart Service.* For information, write to:

> Commodity Research Bureau, Inc.
> One Liberty Plaza
> New York, New York 10006

3. *Hadady-type Professional Commodity Charts.* For information, write to:

> The Professional Chart Service ·
> 61 South Lake Avenue, Suite 309
> Pasadena, California 91101

G.   STOCK CHARTS:

Daily Graphs publishes both stock and stock option charts weekly. For information, write to:

> Daily Graphs
> P.O. Box 24933
> Los Angeles, California 90024

H.   OTHER RECOMMENDED NEWSLETTERS:

1. *The Reaper,* R. E. McMaster, editor, $195 per year. For information, write to:

   > The Reaper
   > P.O. Box 39026
   > Phoenix, AZ 85069

2. *Daily News Digest,* Johnny Johnson, editor, $97 per year. For information, write to:

   > Daily News Digest
   > P.O. Box 39850
   > Phoenix, AZ 85069

3. *Remnant Review,* Gary North, editor, $95 per year. For information, write to:

   > Remnant Review
   > P.O. Box 8204
   > Fort Worth, TX 76112

4. *McAlvany Intelligence Advisor,* Don McAlvany, editor, $77 per year. For information, write to:

   > McAlvany Intelligence Advisor
   > P.O. Box 39810
   > Phoenix, AZ 85069

I.   STOCK MARKET ANALYSIS:

Barron's National Business and Financial Weekly. For subscription information, write to:

> Barron's
> 200 Burnett Road
> Chicopee, Massachusetts 01021

APPENDIX C

CONTACT THE AUTHOR

The following pages give information on other books and services by the author. If you are interested in these or in any of the teaching cassettes, we have included a coupon that you can mail in.

If you would like to contact Jim McKeever, see the last page in this book.

END-TIMES NEWS DIGEST

The *End-Times News Digest* is a newsletter published by Omega Ministries, of which Jim McKeever is president. In it is a main article by him in which he shares his latest thinking on prophecy, world events, the economy and things from the Bible.

The *End-Times News Digest* not only reports the news that is important to Christians, much of which they may have missed in our controlled media, but also gives an analysis of it from the perspective of a Spirit-filled Christian. In addition it suggests actions and alternatives that would be appropriate for a Christian to take.

The *End-Times News Digest* also has a physical preparation section which deals with various aspects of a self-supporting life-style. The spiritual preparation section deals with issues of importance to both the individual Christian and the body of believers.

All of the contributing writers to this newsletter are Spirit-filled Christians. Jim McKeever is the editor and major contributing writer. God gives him insights that will help you, open your eyes to new things and lift you up spiritually.

This monthly newsletter is sent to anyone who contributes at least $20 per year to Omega Ministries.

- -

Omega Ministries   BC-092
P.O. Box 1788
Medford, OR 97501

☐ Enclosed is a $20 contribution. Please send me *End-Times News Digest* for a year.

☐ Enclosed is $10 for six months.

Name _____

Address _____

City, State _____ Zip _____

CASSETTES BY JIM McKEEVER

CASSETTE ALBUMS

Qty Contribution

__ $_____ Becoming an Overcomer (6 tapes) $30

__ _____ Omega World Convention 1983
              St. Louis (6 tapes) $40

__ _____ Annual End-Times Conference 1982
              St. Louis (6 tapes) $30

__ _____ Annual End-Times Conference 1981
              Medford (6 tapes) $30

__ _____ The Book of Revelation is Understandable
              (16 tapes) $60

__ _____ How to Avoid the Mark of the Beast*
              (4 tapes) $20

__ _____ Highlights of Revelation*
              (4 tapes) $20

__ _____ Rapture and the Tribulation*
              (4 tapes) $20

*From radio program END TIMES PERSPECTIVE

__ _____ TOTAL ENCLOSED FOR CASSETTE
              ALBUMS

__ _____ Additional Gift for Omega Ministries

- -

Omega Ministries   BC-092
P.O. Box 1788
Medford, OR 97501

Please ship me the cassettes indicated above.

Name _____

Address _____

City, State _____ Zip _____

YOU CAN OVERCOME

by Jim McKeever

By far the most important preparation for Christians to make for the difficult days ahead is spiritual preparation. This third book by Jim McKeever entitled YOU CAN OVERCOME deals with the spiritual preparation for the end times.

The author feels that this is likely the most important book that he will ever write. In each of Christ's letters to the seven churches in the book of Revelation, special rewards are promised to the "overcomers." Christians in general have read this and would like to become overcomers, but they don't understand what it really means to be an overcomer, nor how to go about it according to the Bible.

A term in the New Testament that is equivalent to overcomer is "bondslave" of Jesus Christ. This book explains what a bondslave is and how one becomes a bondslave of Christ.

Many Christians are concerned about the "mark of the beast." The Bible says that God is going to seal his bondslaves in their foreheads. Neither Satan nor the beast, nor anyone else, could remove God's seal from the bondslaves' forehead and replace it with the mark of the beast.

Thus, if you become a bondslave, an overcomer, and are sealed of God in your forehead, it will be impossible for you to take on the mark of the beast! Also, those who are sealed in their forehead by God are protected from much that's coming upon the earth.

Not all Christians are bondslaves of God. In the end times of this age, becoming a bondslave, an overcomer, is absolutely essential. This book tells you how. Please don't miss this incredible book.

(You may use the convenient order form on pages 319–320 to order this book.)

REVELATION FOR LAYMEN

by Jim McKeever

At last! . . . A clear, readable study of the Book of Revelation, geared for plain folks.

In past times, understanding the book of Revelation was almost optional. But, in the light of recent world events, the understanding of this essential book is urgently needed.

God says, "Blessed is he who heeds the words of the prophecy of this book." (Revelation 22:7) And if we are to heed the words we must understand them. God would not ask you to heed them unless it were possible.

Satan wants you not to read the book of Revelation. He wants you to be confused by the conflicting interpretations of it. But God wants you to read it, to understand it, *and to act on what it says.*

McKeever makes Revelation an exciting and understandable book, and an essential guide to survival in these end times.

(You may use the convenient order form on pages 319-320 to order this book.)

CHRISTIANS WILL GO THROUGH THE TRIBULATION
—and how to prepare for it

by Jim McKeever

This book could affect every major decision that you make!

Most Christians have only heard about a pre-Tribulation Rapture, and probably believe in it because they have not heard a viable alternative presented intelligently. This book is solidly based on the word of God and shows clearly why Christians will go through all, or at least part, of the Tribulation.

If a Christian believes that we are indeed going through the Tribulation, the next question is, how near is it? If the Tribulation is thousands of years away, there is no need to prepare for it. On the other hand, if we are living in the end times, preparation to go through the Tribulation is essential.

This book goes on to discuss both physical and spiritual preparation for the Tribulation. It gives practical, "how to" suggestions for preparation.

PRAY ABOUT ORDERING THIS VITAL BOOK

In times past God did not remove His people from trials, but allowed them to go through them victoriously (Daniel in the lion's den, the three Hebrews in the fiery furnace, the children of Israel in the Egyptian plagues). It is possible that you will go through the Tribulation. The Holy Spirit can use this book to help you understand and prepare.

(You may use the convenient order form on pages 319–320 to order this book.)

THE COMING CLIMAX OF HISTORY

by Jim McKeever

Most major works that deal with an analysis of prophecy and the end times take one small slice out of the broad prophetic spectrum. Until this book, THE COMING CLIMAX OF HISTORY, there has never been a work that beautifully integrates the prophetic works of the Old Testament and the New Testament. Other works have left many questions unresolved such as exactly where did the dry bones of Ezekiel fit in and at what point is the sun darkened and the moon turned to blood? In this book Jim McKeever pulls together many of those loose ends with startling insights into the way that all these prophecies fit together. Yet the concepts that he outlines are backed up one hundred percent by the Scriptures.

He lays out the timetable that God has for the remainder of this age and for the periods of time yet to come. This book will force Christian teachers and thinkers to re-examine many of their concepts placed against his outline of future events. One of the beautiful things about the extraordinary book is that it is written in such a way that the average reader cannot only read it but actually understand it. The logic of this book is very clear so that anyone can follow the author easily. You can see why he arrives at these conclusions from the Bible passages.

As the return of Jesus Christ grows nigh, it is incredibly important for every Christian to understand how this age will end. This book will be most helpful to Christians in this capacity.

(You may use the convenient order form on pages 319-320 to order this book.)

DEEPER LIFE BOOKLETS
by Jim McKeever

HOW YOU CAN KNOW THE WILL OF GOD

One of the most frequent questions asked of Christian leaders by believers is some form of "How can I know the will of God?"

In this excellent booklet, of the Deeper Life series, Jim McKeever gives a clear and Biblical answer to that.

He first discusses the reasons why God may not be guiding an individual. He then discusses the five ways that God guides a Christian: 1) multitude of counselors, 2) circumstances, 3) the Scriptures, 4) direct revelation, and 5) peace in your heart.

This booklet shows how a Christian can recognize and be tuned into these different ways that God can guide him.

ONLY ONE WORD

In this booklet the author gives a profound insight into how to establish a deep and exciting relationship with Christ. One pastor said of this booklet, "Everybody in the church should review this booklet constantly. It should be reread until it is memorized and becomes a part of each believer." Hundreds of Christians have written saying that this booklet provided the key for greater fulfillment and happiness in their Christian life.

KNOWLEDGE OF GOOD AND EVIL

In the garden of Eden, God gave His first commandment to man by instructing Adam and Eve not to eat of the Tree of the Knowledge of Good and Evil. Does that commandment have any implications for us today? The teaching of this biblically-based booklet is that God still does not want man to have the knowledge of good and evil. The author explains how we can have God guide our decision making rather than to "lean" on our own understanding or logic.

WHY WERE YOU CREATED?

The message of this outstanding devotional booklet is that everything in nature does what it was created to do except man. People, even Christians, do not know what the Bible says they were created to do. This produces conflict and purposelessness in the lives of multitudes of Christians. The booklet explains why we were created and tells what we must do to be in tune with God's creative purposes.

(You may use the convenient order form on pages 319–320 to order these booklets.)

TO THE AUTHOR

The various services and materials available from Mr. McKeever are shown in summary form on the reverse side. Please indicate your area of interest, *remove this page and mail it to him.*

Mr. McKeever would appreciate hearing any personal thoughts from you. If you wish to comment, write your remarks below on this reply form.

Comments:

Attach
Here

Place
Stamp
Here

TO:
 JIM McKEEVER
 P.O. BOX 1788
 MEDFORD, OR 97501

- - - - - - - - - - - - - Fold Here - - - - - - - - - - - - -

BC-092

NAME _____ PHONE _____

ADDRESS _____

CITY _____ STATE _____ ZIP _____

Dear Jim,

Please send me information on:

☐ Your Christian newsletter, *End-Times News Digest (END)*.

☐ Your Christian Seminars.

☐ Your speaking at our church or Christian conference.

☐ Teaching cassettes.

☐ Video teaching series ("Coming Climax of History").

☐ I'm enclosing a contribution for your ministry (please make check payable to Omega Ministries) for: $_____ .

☐ Please read the comments on the other side.

DETAILED OUTLINE
AND INDEX

REQUEST FORM

BC-093

Omega Publications
P.O. Box 4130
Medford, OR 97501

Please send me more information about:

☐ Other books by James McKeever

☐ Your newsletter for investors, THE
MCKEEVER STRATEGY LETTER

☐ Your Christian newsletter, END TIMES
NEWS DIGEST

☐ Dr. McKeever speaking at our church or
Christian conference